01/01

From Bordello to Ballot Box

From Bordello to Ballot Box

A First-Hand Account of Legal Prostitution and Political Corruption

An Autobiography by

Jessi Winchester

with W. Lane Startin

BAINBRIDGEBOOKS
Philadelphia

Published January 2001
By
BainBridgeBooks
an imprint of
Trans-Atlantic Publications Inc.
Philadelphia PA

Website: www.transatlanticpub.com

PRINTED IN THE UNITED STATES OF AMERICA

ISBN: 1-891696-17-3

Library of Congress Cataloging-in-Publication Data

Winchester, Jessi, 1943 –
        From bordello to ballot box: a first-hand account of legal prostitu-
tion and political corruption: an autobiography / by Jessi Winchester ; with
W. Lane Startin
        p. cm.
    ISBN 1-891696-17-3
Prostitution—Nevada. 2. Nevada—Politics and government. 3. Political
    Corruption—Nevada. I. Startin, W. Lane, 1973- II. Title.

HQ145.N3 W56 2000
306.74'09793—dc21

                                        00-044492

*Special dedication to
the memory of my father*

Dedicated To:

- Taking back America and restoring it to the vision of individual freedom and pride our Founding Fathers had for our great nation, and

- The bureaucratic pawns who died as a result of the political pursuit of others, and

- Shedding light on a little understood legal industry and bringing it out of the dark ages, and

- To my family for loving and accepting me for who I am despite society's small minded judgmental attitude, and

- To my father for teaching me solid country values, love of family, a strong sense of justice and honor, and

- To my publisher for having the courage to see the public gets the truth.

CONTENTS

PART ONE

For Better or For Worse. 11

Through Innocent Eyes. 20

Where Corn Don't Grow 29

Lights, Camera, Action!. 38

Where Evil Lives 47

Mustang and Old Bridge Ranch 56

The Dark Side 80

Company, Ladies!. 99

Mirror, Mirror. 120

Attitude Adjustment. 130

PART TWO

Land Mines 147

Donkeys and Jackasses 160

The Weeble and the Devious Duchess 173

Integrity – Las Vegas Style. 192

The Political Waltz 209

A Time to Debrief. 234

PART ONE

For Better or For Worse

I began working as a legal prostitute almost on a lark. What started out as a joke between my second husband and me wound up changing my life forever.

I met Michael when he lived next door to me in Los Angeles. A union electrician from Las Vegas, he was working a temporary assignment for the L.A. Department of Water and Power.

We exchanged cordial greetings whenever we saw each other but both of us tended to keep to ourselves. It was obvious we were both single as neither of us was ever in the company of the opposite sex. I didn't want to complicate matters by dating a neighbor, so I just looked.

Michael is a fine-looking man, a John Wayne he-man type. Tall, muscular, dark hair, beard, and a handsome face that made me look longer than I should. When he wasn't working, he wore a Western cut shirt, snakeskin boots, a belt with his name on it, a big rodeo buckle, a Western cut blazer and a Stetson hat.

My best friend, Kathy, caught me stealing a glance outside the window a few times as Michael left his house and decided it was her calling to play matchmaker. She knew Michael from the neighborhood grocery store where she worked as a checker. Casually, she mentioned to him she was having a barbecue that weekend to celebrate my daughter Rebecca's birthday and he was welcome to attend. When he accepted, she excitedly informed me that she was going to host a party and I had to attend since the guest of honor was my daughter. I knew she was up to something; I just didn't know what.

The evening of Rebecca's birthday, we arrived at Kathy's to find a half dozen of Becky's friends, along with a few of Kathy's neighbors, in the backyard barbecuing. We had only been there a few minutes

11

when I heard the roar of Michael's race engine out front. Something told me Kathy had been cooking up more than hamburgers.

Her little scheme worked. Michael and I were the last to leave and we made plans to share dinner the following weekend. I learned he was a Nevada native and had worked in some really fascinating professions. Being a sparring partner to many top fighters is not terribly unusual for someone who grew up in Las Vegas, nor did anyone think twice about his employment as a casino enforcer. Michael had a passion for racing and continued to drive the black pre-runner race truck he built long after it participated in the Mint 400 and the Baja 1000. Employment on a Montana ranch as a working cowboy remains one of his favorite former occupations. He was raised in the city but loves country life as much as I do. We both share a fondness for country music and two-stepping that made me interested in getting to know him further.

The fascinating thing about him is the contrast between the appearance he projects and the elements of his personality. He can hit the bull's-eye of a target three football fields away with a Sharps rifle, yet also identify any classical concerto within the first few notes because he grew up with a mother who was a concert pianist. He can be as annoying as the other guys during "Monday Night Football" and then recite entire histories of Greek mythology. There isn't an engine built that he can't repair, but he can also chronicle each American Indian tribe, their leaders, and the background of their lifestyles and bravery. He is well versed regarding the injustices Native Americans have suffered at the hands of those who helped establish our country as well as current leaders who fail to acknowledge the rights of the American Indian. This rugged cowboy is an intellectual whose wealth of knowledge on many diverse subjects keep me mesmerized and coming back for more.

Slowly, over time, he became an indispensable friend. I couldn't say when friendship eventually turned to love. I just knew my life was happier and more interesting with him in it and I would really miss our long discussions and companionship if our paths were to part. Clearly, he felt the same way.

My house was in escrow and in just a few short weeks, I would have to move out. Emotions were beginning to cloud my decision to leave.

Fate seemed determined to make decisions for us. About the time my escrow closed, Michael's assignment at DWP was completed and he was sent back to Las Vegas. He asked me to reconsider my earlier plan to spend a year traveling with the rodeo circuit and move to Las Vegas instead. I had since lost interest in rodeo plans but I hated Las Vegas and reluctantly told him I wouldn't move there.

A few days later, Michael was gone. We talked daily. It was clear both of us were miserable but my mind was made up. I had no intention whatsoever to while away my days at a slot machine in Glitter Gulch, suffering through 100-degree plus temperatures and surrounded by obnoxious tourists. I had been an independent woman for 13 years and there was no reason to think that should change now.

After a couple of weeks the phone calls stopped. When I called his number, I always got the answering machine. I spent many nights crying myself to sleep. This was when I first realized I loved this man. Obviously, his silence told me he didn't feel the same.

Several days later, the phone rang and his familiar voice said, "OK, you've had a few days of silence to feel what it will be like without each other. I already know I don't want to live the rest of my life without you. If you feel the same, marry me this weekend."

My head was spinning. Did I really want to give up being single? Did I really want to give up Michael? He was insistent that the only option was marriage. I couldn't have both.

A hasty hodgepodge of wedding guests assembled and two days later we were married in a beautiful ceremony at The Little Brown Church in Las Vegas. My children and sister came despite awful heat to witness our marriage and help us celebrate.

We settled into life in tiny Virginia City, a hamlet in the northern Nevada mountains between Reno and Carson City. At first, the rustic Wild West lifestyle was a perfect fit for us both. Becky moved into her own place two doors from us and my sons, Steven and Reed, soon followed. I had a wonderful new husband who treated me like a queen. We lived in an extraordinary country location, and my children were close by. Life couldn't get any better. However, it was about to drastically change.

Only a few months after we were married, Michael was injured and unable to work for an extended period of time. It was up to me to support the family.

Nevada is a right-to-work state, which essentially means employers have the right to offer slave wages and actually expect employees to be cheerful, dedicated, and volunteer to work extra hours. I had just come from a well-paying upper management position with the movie studios, but there was almost no employment in Nevada that matched my qualifications. Entertainment director positions with hotel/casinos in northern Nevada were filled. I was appalled at the pitiful wages offered for those positions, as well as other job classifications, but I needed a paycheck. Until an entertainment position opened up, I decided to work through a temp agency.

On one job, I was sent to city hall to transcribe minutes of council meetings. I enjoyed the work and the people but sitting in front of a computer all day drove me nuts. The eyestrain wasn't the only thing killing me; staying in one place all those hours was torture. I felt like a caged animal.

At the time, brothels were allowed to advertise for working girls. It became a Sunday joke for Michael to read the Mustang Ranch ad and kid me about being able to make more money as a legal hooker than as a transcriber. He ribbed me about being a "natural," but any special talent I possessed sexually was due to his expert teachings. The man is a carnal artist, and I had learned some pretty amazing things that awakened a wild side of me I never knew existed.

Each Sunday, we had the same irritating jest session. He grew up in Nevada and was used to brothels, so he thought it was funny. I had never even talked to a "ho," let alone *been* one! He was just kidding, but I was insulted.

Finally, I told him that if he brought it up one more time, I was going to put on my spandex and go out to Mustang and apply. As a woman in her 40s, I figured they would laugh me out of there. That would be the end of the discussion.

He called my bluff the following Sunday, so I had to keep my word. I phoned Mustang for an appointment, did my hair up wild, put on my spandex and spiked heels and – with much trepidation – drove to the ranch.

The house was surrounded by a high fence with a gate that had to be buzzed from inside to gain entry. As I slowly walked up the sidewalk to the front door, I heard the gate clang shut behind me. Now I knew how prisoners felt. Fear gripped me as I opened the front door.

Music blared from the jukebox and several ladies who were in the parlor smiled warmly as I walked past them. The bar was straight ahead and the bartender waved and pointed toward the office. I hadn't expected to find happy people there.

Charmaine stood up and shook my hand. She was a full-figured woman with a cheerful demeanor. "Let's go to the kitchen and have a cup of coffee. It's quieter there," she offered. I immediately felt at ease.

The kitchen was large and dominated by a long table where the ladies obviously dined family style. Charmaine described the routine and explained the shifts as various ladies drifted in and out of the kitchen to grab snacks. They were all pleasant and I was surprised to note they didn't fit my expectation of a hooker. They all looked so normal.

Finally, Charmaine stood up and guided me back out to the office. "We have a Bette Midler and Cher look alike, Jessi. You resemble Ann-Margaret and it would be fun to add you to the collection. You've got a terrific figure and pleasing personality. I'm sure you would work out nicely here. Let's go figure out which shift you will work and your start date."

I was in shock. This wasn't supposed to happen. What should I do now? I wasn't about to confess this was only a joke to call my husband's bluff and be able to see the inside of a famous bordello. I decided to go home and think everything over.

Charmaine gave me a list of supplies I would need to bring with me since the probation period was 21 days for the first shift and I couldn't leave during that time. We chose a start date and shift and then she walked me to the door. I went back down the sidewalk and out the gate in a daze.

I burst into tears as soon as I got home. Michael looked alarmed. When I told him what happened, he was as stunned as I was. After the shock wore off, we spent many hours in soul searching and talking it all out.

In the end, I decided my maturity would shield me from perceived trauma and my curiosity made me want to find out what goes on behind the walls of those fabled establishments. The pay would be better than the temp agency and I was certain it wouldn't be boring.

Michael put his head in his hands and vowed he would never again tease me about anything he really didn't want to happen.

Nevertheless, my children were grown, we needed the income and the job was legal. There was no reason *not* to give this a try. I would go through the three-week probationary period, after which we would talk everything out and decide if both of us could handle it. Ultimately, entering the world of legal prostitution was simply a pragmatic decision based on the need to circumvent low wages routinely offered by other Nevada vocations.

I reported to work with all the stereotypes others imagine of a "house of ill repute." But after my 21-day probation was over, they had all been proven false. The house was comfortable, clients treated the ladies with great respect, and the women were wonderful. I hoped Michael could accept and adjust to this unusual line of work, because I wanted to go back.

Michael's adjustment to my first year in the brothels was just as complex as mine, but we are very close emotionally and our relationship is set in stone. That's something most folks don't understand. We're the first to admit it is unusual, but overall our lives are obnoxiously normal and much the same as those of other working couples. He's my soul mate and nothing could ever ruin the bond we share.

In the sex industry, most girls choose a "stage name" to imply their personality – but more importantly – to allow them safety and anonymity due to the nature of their work. The bordellos were certainly no exception. Nine out of 10 ladies I worked with did this. I didn't.

The reason? I had nothing to hide. My family knew, my kids were grown, I didn't care if anyone knew where I worked, I live in a state where prostitution is part of Western history, and I'm a country girl—so my name already represented my personality. There just was no need for me to change it, so I didn't.

Most of my co-workers were single mothers determined to provide well for their children. In the houses, they could work two weeks out of the month and make what they would have earned in a full month at most other jobs. That gave them the other half of the month to be home with their children. That kind of quality time is not available to them in most other professions and is a common determining factor in their decision to go into this line of work.

Prostitutes have always been an easy target for those who see themselves as champions of family values, but the definition of good family values depends on the person. The motive for many of the women is to earn a wage that supports their children well and allows them to be able to spend more time with them than most working mothers. I find this logic hard to fault.

As a happily married woman, I was definitely an exception in the houses. Nearly all the ladies are single. Relationships are difficult – if not impossible – to maintain given the nature of the industry. Male jealousy usually ends them. This is not a business that nurtures trust. If a lady marries a client, which happens from time to time, the union is almost doomed from the start. I saw many women pack up and leave with a client, only to return disillusioned weeks or even days later.

Inevitably, those who got involved told similar versions of the same story. They were put on a pedestal by the client, but outside the bordello he couldn't cope with seeing his fantasy as an everyday person. Without the makeup, dramatic hair and fancy costumes, she was no longer his dream. The first serious fight always seemed to end with him calling her a whore. Bags packed, she came back to her sisters and the only environment where she knew she would be accepted, understood, and treated with care.

In rare instances, a husband or boyfriend is able to successfully work it out in his head and cope with the nature of his wife or girlfriend's work. Michael was among them. We have a rock-solid relationship with open communication, friendship, respect, sensitivity for each other's feelings, a mature approach to problems, and a firm desire to make our marriage work. We adore each other.

Michael understood my job was simply that, my job. My heart and emotions remained at home with him. That was what made the difference for him. He never saw me waver from my intense devotion to family and his trust in me to be faithful to him outside of work was unquestioned. In the entire time I worked in the brothels, not once did I see a client off-duty. As soon as I was off the clock, I was back with my family.

Admittedly, Michael never got used to sharing me, but he took comfort in knowing my emotions and heart were reserved only for him. Perhaps because I genuinely enjoyed the company of many of my clients, Michael always had a nagging worry in the back of his mind that someone richer, better looking, or sexier might ride off into the sunset with me. Not a chance. I just laughed and gave him a reassuring hug. He is my hero.

Pimps have no role in legal prostitution, so it was ludicrous when television talk show audiences accused Michael of being one. It's just another myth that has no merit. He has his own career which has absolutely nothing to do with the houses. I married him before entering brothel life. Later on, when I appeared on talk shows, I explained to the audiences that we both worked and put our money into a joint account just as millions of other working couples do. Since our money was co-mingled, he spent some of my money and I spent some of his. He's an electrician, but if I spend the money he made that doesn't make me an electrician. Conversely, if he spends the money I made in the bordellos, that doesn't make him a pimp. He received a lot of unfair abuse.

Michael's family was very distressed with my vocation. It spilled over into how they treated him. His mother died when he was young and his father, brothers and sisters ranged from tolerant to downright hostile.

Ironically, Las Vegas is an extremely conservative city. There are nearly as many churches as there are casinos and strip clubs. Witch hunts are more prevalent than bingo games. Denial and double-standard judgment of others are ways of life in this city of cons and corruption. Growing up in this town must have been a confusing contradiction of two sides to every issue for Michael: there was the right way … and the Las Vegas way. Trying to live a normal life in this twisted city falls light years away from Main Street USA.

Michael's family fell firmly within the description of dysfunctional. His parents married and divorced several times, and not necessarily to each other. His mother was a beautiful, intelligent, strong willed, independent, yet emotionally needy woman. His father was involved with black market items and selling booze to dry states when he was in the Army during World War II. After he got out, associations made over the years led to his move to Las Vegas to help open and operate Benjamin "Bugsy" Siegel's Flamingo Hilton. He is a pleasant but passive, emotionally distant man with many secrets, who prefers not to communicate.

Michael was used to dancing around issues and tended to avoid dealing with reality. I've always been a no-nonsense woman who believed in dealing with everything head on and talking everything out until it was resolved. He liked being unreachable, different, aloof and intimidating. It frustrated him that he didn't intimidate me. I seemed to have direct insight into his mind and soul. He wanted to run as far away from me as he could but he remained by my side.

I insisted on counseling to get past the carnage of his childhood and to make peace with my mother. He didn't want anyone prying into his private thoughts but he went. In the long run, he was glad he continued with the counseling as it enabled him to move forward and enjoy a happy healthy adulthood.

When I began working in the brothels, it would be the counseling that helped us work through the adjustments, remain close, bonded and committed to each other and our marriage.

My sons, daughter, and daughter-in-law showed unconditional acceptance of me regardless of occupation or lifestyle. They loved and supported me 100 percent. There was never an unkind word from any of them. No matter what my line of work, I am always there for my children. I was always Mom; a devoted mother who adored my children and grandchildren. My job didn't change who I was and they knew that. I have been incredibly blessed with remarkable children and we have always been very close.

I felt my life was testament to the fact that normal everyday girls grow up to choose some form of the sex industry for a variety of mundane reasons. Some want more time with their children than a nine-to-five job allows, others are bored with nine-to-five jobs and want better pay and fewer hours, some are attracted by the unconventional lifestyle, a few are hiding from abusive partners, and one or two are addicted to sex and have found an acceptable way to deal with it.

Each woman has her own reason for choosing a career in the sex industry, but the overall stability of women working in the brothels is not out of line with women in any other legal occupation. The American divorce rate seems to indicate marriage is a sexual barter system in which you'll find a higher degree of instability, and a lot less honesty.

Through Innocent Eyes

I remember job fair day at my old junior high school. I remember talking to those manning the booths but I never found a profession that interested me. I wanted to race cars at Indianapolis, Daytona or LeMans. I wanted adventure. I wanted to be different. The one thing I did know for certain, however, was that my future wasn't in the farmlands of Iowa.

Considering my childhood ambition to invade male professions, I wondered how I wound up in an occupation about as female-oriented as they come. More than likely I was comfortable working in the bordellos because of my rural upbringing, which formed my acceptance of sex as a natural part of life. Or maybe it was because sex is the ultimate control of men and calling the shots and making them pay for it is the supreme revenge on male domination. Or perhaps because Nevada is a right-to-work state with extremely low wages – especially for women – where socioeconomic circumstances create a ripe environment for women to choose the high paying sex industry as an alternative. Or possibly out of curiosity to thumb my nose at society's double standards and hypocrisy. Whatever the reason, I know I didn't sit down as a young girl and make a conscious decision to become a prostitute when I grew up. So how did I wind up doing just that? Was it upbringing, environment, or both?

Growing up in a stifling atmosphere of moral constraint and public scrutiny was typical of life in Middle America. Most of us grew up on ranches, farms or in small rural towns. Everyone knew everyone else from early childhood. Family roots could be traced back to the same area for generations and children were expected to continue family businesses. Daily life consisted of school, church, family life, chores, sporting events, the roller rink, sock hops and cruising Main. We had no clue about the world beyond our narrow boundaries.

It was the 50s and early 60s, one of the few times in America that were relatively free of stress. We didn't have to worry about a failing economy, war, gangs, AIDS or drugs. Elvis made our hearts flutter and we giggled about which guys had the hottest cars and how we could get a date with them. Daily lifestyle and occupations were clearly allocated according to gender. Even as a kid I hated labels. They just made me more determined to do what society said I shouldn't. I was always a rebel and stubborn enough to know I would try.

I always felt I could do whatever the guys did and be whatever they were, physical restrictions considered. I pitched in right along with the men to get the work done. On the family farm, work is work and gender never enters into it. It requires long hours of labor, and children start helping at an early age. Both parents were always busy. Children entertained themselves when chores were done.

We raised Black Angus cattle as well as crops, primarily corn, soybeans, wheat and alfalfa. My father spent long hours in the fields tending alfalfa to feed the cattle, milking cows, planting and harvesting. My mother was always in the kitchen fixing meals for hungry ranch hands. We had a huge vegetable garden and a well-stocked freezer with beef, pork and chicken from our own ranch. Mom fixed three huge meals a day, ringing the big ranch bell just outside the back door to summon the hands when the meal was ready. As soon as they left the table, she cleaned up after them and began preparing for the next meal. In between she did her regular housekeeping chores. A sun-up to well past sundown schedule was required just to get by, so it left precious little time to spend with children.

My sister, Nancy, is a year-and-a-half younger than I and we spent all our time together. We each had our own assigned daily chores. Nancy had to feed the pigs and clean their pens. I was subjected to hens pecking my hands until they bled as I gathered the freshly laid eggs they were sitting on.

Growing up around animals I often witnessed the innocence of sex and birth. I simply accepted it as a natural part of life. Even as a child I wasn't uptight about sex, unlike my friends who lived in town. They didn't see nature on a daily basis and were much more preoccupied about the mystery surrounding it than I was. Sunday school and church with its fire and brimstone brand of old-time religion, lack of sex education in public school, parental discomfort about discussing sex, the times, and especially living in the Midwest, left many town dwellers with lifelong inhibitions that most of us who lived in the country never developed.

I can't imagine a better childhood. Growing up in the country plants a child's feet firmly on the ground, instills common sense, and provides a down-to-earth view of life. My childhood years were, quite simply, unremarkable. Many cherished memories stem from those carefree years in the protected environment of the land and the simple lifestyle it offered.

A staunch, lifelong Republican, Daddy plowed "I Like Ike" in the dry pond bed on our property the year we had a drought. Somewhere along the line, a photographer took an aerial shot of it that wound up in *Life* magazine.

Daddy was faithful about making his voice heard at the ballot box during elections and took my sister and me with him to the little one-room schoolhouse a mile from our ranch where he cast his vote. Those vivid memories probably laid dormant in the deep recesses of my subconscious, only to spring alive at the injustices I saw while working in the brothels. Seeds planted in that little schoolhouse at election time were to be harvested many years later in a most unusual fashion.

We had many political discussions around the dinner table. Mostly about subsidies to farmers and how the government was squeezing them out of business. It was adult talk that Nancy and I were too young to understand but we could see Daddy was upset and worried.

Our ranch had been in the family for generations and my father wanted it to remain that way. He had a strong reverence for the soil and animals and possessed solid country values. He taught us that family always came first and that our word was our honor. His life was based in the simplest of lifestyles: providing food for our country and ourselves.

Each year is a gamble in farming and ranching. Families learn to save during the good years and stretch the budget even further during the lean ones. After a particularly meager season, they were sometimes forced to swallow their pride and ask the local bank for a loan. That was always a last resort.

* * *

The maple leaves were turning shades of yellow and deep crimson. I loved the crunching sound they made as my father, sister and I walked through them toward the bank. Summer and winter were boring, bland seasons of the year to me, lacking the drama and beauty of spring and, especially, fall. Spring may have symbolized beginnings and fall endings, but both felt like a promise for the future to my youthful reasoning. Autumn held a special magic, a visual splendor, an appreciation of being alive, and an electricity you could feel in the crisp air. Nowhere was nature more stunning, and I was grateful to have been given the gift of living in a region so blessed with beauty.

The bank stood alone at the corner of the block. The old wooden hardware store next door burned down months earlier, leaving the block looking like a smile with a tooth missing. It was a sturdy two-story structure made of large gray stone with huge granite steps that posed a challenge to my short legs. It was set back from the street and surrounded by an ornate black wrought iron fence that encased magnificent huge old trees and a grass yard that was beginning to surrender its emerald green tint to autumn brown.

Daddy took a small hand in each of his as he assisted my sister and me up the steep steps. He pushed open the heavy wooden door and we listened to the echo as we walked across the marble floor of the stark interior toward Mr. Vance's office.

Mr. Vance was the bank president. He was a large man with a full head of snow white hair and kind eyes. He wore a gray suit and shiny black shoes. We knew his whole family from potluck dinners at church.

He stood up and shook my father's hand and indicated a well padded chair that my father should occupy. Then he turned toward his big roll top desk and began to open a drawer. Nancy and I ran around to where he sat. We knew he wouldn't disappoint us. Each time we visited the bank, Mr. Vance always got a mischievous smile on his face as we huddled around his desk drawer in anticipation of the tootsie roll he would pull out for each of us. Then he would always say the same thing: "Now don't y'all tell your papa I spoiled your supper, girls." We'd laugh and run out of the room to enjoy our treat while Daddy and Mr. Vance talked business.

This had been one of the more barren years. Bloat had killed some of our cattle and flooding had ruined most of our crops. Daddy needed a loan to get us through the winter and to start up again in the spring. After discussing it, Mr. Vance simply got up and went out to the teller's cage and returned with the needed cash. My father shook his hand as he took the money and gathered us up for the journey back down the steep steps.

No contract or written agreement was signed. Mr. Vance knew my father's word and handshake were his honor. He knew the money would be repaid. He also knew there would be a special "thank you" package of Daddy's thick sirloin steaks with the repayment.

This era of honor, trust and integrity was to disappear for good as our country began to lose its character and soul over the coming decades but it left an indelible impression on me that was to last a lifetime and contributed to my finely tuned sense of respect for keeping one's word.

*　*　*

There were only a handful of ranches within a five mile radius of ours. The only other children our age there were boys. Two neighbor boys were in my grade; another was a year ahead of me. Mom wanted us out of the house and out of her way so we either entertained ourselves or played with the neighbor boys if they would tolerate us. If Nancy and I wanted playmates, we had little choice but to become tomboys.

Bruce lived across the road. His mother and father were as busy on their ranch as my folks were so we had little or no supervision during daylight hours. We were left to entertain ourselves when we weren't doing chores. Usually the two of us rode bikes, but one rainy day when we were about seven, we were playing with a doctor kit on Bruce's enclosed back porch.

I was the nurse and he was a patient with a bad tummy ache. My eyes popped when he pulled his jeans down for me to hear his stomach with the stethoscope.

"Bruce," I cried as I pointed to his penis, "What's that? Something is really wrong with you! We'd better tell your mother."

I remember being amazed when he told me that was how he went to the bathroom. "That can't be," I exclaimed. "I don't have one and I can go to the bathroom."

"You can?" Bruce said with much curiosity. "Let's see."

The show-and-tell that followed led to hysterical laughter decades later at high school reunions when Bruce and I reminisced about our childhoods.

After that discovery, I excitedly confided to my girlfriends at school. They told me about a page in the dictionary that featured Adonis wearing only a fig leaf. I spent a lot of time after that looking up Adonis and dreaming about what was behind that leaf!

My sister and I spent most of each summer with relatives. Mother looked forward to a three-month reprieve from care taking. Time away from home unlocked the protected cocoon of Middle America, in which Nancy and I lived.

Uncle Roy was my father's older brother and a top executive with the railroad in Chicago. They never had children so their cosmopolitan country club lifestyle revolved around their social circle. It was a constant reminder to my mother of the station in life she would never achieve. She was openly resentful and jealous of my aunt.

Despite the vast difference between my aunt and uncle's urban affluence and our modest rural existence, there was a strong brotherly bond between my father and uncle that transcended differences in lifestyle.

Nancy spent summers with my uncle and aunt in Chicago while I went to Tennessee to stay with my paternal grandparents. My aunt and uncle were crazy about Nancy and looked forward to the summers she spent with them. They exposed her to museums, symphonies, ballet, fine dining, and a life totally foreign to the one she lived the remainder of the year. Even better, she was the sole focus of their attention and she basked in that warmth.

Nancy spent more summers in Chicago than I did in Tennessee as a result of her obvious art talent which was encouraged by my aunt and uncle. Chicago has an acclaimed art institute and, when my sister reached her early teens, my aunt and uncle financed her training there for several summers.

Had she received additional encouragement from Mother to pursue her dream of becoming a comic strip artist, my sister's adult life would have likely taken a totally different route. Passive by nature, she gave in to my mother's insistence that she get a college degree and teach home economics. She spent four years in college but never received a degree. Instead, she spent several decades working at Los Angeles International Airport. Potential talent was pushed aside as she rarely had time to paint or draw.

Meanwhile, I stayed at my paternal grandparents' tiny farm in southern Tennessee. My father's parents were simple country folks but I loved the time I spent there. My grandfather died when I was in grade school, so Grandma was always happy to have the company of a lively grandchild. She was a stern woman; aloof and not prone to affection, but I knew she loved me just the same.

Life was tedious in rural Tennessee, and Grandma's daily chores on her small acreage kept her busy. I followed her around, feeding the chickens, weeding the garden and exploring unfamiliar territory. She lived on the edge of a tiny town located only a few minutes north of the Alabama border. We often walked into town for supplies.

Downtown consisted of only two blocks of stark red brick buildings. The feedstore, bank, dress shop, meat market, drugstore and beauty parlor were run by predominately plain women who had spent their entire lives within the boundaries of this tiny hamlet. I loved their gracious manner, deep melodious southern drawl and backwoods way of describing things. By the time I returned home each fall, I too had become a "southern belle." After a half dozen summers in the Deep South, my Tennessee drawl merged with an Iowa twang to form an unusual lifelong combination.

Sunday was my favorite day in Tennessee. Religion played a big part in growing up, both in the Midwest and South. Church in Iowa was an expected part of life. Because all my friends were also forced to attend services and social events, I tolerated it, but mainly because it provided a gathering place to spend time with them.

While I found religion for white people in the South similar to that of Iowa, religion for blacks was passionate and consuming. One Sunday I stumbled across an old Baptist church a quarter mile from Grandma's house. I could hear the music from her front porch and it pulled me like a magnet. I had never heard music like that before.

Grandma explained it was a Negro church. I didn't know what that meant. I just knew I loved the music and that was where I wanted to be each Sunday morning.

It was hot and humid so the church doors were open for ventilation. I instinctively knew I shouldn't go in, so I sat down on the front steps all by myself to just listen. The sounds coming from within the church filled the air with excitement. I could barely sit still. Suddenly I became aware of someone sitting next to me.

Latisha smiled at me. "What's your name?" she asked. I smiled back at the dark cherubic face looking at me and told her my name.

It was the early 50s in the Deep South. We were only little girls. We didn't know it was taboo for us to be playmates and friends. We talked and giggled and danced to the music. When the service was over, Latisha's mother emerged. A plump woman with warm eyes, she stood with her hands on her hips watching us. "You come along now," she said to Latisha as she reached for her hand, "and you'd best scoot on home now, chil'," she said to me.

Grandma explained why Latisha and I couldn't play together but her explanation made no sense to me. It made me sad. We were just little girls looking for playmates. The following Sunday I ran the short distance to the church when I heard the music begin. Latisha was already sitting on the steps waiting for me. It became a weekly ritual that ignored color and simply united two little friends for an hour each week.

It also fostered a deep love of gospel music that led into a passion for rock n' roll years later that would drive my parents crazy. My interwoven choice of country, gospel, and rock n' roll convinced my mother I was incorrigible and beyond redemption. She often blamed my grandmother for corrupting my mind.

One summer when I was about 10, Grandma surprised me with the announcement that we were going to spend a couple of days in Nashville. She made the trip by bus once a year to shop in the big city and purchase things she couldn't find back home. This time, she was going to take me to the Grand Ole Opry. I was heady with anticipation. It was a hundred mile trip by bus and felt like we would never reach our destination.

The Ryman Auditorium was kitty-corner from the bus station, so it was the first thing I saw when I got off the bus. My heart stopped.

It was a huge red brick building with white trim and a million big steps. Inside was the stage where my heroes gathered to make musical history, and we were going to be part of that for an evening. I could hardly stand the excitement. As Grandma watched me, it was one of the few times I saw her enjoy a hearty laugh.

I wanted to walk down 16th Avenue and look at all the wonderful old houses that had such southern character and were home to the recording studios of artists I had loved for years on the radio.

The glitter and glamour of the busy streets downtown were almost more than I could bear. Grandma bought me a new hat to wear to the Opry; a felt cowgirl hat; the first time I ever owned a hat that wasn't straw. I felt so important and special.

The Opry was a dream come true. It was all we could talk about on the ride home. Nashville ignited a desire in me to be part of an exciting lifestyle when I grew up; in particular, the country music scene. Unfortunately, I couldn't sing so that dream was never to be. The memory, though, of that special time with my grandmother has remained safely tucked away in my heart.

It was to be my last summer with her. She died of a heart attack Christmas shopping later that year. A tiny leather suitcase containing a manicure set was in her bag for me.

Where Corn Don't Grow

In my late teens I left the monotony of Iowa for the excitement of the west coast. Years earlier, I had resolved to leave Iowa for good after high school. As it turned out, my whole family went.

Our ranch had been in the family for generations but as each year passed, government regulations and newly enacted foreign and domestic policies aimed at deliberately making it harder and harder for small farmers and ranchers to stay in business forced thousands to give up a way of life that was part of their very being. Government simply waited out the farmers, knowing it was only a matter of time before they went under. Just as it had done with the American Indians earlier in our history, our government ended a way of life for thousands without conscience or consequence on the part of those making the life altering decisions.

All over the heartland, the gut-wrenching scene repeated itself. Proud men and women entrusted with the important task of providing food for the nation were being reduced to a fellowship of broken spirits by their own government. Foreclosure signs posted at the entrance to farm driveways were evident all over the region. Heartbreaking machinery auctions became weekly events. Neighboring farmers and complete strangers alike gathered like vultures to pluck bare years of hard-earned gain, leaving the owner in tears and feeling like their limbs had been amputated. Worse, the government stole a way of life along with a person's very soul and reason for being.

My father was an honorable man who served his country during wartime, worked hard all his life, paid his taxes without complaint, gave back to his community, helped his neighbors, got misty eyed during the Pledge of Allegiance and "The Star-Spangled Banner," and taught his children to honor their country and those who ran it. In return, bureaucratic greed, absence of integrity and an inhumane lack of concern for those who displayed lifelong loyalty to their country, destroyed him. I loved my father so much and I hurt for him. I loved our ranch too and knew those responsible for running government agencies could find a way to avoid ruining thousands of families if they wanted to. Their sickening focus on the almighty buck at the expense of human lives turned my pride in our country's leaders into disgust and loathing.

Losing the ranch was devastating. Daddy did his best to avoid the inevitable but when it happened, it was heartbreaking to hear his pitiful sobs and see the unbearable sadness in his eyes. That devastation reached far beyond fiscal accounting by government agencies; it not only ended a way of life, it ended lives literally, as many displaced farmers committed suicide out of depression and desperation. Many had no other vocation to turn to and couldn't face living in town. Others developed life threatening stress-related illnesses, or simply gave up on living entirely.

The cold-hearted bureaucrats didn't care that they were ripping the very heart out of human beings whose lives for generations had revolved around the soil. They were urban yuppies who only cared about the bottom line and making cuts that would gain them prestige in the eyes of their bureaucratic bosses along with a big promotion and raise. Human beings meant nothing to them.

Losing the ranch was my first experience with out-of-control federal agencies. That devastating experience formed a strong and lasting impression of an indifferent government driven by elitist greed that exhibited no remorse, accountability, or sense of right and wrong as a result of the human suffering caused by their decisions and actions. Government's total lack of humanity formed the basis for my intense dislike and distrust of the system and those who run it.

The Midwest and South were the only homes my parents knew. They were forced to leave a sheltered part of the nation where residents always looked out for each other. They were saying goodbye to friends they had known since they were toddlers. They were leaving family behind. Worst of all, they were driving away from a way of life that was safe and secure, toward an unfamiliar life filled with unknown challenges.

Driving down our lane for the last time left my father a broken man, but he was actually one of the lucky ones. He had a teaching credential to fall back on that would help him pull the unraveled strings of his life back together and be able to support his family.

Moving to Santa Barbara, California, proved to be culture shock that was swift and sure for all of us. After my insulated upbringing, it was like being dropped into the middle of a foreign world. It made our heads swim with confusion and overload.

Santa Barbara is a sea of modern Mediterranean-style shopping malls filled with an overwhelming amount of expensive choices in every category imaginable. It was a stark contrast to small-town Iowa, which offered only a short main street of individual buildings with a limited choice of bland basics.

Southern California is a world of expensive homes featured in architectural magazines, designer clothes, idyllic beaches, palm trees, and men and women in brief swim wear. In Iowa, we were used to modest farm houses that were often over 100 years old and in need of paint, corn as far as the eye could see, coveralls and work boots that came from the Sears catalog, and women dressed in a prudent modest manner. I felt like the proverbial country bumpkin.

I attended Santa Barbara City College and found out the parties they threw were a whole lot wilder than those we had in Iowa. It was my first exposure to drugs and random sex. One California party was enough for me. The heartland's idea of a great party consisted of barbecue and beer. All during high school, I never knew anyone who did drugs. It was never even discussed, let alone done. But by 1996, the Office on National Drug Control Policy listed Iowa as one of the nation's top eight states with a serious methamphetamine problem.

Some Californians were superficial with little character or soul. They obsessed over money; we had none. We were rich in family. In Iowa, our neighbors would help us rebuild our barn if it burned down without ever having to be asked. We never knew or spoke to our neighbors in California. We were really square, but we had solid values, so tangible you could almost hold them in the palm of your hand.

Daddy was offered a position teaching high school in central California where life more closely resembles the Midwest. But I was entranced with the coastal area and decided to stay and learn the secrets of the glitzy big city way of life.

During the 1960s, it seemed that government didn't intrude into every area of citizen's private lives. Big Brother hadn't yet decided America's population was too stupid to make their own decisions and needed a 'Political Parent' to regulate every area of their lives. Nor did they feel the need to preface each law or regulation with a threat to intimidate citizens into obeying.

During that time of blissful freedom, it was easy to get an apartment simply by finding the one I wanted and paying the first month's rent. There were no requirements for first, last, deposit and credit check. If you failed to pay your rent on the first of each month, you were simply without a place to live.

Jobs were also easy to find. I wanted to be a dental assistant so I typed up a resume and cover letter and mailed them to every dentist in Santa Barbara. Within a week I had several offers.

I was spreading my wings for the first time and loving it. I spent a lot of time on the beach, in beatnik coffee houses, or just breathing the exhilarating scent of being on my own. While still at the city college, I worked as a dental assistant for a couple of years before meeting and marrying a police officer.

Jim's blond good looks were reminiscent of John Schneider from the TV show *Dukes of Hazzard*. He had that fresh-scrubbed, innocent, lost little boy look with dazzling blue eyes that melted your heart. His wavy blonde hair framed a fair skinned face that made women want to put their arms around him and mother him. His tanned body didn't have an ounce of fat on it. He dressed immaculately.

At 5'10", he was one of the smallest officers on the department. But he made up for that with his confident, take-charge personality, which sent a strong message to potential enemies that he was well-equipped to defend himself. In uniform, that message was irresistible to women.

I met him on the beach in Santa Barbara on the Fourth of July. A struggling dental assistant, I had the day off and decided to relax by the water and get a tan. As I looked for enough sand space to spread out a towel in the sea of humanity that obviously had the same idea,

I finally spotted an opening. It was a warm day but the ocean breeze caressed my skin as I lay there listening to the sea gulls above.

"You'll be really burned at the end of the day if you don't put on some suntan lotion," he said.

I opened my eyes. The young man on the towel next to me smiled as he extended the lotion. We spent the whole day talking, and I offered to show him the fireworks that evening from a spot the locals knew about on the hill above the Mission. It was a wonderful evening that ignited more fireworks than the ones we watched that night.

He worked in a neighboring county so we soon began spending every weekend together. He was caring and considerate and the more time we spent together, the more we realized a special relationship was developing. It wasn't long before we were married.

But somewhere between our wedding and the birth of our first son, the training instilled in police officers to disassociate themselves from their surroundings in order to cope with the things they dealt with in the line of duty kicked in. Big time.

Gone was the tender person that put his arms around me and comforted me for insignificant little issues that seemed important to me at the time. He had become an unemotional and unresponsive person with little patience for the onslaught of intense psychological circumstances of pregnancy. I frequently left the house to sit dejectedly on the curb with my back against a telephone pole and my huge tummy under my chin and cried my eyes out. Alone.

Jim was a good father during the first few years he was involved in his children's lives, but he was too self-absorbed and emotionally distant to form the close bond that I have with them. More and more, we began to go our own directions.

A policeman's number is always unlisted, yet I would answer the phone and women I didn't know would be on the other end. They would hang up without leaving their names when told he wasn't there.

It was evident my marriage was in trouble, but I had small children, no career and no money. Like millions of other women trapped by such circumstances and in a relationship that was no longer happy or fulfilling, I felt I had no option but to make the best of the situation and find other things to fill the void.

An article in the paper about foster parents caught our attention. Jim was seeking something to help balance the daily suffering he was exposed to at work. I adore children. My children were too young for me to work outside the home, so taking newborns from the hospital as foster children until they were placed with adoptive families was a fun and natural step to take.

Those were wonderful and fulfilling years. The feeling of awe when those brand new, tiny little miracles were placed in my arms never dimmed. They were the embodiment of trust and innocence. They looked to me for their very survival. It was an awesome and humbling five years.

Even Jim allowed a tender side to peek through that cold stone wall of protection he had developed over the years. He would work a full shift and then come home and occasionally get up in the middle of the night to bottle feed an infant. There simply was no way to prevent falling in love with each and every miracle entrusted to our care. Both of us felt a lump in our throat each time we handed our most recent baby into the eager waiting arms of its adoptive parents.

Rebecca came to us at six weeks of age. The county told us she would be in long term care because she had neurofibromatosis, also known as NF, von Recklinghausen disease or Elephant Man's Disease. It is a rare condition in which tumors grow all over the body. Not only is it incurable, it is cruel and unpredictable because one never knows how the condition will manifest itself. That depends on where the tumors grow. Modern medical science has improved the quality and life expectation with modern marvels like MRI scans which allow doctors to chart tumor growth but because of the uncertainty of the progression and the incurable nature of neurofibromatosis, the county had been unable to find adoptive parents for her.

Her sunny nature and intense attachment to us made any future thought of parting with her unbearable. Foster parents were just beginning to be considered as adoptive parents for hard to place children. We were crazy about this special little girl. We wanted to adopt her but were afraid if we asked, she would be removed from our home because we had become too attached to her. With a lump in our throats, we approached the adoption agency with our request. To our immense relief, they were delighted. After the required adoption placement investigation, Becky became our lawful daughter and has grown into a loving, delightful young woman who loves and lives life to the fullest and is intensely independent despite her disabilities.

Several months after adopting Becky, a conglomerate of doctors were looking for a family to live in the rambling ranch house on top of a mountain on the thousand acre citrus ranch they owned in rural Ventura County. We jumped at the chance and the owners were thrilled to have a law enforcement family to maintain security on their property. It was an incredibly breathtaking location and peaceful lifestyle.

It was also one of the best times of my 12-year marriage. I grew up in the country and that lifestyle always calms and soothes me. Jim enjoyed it too so it suited us both.

Living in a remote area prevented my small children from having playmates so I opened a licensed day care center that catered to the families of doctors and lawyers who lived around the golf course just down the road. I had also hoped the added income would discourage Jim from working a second job in security during his off-duty time. He tired of finding his home filled with noisy, active children and decided to take the extra job and began spending more and more time away from home.

The biggest tip-off that my marriage was all but over came one day when a drug deal went bad and two suspects took a victim into our isolated orchard to kill him. An eyewitness driving along the road saw the victim herded into the orchard at gunpoint and called authorities. Police units, tracking dogs and a helicopter arrived. One suspect was caught but the other remained at large in the thousand acres of citrus in which we lived.

Jim was scheduled to go on duty at 3:00 p.m., so he removed the distributor cap from my vehicle so the suspect couldn't steal my car, gave me a rifle to defend myself and our children in case the suspect came up to the house, and left for work. I never found out what transpired at the station when he arrived but a police unit showed up at my door within minutes of Jim reporting to work with instructions to stay with us until Jim could return home to protect his family. Eventually the suspect was apprehended but the experience left me with a permanent feeling of being abandoned and unloved.

Not long after that trauma, a major brushfire burned within yards of the ranch house and convinced us to move into a rural, but less remote, area of Lake Sherwood in Ventura County. We built a home down the road from Dean Martin, Clark Gable's widow, Kay, and Eve Arden. I loved taking my children for horseback rides along the country roads past their grand estates when the air was crisp and we could see the ranch hands bailing hay in the fields.

Unfortunately, the move did nothing to improve our marriage. Within six months, Jim became involved in a long term affair with a married woman he worked with in his off-duty security time.

Neither of us were bad people who set out to make each other miserable. As happens with millions of other couples, we were simply poorly matched. Our personalities were total opposites. Jim was void of emotion; I was warm and demonstrative. He was an introvert; I was out-going. He thought with his head; I felt with my heart. He avoided dealing with personal problems; I dealt with them head-on. He kept his thoughts to himself; I was outspoken. He conformed; I rebelled. He was urban; I was country. He was yuppie; I was down-to-earth.

We were very young when we married. Our personalities, outlooks, likes and dislikes, and approach to life were very different and became even more apparent as time went by. As we got older our differences took us in separate directions. The sad reality was, we became strangers and simply had nothing in common any longer. The only thing holding us together was our children. It was inevitable that the relationship would end.

My husband's many affairs certainly contributed to, but were not the catalyst for, the final chapter of our marriage. The end came not only with another woman but with a motorcycle as well.

From the time I was a child, I had always been a rebel. I had a high energy level and a low tolerance for boredom. I found those who conformed in society uninteresting and saw them as invisible in a faceless crowd. My inborn, headstrong nature made me determined to be different so it doesn't surprise me that many years later I chose to work in professions that raised eyebrows.

It came as no shock, therefore, that I began riding motorcycles in the 1970s when it wasn't fashionable for women to be so blatantly brazen. Eventually I used them in stunt work. Motorcycles and stunt work at that time were almost exclusively male territory. It was a new avenue for females, and they were resented and barely tolerated by male colleagues. Nevertheless, times were changing and women were beginning to gain baby steps of acceptability in roles normally assigned to men.

Mr. Macho had worked many different divisions within the sheriff's department but motorcycle patrol wasn't one of them. He didn't want his wife outdoing him so he put his foot down: the bike or him. Shouldn't give a redhead an ultimatum!

I helped my husband pack and then went out and bought a new Kawasaki 1000 LTD street bike. I loved that bike and rode it to the Hollywood studio I worked in each day. Women rode as passengers at that time; not as the driver! I enjoyed the stares I got on the freeway. But then, I was *always* unconventional.

Lights, Camera, Action!

The guards at the studio's main gate were used to seeing me pull up on my bike and no longer ribbed me. They knew I could handle a motorcycle as well as any man.

On any given weekday, the studio had an average of 3,000 employees on the main lot, but there were only around 300 parking spaces. Only a chosen few were lucky enough not to have to park outside the studio in a lot several blocks away and walk. I was upper management and, therefore, had my own assigned parking space on the lot.

Parking spaces were anywhere they could fit them but most were along the sides of the huge buildings in which the film sets were located. Names were prominently posted so no one would infringe on an assigned spot. When that happened, security removed them.

My space was beside the entrance of the *Hart to Hart* set, not far from the west entrance gate. I had the luxury of sleeping an extra 10 minutes in the morning because when the guards saw my bike make the turn into the studio entrance, they simply raised the security arm and I whizzed through and into my space without delay.

Just around the corner was Stephanie Powers' Jeep, parked on the sidewalk just before the dressing rooms. She was beautiful, feminine, a star, and, in my view, one of the few "real" people in Hollywood.

I spent nearly all of the 1980s working at the studio. It was a sad time of transition and major change in philosophy within the film industry that took the history of great art and classic film legends into an age of baby boomer greed. Mediocre actors were made to look larger than life by increasingly more spectacular special effects. In addition, they were hyped by public relations and research specialists whose job it was to promote a product that did little more than part the movie-going public from their money.

For decades, the major studios had been run by executives from the creative sector of the film community. They were people who were firmly rooted within the industry, occasionally having worked their way up the ladder by spending a great deal of time in various film departments. This gave them a good understanding of the whole picture as opposed to simply waltzing into the executive offices and trying to run the business.

It was also an education in managing temperamental personalities, unique to the industry, that gave this brand of executive an advantage in knowing how to extract the best the eclectic blend of talent had to give, both in front of and behind the camera.

The studio was a fascinating study in human nature. I greatly admired the top brass who possessed the understanding and ability to coax and encourage each unique artistic contribution from those who helped make film the remarkable art it has always been.

But times in the industry were changing during the 80s, and not for the better. Knowledgeable executives who concentrated on creative results were being replaced by bottom-line oriented bookkeepers and lawyers. Often this new breed of executive had little or no experience with the creative product. Morale toppled within the ranks; movies lost their glamour and class. Film became a battle of the spectacular to see whose special effects department could outdo the other and create bigger and better returns at the box office. The emphasis is no longer on heroes or role models; the only hero in Hollywood now is the dollar bill. That part of the experience left a bad taste in my mouth. The feeling was reinforced many years later when I encountered the same behavior from within the political process. What I saw in both professions made me determined I would somehow work in the future to put people first.

Once in a while, legends such as Bette Davis and Elizabeth Taylor gifted the studio with guest appearances, reminding everyone of film's past glory days, its romance, charm, and elegance. When that happened, the air was filled with reverence and awe. You just knew and felt something very special and out of the ordinary was happening on the set.

A normal shoot involves around 150 behind-the-scenes crew members to move scenery, oversee lighting, operate cameras, apply make-up, adjust costumes, make on-set script revisions, and dozens of other behind-the-scenes functions that keep cameras rolling. It's a madhouse of activity and the sound level is deafening. Usually the commotion continues right up until the director yells, "Quiet on the set!"

Bette Davis originated the starring role on *Hotel*, whose sound stage was kitty-corner from my office. The complete hush as she entered the room left no doubt that a legendary queen of Hollywood's heyday had arrived. Even the most unrefined crew member was silent and removed his hat in tribute and respect. Watching a much-loved icon of film apply her craft, briefly treated those present to art at its professional best. Although she taped the pilot, by the time shooting started on the series, her health had greatly deteriorated and she ultimately had to relinquish her role.

Hotel seemed to host more than its share of legendary guest stars. Elizabeth Taylor was scheduled to tape an episode. She arrived in true star tradition but was no prima donna. With a dazzling smile and a wave of her arm, Miss Taylor said, "Good morning, everyone," and the set started humming with normal activity.

She was a tiny little thing. She was a larger-than-life legend so I expected her to be much taller than she was. Although she is one of the few remaining legendary greats, the remarkable thing about this woman is her dedication to humanity. Instead of being full of herself, she thought of others. A crew member showed me a special key ring she presented to each member of the crew as a remembrance of her visit, which was a most unusual gesture for a star. She is well-known for her fight against AIDS and has earned respect and love, not only for her immense talent, but for her contribution as a community activist as well.

While I was there, the studio housed three separate companies who all worked independently, yet together. The west portion of the lot housed Warner Brothers and some independent production offices such as Clint Eastwood's Malpaso Productions. The grand old Warner Building that housed the offices of Jack Warner during Hollywood's heyday is located on the north edge of the lot. Just outside the studio walls and across Olive Avenue is the studio's "glass building," where most of Warner Brothers business offices were located.

Columbia Pictures had most of their facilities on the east side near the back lot outdoor film sets. Towards the end of the decade, Columbia moved to their own separate lot.

The studio was called The Burbank Studios, or TBS, during this time which was also the name of the third company on the lot. TBS was the main liaison between Warner Brothers and Columbia Pictures. Its primary responsibility was to see the entire studio ran smoothly.

Film production companies like Warner Brothers and Columbia Pictures deal with "above-the-line" unions, which are composed of mainly talent, producers, writers and directors. TBS was responsible for "below-the-line" unions, which include people working with cameras, lighting, set construction, special effects, costumes, make-up, grips, electrical, set painting, transportation, post-production and many more.

Originally I had hoped to do motorcycle stunts as a full-time living, but in the film industry they say you should "keep your day job." As it turned out, that was sound advice, as stunt work wasn't frequent enough to pay all the bills.

So at TBS, I worked for the vice president of labor relations. It was our office's responsibility to coordinate the collective bargaining agreements each of the unions had with the major studios and isolate and resolve any problems that occurred. Each contract had meticulous and very explicit boundaries that could not be crossed by another union. Violations often resulted in situations that ground filming to a halt, causing expensive grievances that often had to be arbitrated. With nearly 40 separate unions to deal with, it required a lot of attention.

TBS worked hand-in-hand with Jay Ballance of Warner Brothers labor relations and Tony Vaughn of Columbia labor relations even though each company's organization was separate and distinct. It is a very stressful and cutthroat business which helped instill the personal strength I later needed to run for public office.

Vince Soukup was vice president when I was hired. He was a wonderful man who didn't subscribe to the prevalent "men only" attitude. He patiently taught me everything I needed to know to run the entire department if necessary. I found it hard to believe it was my job to work on a daily basis with famous personalities and actually get paid to do it.

Some sets were friendlier than others. I often took an early lunch so I could spend time on the *Fantasy Island* set when they were filming on the main lot. They had an exterior set about a half mile from the studio on the Columbia Ranch which housed "de plane" but most filming was done on a stage near the commissary. Cast and crew were close knit and it was one of the most relaxed sets on the lot.

Tanya Tucker, the wild girl of country music, was a guest star for one episode. I was rarely in awe of actors, but country music artists were a different matter. I admired the way Tanya lived her life on her own terms, despite living in a fishbowl with the inevitable criticism it drew. I wanted to watch how she interacted with cast and crew so I slipped in and sat down to watch.

She was having a great time and really seemed to enjoy her role. Normally, when shooting stops, talent doesn't mingle with the crew; they go outside to their dressing room trailers. Not Tanya. She turned to a crew member and asked where his cards were. He grinned and pulled them out while other crew members gathered. Then Tanya and the crew sat down on the floor to play a little poker. Watching that scene made me realize why I love country folks so much.

One of the funniest experiences happened during the filming of *Ghostbusters*. The set was huge, so it was filmed on Stage 13, the largest sound stage in the nation. Originally, the stage was built for Esther Williams by Howard Hughes for her famous aquatic roles. The gigantic floor is removable, designed to become a swimming pool, lake or ocean as needed.

Stage 13 was just around the corner from my office and a myriad of problems on the set kept me busy going back and forth. It was the problem off the set that nearly caused panic, however.

Sound stages are insulated against outside noise but car engines often penetrate the protective cushioning and cause unwanted noise on film, so studio personnel get around the huge lot by foot or on bicycle.

Ghostbusters was filming during the winter, very close to the holidays. Shortly after lunch break, cast and crew returned to Stage 13 but Dan Ackroyd was missing. He had been riding a bike on the way back to the set, right behind Bill Murray, but only Murray arrived. They looked everywhere for Ackroyd with no luck.

Security was called in and began an extensive search of the lot. After 45 minutes, sheer panic set in. A major star had disappeared into thin air. Security was nearly ready to call in the Burbank police.

Suddenly, there was a commotion in front of the fire department across the street from my office. Security emerged with a group of festive firemen ... and Dan Ackroyd. Not another word was said about Ackroyd's disappearance but a fireman later told me Ackroyd heard music as he rode past the fire station and went in to see what was going on. A belly dancer entertaining the firemen during a holiday party sidetracked Ackroyd and he simply "forgot" to return to the set.

It was a extraordinary time of doing a job I loved, working with people I liked, and being exposed to a world others only watch on screen. Much of the satisfaction I enjoyed in my job was due to Vince's exceptional nature. He treated me with great respect and kindness. Eventually, however, Vince left to run a prestigious industry related organization and I was left to run the department alone until a new vice president could be found.

Even though I proved myself capable of running the department during the brief vacancy, I lacked a college degree and was excluded from consideration for the position of vice president. Privately, I also felt gender worked against me but that type of opinion is always next to impossible to substantiate. I resigned myself to the fact I would be training a new vice president and felt content and blessed to be working in a job I loved that supported my children well.

A couple of months later, Hank was hired to replace Vince. He was in his late 30s or early 40s, pleasant looking, trendy dresser, the right credentials, quiet, detached, intellectual and was the epitome of the successful baby boomer. His wife was a professional, they had a terrific house, politically correct vehicles, a baby on the way, and friends in high places.

We couldn't have been more different. Hank attended Shakespearean festivals; I went to George Jones concerts. Hank enjoyed philosophical discussions with highbrow colleagues; I preferred the company of crew members and their behind-the-scenes revelations. Hank drove a Lincoln Town Car; I drove a truck and a motorcycle. Fine dining in a chic restaurant suited Hank; I love down-home barbecue. I prefer historical or biographical reading; Hank liked the classics.

Little things got on each of our nerves and Hank's actions, body language, and attitude toward me always made me feel just not quite good enough. He hated the Elvis picture in my office and I had little patience for his aversion to germs. We did our best to keep the atmosphere cordial, polite and professional. We inherited each other without the luxury of interviewing or choosing, so we tried to create the best working relationship possible under the circumstances. In spite of our differences, we developed a professional style that worked for us both, but it seemed to me that females in business always had to be the ones to make concessions.

Over the years, the atmosphere never really improved and we were never able to develop a comfort level between us. An unspoken strain always hung in the air. We were both unhappy. I could see the writing on the wall: one of us would eventually have to leave, and it would be me.

Aside from the stress in the office, filming involved long days. It wasn't uncommon to go to work in the dark and return home in the dark. Consequently, there was little time for a social life. So the studio became both a means of support and a social gathering place. Time spent on the film sets over the years put me on a first name basis with both cast and crew of most sets.

As a tomboy, I could relate well to the crews. While differences in class station were recognized, no one considered themselves better than anyone else, so I was never awestruck by famous talent. Most actors were fascinated that a tiny redheaded female could put a several hundred pound motorcycle through its paces and rarely come out with broken bones. Directors gnashed their teeth when one of their actors jumped on the back of my bike for a "spin around the block." I was just one of the guys. Well, not always!

Actors collected women the way I collected splints for the toes I was always breaking. I could usually fend off their passes with humor. The studio was like a candy store of good looking men, however, and sometimes I did indulge my sweet tooth. Thirteen years is a long time to be single! Every so often, a girl's gotta do what a girl's gotta do.

I raised my children alone those 13 years. They would often accompany me to work so we could spend time together. As the years went by and they grew into young adulthood they began to work there themselves. Steven was a crew member on *Blue Thunder*, *Dukes of Hazzard* and *T.J. Hooker*. Reed had a bit part on an episode of *Alice* and became interested in a career in camera work.

Both my boys shared with me the enormous feeling of loss the day when the set John Wayne shot portions of his final film, *The Shootist*, burned to the ground. Wayne was a much loved Hollywood hero, so *The Shootist* set was a revered spot on the lot. I reacted with disbelief to the phone call telling me the set had burned to the ground. I couldn't stand to watch it on the six o'clock news, and it took me nearly a week to gather the courage to go over to the set.

By that time, investigators determined it was arson. Not only did it destroy an irreplaceable part of film history, it nearly spread to a huge storeroom nearby that contained costumes used in decades of famous films.

Eventually, investigators determined the culprit responsible was a construction employee who was about to be laid off and apparently decided to "create" more work by burning down the set so another would have to be built.

Fortunately, the fire was extinguished before it could harm the neighboring outdoor set of *The Dukes of Hazzard*. Both my sons and I spent a great deal of time working on the "Dukes" set and were glad when it became the scene of a happier event.

Tawny Little was a television reporter who interviewed John Schneider regarding his role on "Dukes." That interview led to a budding romance which culminated in a breathtaking wedding in the gazebo that dominated the center of the *The Dukes of Hazzard* exterior set. It was a happy event that helped ease the black cloud that continued to hang over the John Wayne set nearby.

Working in a man's world at the studio contributed significantly to the steel in my backbone and the extra layer of skin I developed. If I had been the fragile little female, I would have been chewed up and spit out. I learned to be tough but I did it with humor and fairness and remained very much a female in the process. It was an unpopular and stressful job and as a woman, I had to work twice as hard for half the credit. It not only taught me strength in the workplace, it also whetted my appetite to fight for equality for women in all work situations. My sense of fairness was assaulted nearly on a daily basis at the studio. That came to a head years later in the bordellos.

A year before I left the studio, I was diagnosed with cancer. It was, of course, a frightening experience but I didn't allow myself to dwell on it. I didn't have time to. I was a single mother. I spent my medical leave building up my strength and spending time with my children, but it went by quickly.

Soon I returned to a 40-minute commute to the studio each way, long work days and sandwiching in all the domestic responsibilities at home. My children knew I would be all right but the experience made us all realize and appreciate how fragile life can be.

The surgery and treatments left me with less energy to deal with working full-time under stressful conditions while raising children alone. After a few short weeks back at work, I could feel the strain beginning to take its toll. It was time to make some lifestyle changes.

Not long after, the Writer's Guild went on a lengthy strike. That was the incentive I needed to make a change. I had enjoyed working full-time in management, learning motorcycle stunts from the best in the industry, meeting and working with celebrities as well as those who work behind the scenes, exposing my children to people and experiences others could only dream about and for a job that taught me strength and helped me develop into a strong person that could deal with whatever the future held. Despite that, it was time to make changes in my life that would provide as much tranquility as possible for me and my children.

I spent the months during the writers' strike selling my house in preparation for moving out of California. My boys were now grown and only Rebecca still lived at home. I had worked hard raising my children and they had become remarkable young people. I did my job well and it was time to reward myself with something fun and frivolous. In my usual unconventional style, I planned to take my RV and follow the rodeo circuit for a year.

Little did I know that in only a few short months I would marry Michael, the neighbor I had become friends with, and be working in a Nevada legal bordello instead.

Where Evil Lives

Storey County, Nevada, is a remote and sparsely populated area in the northwestern part of the state, with roughly 3,000 inhabitants. Virginia City, the county's seat and only town of any size, is located between the Storey County brothels to the north and Lyon County bordellos to the south. It was a convenient location to live during my years as a working girl. The houses in which I worked — Mustang Ranch, Old Bridge Ranch and Moonlight Bunnyranch — were all within a short driving distance from home. But while the proximity to work was an advantage, Michael and I became increasingly disillusioned with the town as time wore on.

The deception of Virginia City is that its past has been romanticized to the point that newcomers believe its remote location and Old West charm will offer relief from their former locale. They move to town enamored but leave cynical.

I thought that legacy would be different for me but I was wrong. Michael and I completely fell in love with this hideout on the mountain. We felt we had truly found a place where we fit. We set about getting to know our neighbors and becoming involved in the rhythm of local life. It didn't take long before we discovered it was a town with a false face and unkind nature.

Virginia City is a town time forgot and whose future isn't likely to change. Caught in a limbo between two very different time periods, it's normal to see wannabe gunslingers roam Main Street alongside well-dressed businessmen carrying attaché cases. A long time resident's Model T Ford can be seen parked alongside a brand-new Lexus. Women with bustles and parasols assist shoppers attired in shorts and tennis shoes. If a person suffered from amnesia and was dropped off in the midst of town, they wouldn't have a clue regarding the time period.

The cold wind always blows. It was the one thing I really hated and it eventually came to symbolize the hearts of most residents to me. Nearly at the top of the mountain, the town is nestled into the side of Mt. Davidson. In the winter, the wind whips over the top of the mountain from Lake Tahoe and its cold fingers grab everything in sight. During the summer, it stirs up the cottonwood causing noses to run all over town.

The town's past is rich and colorful. As many know, gold and silver were discovered here in the mid-1800s – the fabled Comstock Lode. When word got out that it was one of the richest discoveries in the territory, professional miners and novices alike seeking their fortune converged on the area like locusts. Tents and shacks dotted the steep hillside and silver barons began constructing mansions.

Saloons popped up every few feet to give the miners respite from their backbreaking labor and help separate them from the good wages they made. After a few hours of drinking and carousing with their co-workers, many miners would gamble their earnings on faro, a card game that was far and away the most popular game of chance of the time. Many entertained visions of immediate wealth and gambled thousands, sometimes their entire savings. If they won, they reasoned, they would be able to build a fine house and send for their family. If they lost, a few despondent men solved their problem with a bullet or started a fight that terminated in a shootout. Life was hard and wild in the isolated terrain of this booming mineral town and miners longed for a gentle escape.

Before long, "soiled doves" began arriving by the dozens. Women were expected to marry and stay at home in the 19th Century. Those who worked were not respected. Poverty wages and limited employment opportunities for women made prostitution a practical choice. It provided good pay, food, shelter, a safe environment and the friendship of the other ladies, all of which helped ease the isolation and rejection experienced at the hands of "proper" society.

In the early days of these mining camps, when prostitutes were the only women present, they were treated as respected members of the community. The comfort they provided in the primitive camps sustained the men who were establishing communities. Seldom are they given credit in history books for their contribution in settling the West.

As was the case in most Western boomtowns, there were no "proper" women in the early camps. They would not arrive for some time, not until the men "civilized" the town and were able to provide a suitable existence for them.

In the meantime, the work associated with mining was dangerous and exhausting. Many died from cave-ins, illness or gunfights. The men longed for the softness of a woman's touch and the lilt of a sweet voice. The brothels became a social center where guests enjoyed live piano entertainment prior to sitting down to a formal dinner with an elegantly dressed female companion. Undoubtedly this was the only incentive for the men to bathe and dress up.

Before long, the town's population grew to 40,000. It was a bustling metropolis, the largest city in Nevada. Its riches helped the Union Army win the Civil War and contributed to the establishment of San Francisco 250 miles to the southwest. Seven hundred miles of tunnels crisscross underneath Virginia City. They are reinforced by thousands of logs that created a patchwork of lumber deep inside the ground. The noon whistle that signaled a shift change in the heyday of this bustling city of commerce still blows today, reminding residents and tourists that history still lives.

The town was founded on greed and violence. Silver and gold often bring out the worst in men and spawn an obsession for instant wealth which annihilates regard for other human beings. The working class spent their days underground making heartless elitists even richer. Men lived and died by the brutal code of the West. Unable to rest in peace, the souls of men crushed underground or killed in a hail of gunfire seemed not to know they were dead. Tormented spirits appeared to rise up to roam restlessly among the living. Tales of ghost sightings are common in several establishments.

A sinister cloud from days past seems to hang over the present-day community. The troubled residents continue to embrace a callousness toward their neighbors. Something evil happens to a place where men care only for themselves with no regard for another.

After 30 years, the mines began to play out and most residents moved to a more hospitable climate. In a scene repeated in the mining boomtowns of virtually every western state, shortly after the 20th

Century began a cloud of quiet enveloped Virginia City as only the most hardy remained. The largest city in Nevada became a virtual ghost town.

Modern times find the town to be so tiny that mail isn't even delivered door-to-door. Folks pick their correspondence up at their postal boxes in the small post office on Main Street. Mail is in the boxes by 11 a.m. and the post office becomes a lunchtime social gathering spot. Everyone catches up on gossip while they retrieve the contents of their boxes.

I love the drive up the mountain from Carson City. Cresting the hill into town, a magnificent view awaits. At dawn or dusk, the huge pillows of clouds softly intertwine with the blue and pink hues of the sky causing the mountains to proudly display the purple tint that was so movingly written about in the song that symbolizes the pride we feel in our country . . . "America the Beautiful."

The center of town looks like the wild west hamlet it portrayed in the *Bonanza* TV series. Main Street is narrow with limited parking. Rails along the sidewalks still remain, where a cowhand can tie his horse reins while he grabs a cool beverage.

The smell of candy fills the air as the steam escapes out the exhaust pipe of the fudge shop. An antique photo gallery, complete with Western costumes, beckons tourists to take a memory home.

A toot of the old V&C Railroad whistle reminds folks they can still take a short trip through history on their ride down the mountain to Gold Hill. Cinders often leave permanent reminders in the clothing of tourists that people have not always traveled by car.

The narrow and winding road down the other side of the mountain offers a spectacular view of Lake Tahoe and its beautiful snow-capped mountains and ski slopes. The entire mountain is a secret wonderland of surprises.

Nighttime is so peaceful that the only sounds heard are the wind, coyotes or the wild horses being herded out of town before residents wake up. Wild horses roam freely all over the mountain. In the winter, they migrate down the mountain to the lower levels where it is warmer and food is more plentiful. During the summer, they graze near the top of the mountain and come into town at night to munch on resident's lawns. The sheriff coaxes them onto Main Street about five in the morning and taps his siren to get them moving. The sound of hoofs clomping along the road down by the cemetery where they run off into the hills, is always music to my ears. Watching those magnificent animals run off to the freedom of their own world ignites a passion for protecting human rights as well.

Michael and I are history buffs who know how historical accounts often twist facts to present a slanted view. History reversed relations between settlers and Native Americans to portray Indians as savage and soldiers as protective heroes when in fact it was more often than not the Indian tribes who wanted to continue living in peace but were constantly hunted down and persecuted by self-serving whites. Indians trusted the white man's word, only to be deceived time and time again. Their culture, freedom, and very lives were tragically ruined by the white man's lies, greed, and total lack of honor. We discovered these same dishonorable traits among Virginia City residents in alarming abundance.

Evil takes root where greed prevails. Man seems destined to never learn from history. Like many before us, we arrived full of respect for the history that built the town and departed sadly realizing the present had not learned from the past.

Since the inception of the infamous Mustang Ranch brothel, its notorious owner, Joe Conforte, was the undisputed king of Storey County. For nearly 40 years, the tiny county has been a Mecca of corruption. "Joe's Boys" included the sheriff, district attorney, county commissioners, and anyone else he deemed necessary for a profitable business arrangement. Crooked officials were considered respectable citizens in Virginia City. Giving away turkeys to the poor at Thanksgiving and paying medical bills for a few Virginia City residents made him the Pied Piper of the county. Whatever Joe wanted, Joe got.

Conforte hated being called a pimp but he was often saddled with that label in newspaper articles. In fact, in 1972, *Rolling Stone* magazine featured Conforte on its cover with the caption, "The Crusading Pimp." He was the main brothel owner to line George Flint's pockets as representative for the brothel association. As that representative, by virtue of his lobbyist paycheck which is derived from brothel owners who obtain their money from prostitutes, it would appear to indirectly place Flint within the same category as well.

Conforte is in exile, Mustang has been shut down, and those connected most closely to Joe's operation are facing prison. While some of his operatives still remain in influential positions, others in Virginia City decided it is time to "clean up" the town's shady reputation.

Not long after Mustang was seized in August 1999, the Storey County Boys decided to revise the county's short brothel ordinance to more closely resemble Nye County's 52-page law, which in turn is patterned after the gambling ordinance. That told me the law would focus only on owners and not address safety, legal, and constitutional issues of the ladies. Flint made sure he was right in the middle of it.

In an article in the Virginia City *Comstock Chronicle* of May 5, 2000, Flint states he "represents Conforte family interests." As a long time representative and lobbyist for brothel owners, the old adage, "You can't play in the mud without getting some of it on you," came to mind when I thought of him.

When he represented Conforte, Flint often spoke out against Conforte's nephew, David Burgess, who owns the competing Old Bridge Ranch just yards from the two Mustang houses. Old Bridge Ranch is now the only brothel open in Storey County and it is for sale.

Storey County commissioners have a hostile past history with Burgess so Flint tried to convince the brothel owner he needed help with the commissioners who would be examining possible new owners for his ranch. Flint undoubtedly saw an additional opportunity to solicit another paycheck in the process. Given the bad blood between rivals Conforte and Burgess, many suspect Flint is still paid by Conforte in an effort to manipulate the county commission into granting Flint's choice for a new owner of Old Bridge Ranch, which without a doubt would be Conforte, well hidden within corporation papers.

With the close of Mustang, it seems Flint is willing to represent any one in the brothel industry who will provide a lucrative paycheck, which makes one wonder who the true prostitutes are.

Flint intended to be the only "authority" listened to by the commissioners on both the issue of potential new brothel ownership and brothel ordinance revision. He was furious when I showed up to tell commissioners how various owners affected the lives of women working in their houses and how those issues had never been addressed in any brothel ordinance. The women live and work in the houses and learn first hand what an outside lobbyist could never know. There are legal and safety violations that directly affect the women. Brothel management doesn't want these issues revealed but the boys have gotten away with them for much too long. I defined for commissioners which potential owners would run their business in a professional manner and which ones had the potential for creating problems for the women, the industry, and Storey County.

I recommended commissioners go to the library and get a copy of *The Nye County Brothel War: A Tale of the New West* by Jeanie Kasindorf. It is a tragic and accurate account of brothel events and corrupt politics in Nye County that mirrors Storey County. Nye County learned little from their disastrous past and took no steps to prevent tragic errors in the future. Brothel and political life goes on as usual. The long ordinance Storey County wants to copy does not address specific safety and freedom issues that would protect the ladies. Reading Kasindorf's book would give Storey County's inane commission and the banker/wannabe sheriff time to learn.

Flint went ballistic. A pompous, squat, aging man with a limp and a mouth of acid, he screamed and stuck a finger in my face in an attempt to intimidate me into silence. When that didn't work, he disrespected my views and intentions and tried to discredit my credentials. Neither the commissioners nor the sheriff made any attempt to halt his disturbing verbal abuse but everyone in the room got a bird's eye view of how male bullies in the business too often treat the prostitutes.

A favorite control tactic of these tyrants is to bully, intimidate, threaten and degrade the women. Commissioners, as well as the attending public, got to see first hand with Flint's explosive outburst a classic example of how women in the business are often treated, and demonstrated why I felt so passionately about protecting the girls against such abuse. Flint's sorry example unfortunately failed to register with the male commissioners or sheriff, as he prevailed and I was shut out.

Flint publicly stated he favored locking the girls into houses for the duration of their shifts, whether it was a few days or a few weeks.

He said it was to keep the girls from leaving and then working out-side the house. I knew he was afraid owners might miss out on a dime. The women are not inmates, slaves or imbeciles. They are pro-fessional independent contractors. Holding them against their will is not only illegal, it's unconstitutional. I fear for the girls because they have no one to turn to for help and the "boys" always get everything they want.

Commissioners decided they would appoint a panel at the meet-ing the following month to work on a revision. They indicated both Flint and I would be considered, along with others.

Immediately following the meeting, I stayed to talk to a reporter. We found it odd to see Flint and Commissioner Greg Hess huddled in a back pew of the hearing room engrossed in an intense private conversation.

Hess was evidently influenced enough by Flint to announce at the following meeting that the rules had changed and Flint would be the main authority for revising the ordinance. I would not be included.

I have been a brothel working girl, have political experience, and have long been an advocate for brothel worker issues. Denying that kind of input fairly screamed of special interest influence at the commission level, just like the good old days.

If they had nothing to hide, the commissioners had a perfect opportunity to send out a message of honesty that would confirm the county's sincere effort toward dispelling corruption in Storey County by simply by encouraging both Flint and me to serve togeth-er on the panel in an effort to ensure both owner and worker issues were addressed in the revision. Instead, they failed miserably to demonstrate above board conduct and their actions only served to perpetrate the county's age-old shady message. With typical Storey County logic, commissioners also favored input from a local gay businessman to help make decisions for brothel operations.

Hess stated he felt "some people" wanted to be on the panel for publicity so he took it upon himself to decide Flint would be the main person to work on the revision. I realized I was dealing with a kan-garoo commission that was simply incapable of understanding that a person could unselfishly care about, and want to protect, another human being.

I put on my coat and stormed out, slamming the door to the hearing room so hard it was still vibrating by the time I reached the bottom of the stairs. Corruption and total disregard for others still appeared to be priorities in Storey County. Tragically, my sisters will be the ones to suffer.

In the end, the commission approved the brothel ordinance in July, 2000, minus deliberation regarding prostitute issues and with no attempt to repair any of the problems brought to their attention by Old Bridge Ranch owner David Burgess or his attorney. It certainly appeared the commission was more concerned with having it their way than with fairness and integrity.

After 10 years, it was time to close the door on conduct that would never change, so Michael and I moved down the hill to Carson City. Years of constant emotional battering and disrespect from my community have taken a toll on my health and soured our outlook on human nature. The town time forgot is one we hope we will. Our efforts will be put to better use in another community.

Mustang and
Old Bridge Ranch

There were three houses on the Mustang Ranch property: Mustang I, Mustang II and Old Bridge Ranch. Several miles east of Reno the "Mustang Exit" sign on Interstate 80 points the way to the secluded Ranch. A winding dirt road leads to the river that divides Washoe and Storey Counties. The bordellos are located on the Storey County side where they are legal, literally feet from the river.

Nevada brothels have a history running back almost 50 years. Joe Conforte first came to Nevada to begin building his bordello empire in 1955. That year, he opened an illegal operation called Triangle River Ranch near the small rural town of Wadsworth. The brothel consisted of moveable trailers on a site where Washoe, Lyon and Storey Counties meet. When the law went after Conforte in one county, he simply moved the trailers into one of the other counties and out of their jurisdiction. He spent freely to avoid doing that often, making sure police and local politicians were abundantly supplied with cigars wrapped in currency.

Bill Raggio was district attorney in Washoe County at that time and a particular thorn in Conforte's side, arresting him repeatedly for vagrancy whenever Conforte showed up in Reno with his ladies. Conforte vowed revenge and hatched a scheme to set up the DA. An underage woman who looked older was sent to Raggio's private practice on the pretense of obtaining a divorce. She was to lure Raggio into a compromising position, which would provide Conforte with the leverage he needed to have his pending criminal charge dismissed. But the plan backfired when Raggio asked a friend to accompany him to the woman's room. In a 1986 interview, Raggio revealed

Conforte threatened him over the alleged incident. Raggio subsequently filed extortion charges resulting in a jail sentence for Conforte and perjury charges against the woman.

In 1960, the Storey County Commission declared the Triangle River Ranch a public nuisance. Raggio appeared to allow retribution for a personal vendetta to cloud his ability to be fair and impartial when he joined other officials in a pompous display of male blustering to pose for pictures as the ranch burned. Stating, "You have to understand Conforte has flaunted the law," it took on the ominous look of a witch hunt. A powerful northern Nevada figure to this day, Raggio was elected to the Nevada Legislature in 1972 and currently serves as majority leader in the state senate.

After serving 22 months for his extortion conviction, Conforte pled guilty to tax evasion charges and spent another two years in federal prison, finally released in December 1965. Two years later, Conforte and his wife Sally opened the Mustang Ranch just across the river in Storey County, where it would remain for the next 32 years.

A district judge ordered the illegal houses shut down and directed Conforte to repay Storey County for law enforcement patrol costs incurred while making sure the houses remained closed. But Conforte was a crafty and cunning individual, and continued to pay the county even after his debt was cleared. He also continued running his business. The county wanted to continue collecting money from Conforte without having to answer tough questions, so in a classic example of the "if-you-can't-beat-'em-join-'em" mentality, the county commission passed the first brothel licensing ordinance in the United States, in 1971, effectively legalizing the Mustang Ranch. Lyon County followed suit the next year. By 1980, five other rural Nevada counties had passed similar ordinances. Three of those counties (Churchill, Mineral and Nye) even secured voter approval to do so.

Plans to put a legal brothel in Las Vegas in the early 70s almost came to fruition as well, but Clark County officials, fearing Conforte's influence and negative repercussions to their all-important gambling interests, nixed it by pushing a bill through the Nevada Legislature that can only be described as bizarre. By state law, no county with a population of more than 200,000 can have legal prostitution. That allows the small rural counties to keep their bordello ordinances on the books if they wish, but also ensures that the large counties of Clark and Washoe (which together account for well over 80 percent of the state's population) don't have to be put in the politically embarrassing situation of insulting the powers that be.

Conforte drew the ire of powerful people with his arrogant flamboyance and flagrant in-your-face attitude towards the law. After the US Supreme Court refused an appeal of another tax evasion conviction in 1980, Conforte fled the country, but returned three years later upon agreeing to testify in a related case. Conforte would fight the IRS and bankruptcy proceedings for another eight years until he announced his "retirement" in August 1991, after which he disappeared again. Conforte hasn't been seen in Nevada in almost a decade; he was even a no-show at his wife's funeral. He is believed to be living in South America, buffeted by illegal wire transfers of millions of dollars from Mustang to a Swiss bank account.

Over the years, problems and social pressure would continue to plague Mustang Ranch. The early days at Mustang Ranch had more than their share of dark sides. Even though Conforte is gone and the Mustang Ranch is closed, reminders of his reign still exist.

The houses at the Ranch had a turbulent history of calamity and misfortune, most of which Conforte brought on himself. He made his own rules and felt he was above anyone else's. His underworld connections, twisted view of life and choices he and his wife made regarding management of the houses often resulted in government intervention, violence and even a lover's triangle that ended in death in the parking lot of the main house at Mustang. While incidents of this nature can happen in any type of business, they become sensational when linked to a bordello.

The ironic thing about the lover's triangle death was the double standards that ruled the relationship of the owners. Conforte was famous for having his own small group of ladies who were at his beck and call. They entertained only high-end clients and dignitaries and were the ones draping his arms when he went out in public.

While Joe promoted the Ranch and played, his wife ran the day-to-day operations. Sally loved boxing and became the manager of Oscar Bonavena, who was at one time a top-ranked heavyweight who fought the likes of Joe Frazier and Muhammad Ali. Joe's macho double standards and ego apparently had trouble handling the love affair that eventually developed between his wife and Bonavena, but the situation reached a climax when the boxer began bragging that he would soon take over Mustang Ranch. He was fatally shot early one morning in May 1976 in the main parking lot. While only a few key people still employed at the Ranch 20 years later knew the real facts, a guard took the blame and served 18 months for voluntary manslaughter.

The Ranch was also in constant trouble with the IRS. While most brothel owners keep legitimate records and present the ladies with 1099 forms at the end of the year for tax purposes, the IRS was well aware of the "creative bookkeeping" that went on at the Ranch and constantly monitored, audited and indicted the establishment. Conforte himself was convicted of tax evasion no less than twice and it was the IRS that finally shut down the Ranch in the summer of 1999.

Despite repeated efforts to obtain a 1099 form, I was never given one by any of the houses on the Mustang property, so I was forced to file estimated taxes according to my own carefully documented records. The Ranch was always in trouble but because I filed estimated taxes, I never was personally. That was one of the main reasons I eventually transferred to a house in Lyon County which engaged in legitimate business practices.

Federal agents have had a decades-old personal vendetta against Conforte for outsmarting them, fleeing the country and being unable to lay a finger on him personally in a court of law. As a result, the government became obsessed with destroying Conforte by forcing forfeiture of the empire he built.

Sex for sale may be considered an unsavory business to some but no matter how the industry is viewed, it is legal in the houses of Nevada. It is part of free enterprise and as such should not be put out of business because of the federal government's personal vendetta with Conforte. In doing that, the government is denying Storey County residents legally obtained revenue that in great measure supports the small county. In fact, when the federal government shut down Mustang Ranch, they not only closed the largest bordello in the county (and the state), they closed the county's largest single employer in any industry.

Although hell-bent on "getting" Conforte at any cost, when it looked doubtful the government could obtain a conviction against him personally, they simply changed the rules as they so often do against the public and went after his operatives instead. In so doing, doesn't the government cross that fine line into criminal activity themselves in order to soothe their own egos and further their own careers? Neither side is innocent and the inevitable outcome is a no-win situation for everyone.

The main house lies straight ahead after crossing the bridge. It is the largest and most famous. The exterior is a salmon colored adobe with a Mediterranean tiled roof and a guard tower. Black wrought iron fencing surrounds the house. Dimly lit, the interior is spacious with lots of plants, a large bar and many comfortable sofas. It fit the image of what people imagine in their minds when they think of a brothel.

The smaller Mustang house is located a few hundred yards to the east. I "TO'd" (turned out) at this house. (T.O. is an industry term which designates where a woman learns her trade and denotes the first time she works as a prostitute). Mustang II is much plainer than the main house and didn't have a chef; ladies' meals were brought over from the main house. The staff was cold and indifferent and the house was run with an assembly-line mentality that caused the ladies to be edgy, more competitive and less bonded. The madam was a Gestapo-mama from hell who took pleasure in bullying the girls. Consequently, turnover was frequent. I worked at Mustang for only a few months before deciding to move over to Old Bridge Ranch.

Old Bridge Ranch, or OBR as it is known locally, is a middle-sized house located on the west side of the property. OBR is owned by Conforte's nephew, David Burgess, but is considered independent of Mustang Ranch and remained open after Mustang was shut down. It has a reputation for friendly girls and a comfortable work environment. The exterior and interior of the house has a look of welcome and a comfortable, lived-in feel lacking in the other two houses. It is one of the few houses where the ladies are free to go home after their shift. Some did but most preferred to sleep at the house rather than drive the eight miles into town when they were dead tired. I immediately felt more relaxed and was sure I had made the right decision.

I nearly always worked day shift, usually from 11 a.m. to 11 p.m. I liked the clients on that shift better. There were too many drunks late at night. My first shift at the new house, I was given a room near the main hall where I could hear the line-up bell better on-duty and yet was far enough away from the parlor noise that I would be able to sleep off-duty. It was a great location, and I wondered why I got it over the girls with seniority. I soon found out.

The room was plain and quite small. Each set of two rooms shares a bathroom and I was happy to see they had bidets. I pushed my trunk into the closet and began to pull out the canopy material, curtains, throw rugs and all the things that would transform the room into a place a gentleman would find comfortable and attractive. I wasn't due on the floor until morning, so I took the opportunity to get the room ready beforehand so I could sleep as late as possible.

As I worked, several girls stopped by to welcome me. Serena asked if I had requested Room 23.

"No, it was assigned to me," I replied. "Why? Did you want it?"

Serena looked at me in amazement. "Hell no, girlfriend! No one wants to stay in here."

I stopped working and looked at her. "Why? What's wrong with this room?"

Prostitutes are a superstitious group, always throwing coins on the ground by the front door to entice good fortune, among other traditions. I figured it was just more of that.

"You really are new, honey, but you'll find out soon enough," Serena said over her shoulder as she wandered off down the hall.

I dismissed it. There was too much to do and my thoughts drifted to the kitchen. I was hungry and had heard the chef was great at this house. I intended to find out shortly.

My room and shower finished, I put on my robe and slippers and padded down the hall. The kitchen was directly ahead. I visited with several of the girls while I ate and then took some of Clint's homemade cookies and went down the main hall toward the Jacuzzi room where the phone was located.

I called Michael. He was glad to hear an upbeat tone in my voice. The other house made me tense and uncomfortable but this one already felt much better. I went back to my room, opened the window a bit for fresh air, turned out the light and fell asleep.

I was cold. I sat straight up in bed. Who had been in my room? The light was on and my covers were on the floor. I could lock the door to the bathroom from my side to keep my bath mate and/or her client from entering my room but doors facing the hall had no lock so security could get in if a lady had a problem with a client. I am a light sleeper and was sure I would have heard anyone who opened my door. Nothing appeared to be missing. Distressed, I looked at the clock. It was 3 a.m. I propped the back of the chair under the doorknob, closed the window and latched it, turned out the light and went back to bed.

The radio suddenly came on. Really afraid now, I jumped out of bed, turned on the light and checked the alarm on the clock radio. It wasn't set. How did the radio go on by itself? I don't drink or do drugs so I knew it wasn't in my head. I don't believe in ghosts either. I didn't know anyone at the house yet so I was sure it wasn't a prank. Everyone would think I was crazy if I said anything. I didn't know what to do.

Parties are never conducted under the sheets. Ladies put a "runner," a large towel that is put in the laundry after each use, on top of their made-up bed. When off shift, the room ladies work out of is also the room they sleep in. The sheets are for their use only.

I had crawled between the sheets expecting a good night's sleep. Now I was too afraid to be confined by the covers. I turned off the radio and the light and laid on top of the bed, lying very still until the fright went away. Just as I began to relax, the light went on again. Grabbing my robe and throwing the chair aside, I ran down the hall yelling for the madam.

"Jessi, what on earth is wrong?" asked the madam as she put her arms around a clearly distraught hooker. I stammered as I quickly tried to tell her about my experience. Several of the girls crowded around to see what was wrong.

"Well no wonder," exclaimed an Amazon-sized blonde. "She's in Room 23."

"What the hell is the matter with Room 23?" I demanded to know. The madam hushed the girls and reassured me that everything was all right and she would check on me often until I was settled in. I had a strong feeling there was more to the story than I had been told but no one seemed willing to talk about it. I told the madam if the situation wasn't better by morning, I wanted a different room.

As I turned to go back down the hall, one of the girls ran up to me and thrust a crucifix into my hand. "Here, honey, put this on your wall above your bed. It will help keep you safe," she said with a concerned look on her face.

Religion always seemed hypocritical to me but I took it anyway and put it up over my bed as she had instructed. When I couldn't sleep, I left my door open and asked the next girl who passed to stop and tell me about Room 23.

Lila came in and sat down. She had been at this ranch for three years and had seen many other occupants run from this room. She cautioned me that what she was about to tell me was simply legend and had never been documented. Despite that, I wanted some kind of explanation for the strange things that seemed to happen inside that room and encouraged her to tell me anyway. According to her, one evening a fire started in the kitchen about 2:00 a.m. The building was old, the timber was very dry and the fire department was a long way off. Soon the house was fully engulfed in flames.

Clients were frantically running toward the exit, as was anyone who was awake and working at that hour. Keith, one of the security guards, ran down the halls banging on the sleeping girls' doors, yelling at them to get up and get out. He methodically went room to room, grabbing each girl by the arm and rushing her outside. He kept going back in despite pleas from everyone not to. He rushed back in one last time just to be sure all the ladies were out. But the roof caved in and Keith was killed in Room 23.

Because it was a house of ill repute the fire was determined to be an accident and the matter was quickly forgotten. After re-opening, Keith's presence could be felt in Room 23. The ladies were sure his spirit protected them; they just didn't want to stay in the room.

I felt the same way. It was nearly dawn when I went out and told the madam I would not spend another night in Room 23. Within the hour I had my trunk packed and ready to move down to the room at the end, which would now be my permanent assignment. Turning around as I left Room 23, I softly said, "Rest well, Keith," as I closed the door.

OBR is a famous Nevada brothel, but management paid little attention to upkeep and the décor inside, which left a lot to be desired. The paint on the walls was chipping and curling. In some rooms, each wall was a different color. "How are we supposed to get premium dollar for parties with a cheap-looking environment?" I often lamented.

It was a frustrating problem, but after I settled into my room I resolved to do something about it. So, I brought in a couple of my antique night tables and lace curtains, created a canopy around the bed, blended lots of plants, wood and copper and hung lingerie on padded hangers alongside paintings of Gold Rush-era "soiled doves" and the map of Nevada bordellos that nearly every working girl had in her room. I replaced the light bulb with a red light that gave the room a warm glow and added a lot of soft touches, such as an old pitcher and antique bowl that gave my room a Victorian hideaway feel while at the same time camouflaging the room's stark, bare walls. It was cozy and inviting and I got a lot of compliments for it.

* * *

A misconception the public has is that the working girls are cold-hearted gold diggers and the bordellos are about nothing except sex. That's simply not the case. Both Phil Donahue and Geraldo Rivera taped shows inside OBR where more than a few clients told a different story. The ladies are so often treated unfairly by society that they develop a keen sense of compassion and can sense things in people that others can't.

Kevin's story is a perfect example of this. On his first visit, I sat on the side of the bed and held my arms out to him. He melted into them, laid his head on my breasts and began to cry. For two hours, he talked and sobbed and I quietly held him and listened, wiping away his tears and brushing the hair back off his forehead as I planted soft kisses on his swollen eyes. My heart broke for him.

Kevin was in his early 30s. A genuinely decent and sensitive man, he adored his two little babies and but simply could no longer take his wife's emotional abuse and the constant fighting. His wife refused counseling and instead, ran off with another man, taking Kevin's children with her. The ensuing divorce was nasty, his wife keeping his children from him as much as she could. It tore a hole in his heart.

Much later, Kevin told me he decided to come to the brothel that night because he had no family and the only friends he had were superficial ones at work. He was at rock bottom and felt like committing suicide. Only thoughts of how that would affect his children kept him from doing something drastic. He had to find someone who would listen and would hold him, even if he had to pay for it. So he made his first visit to a brothel. He was grateful that we were there when he needed us. He didn't know what he might have done if he hadn't had that option at that low moment in his life.

Not feeling up to idle chitchat, he saw a warm smile and picked me right out of line. He instinctively felt I would be nurturing and was thankful I was. He became a regular, coming in once a week for several months and then twice a month for nearly a year. The houses were often about much more than just sex and this was one of those times. It was one human being taking care of another.

For weeks, we spent our time together talking, holding and healing. I spoke to another of my regular clients who was an attorney. He agreed to take Kevin's case at a low fee and help him with the legal work necessary to gain custody of his children.

Gradually Kevin began to heal and became stronger. We started to laugh and have fun. I convinced him to seek counseling and eventually talked him into joining a non-threatening singles club that spent a lot of time in talk groups sorting out the new rules of being single again.

Kevin eventually gained custody of his children. After more than a year of visiting me, he came in with a present just before Thanksgiving. He knew I was country and bought me a beautiful heart shaped belt buckle. Giving me a big hug, he explained he had met a wonderful woman and was ready to start a serious relationship. This would be our last date. I was thrilled for him and we spent our last hour together toasting his good fortune in the Jacuzzi. Every time I wear that buckle, it brings back warm memories. Wherever he is now, I hope the sun is shining on him.

The girls were another source of sunshine. Like in a college dorm, we lived together 24 hours a day. We were close-knit and always kidding each other. I was hired because I resembled Ann-Margret. Clients gave us money to put in the jukebox, and I always played country.

I'm into hard country; George Jones is one of my all-time favorites. The girls ribbed me, saying an Ann-Margret look alike should be playing Elvis records. Anytime the girls heard George or Alan Jackson singing, they knew I was working. They got me through my shifts. They were "home" to me and I could lose myself in the familiar fiddles and George's incredible vocal talent. If I had a bad night, George and Alan were always there to take me away.

I grew up on ranches and country music. It was the one constant in my life that I knew I could trust and that brought me comfort and security. I also took a lot of heat for it. While the other girls listened to rock or rap, Billie and I were the only cowgirls working the three houses at Mustang Ranch at the time. Billie brought her horses out from Tennessee because she planned on staying, but she hated the hard, brown terrain and left, leaving me alone to take the ribbing.

But being country in northern Nevada does have its advantages. The area is home to a lot of cowboys, so naturally cowboys frequently visited the bordellos. Whenever the buzzer rang and there were cowboys outside, the lineup dwindled as the girls wandered off muttering, "This one's Jessi's." I loved it. They were real and they treated me like a queen. They had no use for phony city gals and I understood them. The cowboys always made my shifts happier. And I could play my music with them!

Sometimes it was fun to just watch the girls. They were all so different and had such distinct styles of working.

Veronica had a regular the girls called "Wolf." He was one of those predictable clients that always showed up on the same day of the week, at the same time, looking the same. The first time I saw him, he looked every inch the attorney he was. Ramrod straight, conservative business suit, bland tie, shined shoes, short haircut and immaculate manners. He was 100 percent prep.

Veronica was the only one he ever partied with but he liked to sit in the parlor and visit with the ladies for a half an hour before they went to her room. We all got to know Wolf well during those visits and saw a very different side to the stuffy lawyer most of his clients must have seen.

He seemed genuinely comfortable snuggled down into the marshmallow soft cushions of the couch surrounded by a bevy of beauties hanging on his every word. He clearly enjoyed his visits to the house. He told the ladies they were the only "real" people he got to be around, considering those in his own profession. His sense of humor and upbeat outlook kept us hanging around him out of preference. He made us all laugh. A gentleman, he always bought drinks for everyone and encouraged the women to mingle if they needed to. Wolf was a fun person; we looked forward to his visits.

Veronica was Wolf's opposite. I secretly called her "Amazon Woman." I say secretly because I wanted to continue living. The first time I had a conversation with her, I had only been at OBR a few days. I was sitting at the table in the kitchen when she walked in. A huge individual, I thought she was a male client in drag at first, something which isn't that unusual in the houses. It wasn't an unreasonable assumption, but it was a wrong one.

Well over six feet tall, she had muscles where I didn't even know muscles grew. She wasn't fat, just big. Very big. With her platinum blonde shoulder length hair, tattoos on both back shoulder blades peeking out of her black leather top and her surly demeanor, she was a very intimidating figure indeed.

Her piercing brown eyes fixed on me. "What the hell are you doing in the kitchen right now?" she interrogated.

After hearing her speak, I realized she wasn't male after all. I was puzzled but not about to hassle someone who was two body sizes larger than I was. "Eating?" I answered with a questioning tone.

"I know you're new, so I'll cut you some slack this time," she snarled. "But make sure you don't come in here after your shift and eat before those of us going on night shift. You eat after we're through. Don't let me catch you in here again before my shift. We eat first. Got it?"

Did she really think I was going to argue with her? "No problem," I said as I picked up my plate and headed for my room.

She never got much friendlier than that. She avoided most of the girls and kept to herself. Still, certain clients were very loyal to her. Wolf was one of them.

Veronica would come over to the couch and fetch him after his allotted visiting time with the other ladies. She would strap a leather-studded collar around his neck, hook a leash to it and lead him down the hall to her room. Right on cue, exactly 40 minutes later, you could hear his victorious howl throughout the house.

A few minutes later, dressed again in his business attire and looking like he was headed for his next court appearance, he would appear in the parlor again, wave to the ladies and disappear out the door.

The room was very still. Everyone in the parlor turned to look at Veronica. It was one of the rare times I ever saw her smile. "What can I say?" she said to everyone, "The man is an animal."

Everyone laughed and went back to their noisy chatter. The Ranch was packed.

* * *

As couples wandered off to see the various specialty rooms, Crunch paged me. He normally tended bar, cooked or worked security, but on this occasion he was filling in as night manager. A former professional football player, you knew just looking at him that he could live up to his nickname. But he was a sweetheart and always looked out for the girls.

I went into the office where he introduced me to Wes. Crunch explained that Wes had been a regular of Tiffany's for over a year, but had a bad experience the last time he paid the house a visit. Tiffany was young, rebellious and troubled. She also did drugs. During her last party with Wes, she mutilated him with tweezers by plucking his body hair and digging at his skin. Although he really liked Tiffany, he was understandably afraid to visit her again. Crunch suggested Wes talk to me because I didn't smoke, drink or do drugs. I was also stable and more mature than most of the ladies. He suggested I take Wes to my room and reassure him that good parties were ahead for him.

"Sure, sugar," I cooed as I took his hand. We left the office, walked through the parlor, past the bar and continued on past "night hall" on the left, "mid-shift hall" on the right and down the corridor. "Day hall" where my room was located was on the left just past the kitchen. I stopped and asked Wes if he'd like to sit at the table and have a cup of coffee and a piece of pie and visit for awhile.

He smiled. "I guess I am a little nervous and uptight. That would be nice."

He told me he was a ranch hand at the Bar-W a few miles down the road. He liked all three houses at Mustang Ranch and considered the staff and ladies almost extended family since he had none. A quiet, well-mannered man, he was almost apologetic about complaining about Tiffany. When we finished our dessert, I stood up and took his hand again. We continued to my room, the last one at the far end of day hall.

I motioned for him to sit in the comfortable chair by the bed. I sat across from him stroking his hand. He took off his shirt and showed me the welts and scratches from Tiffany's drug-induced frenzy. I winced.

"Wes, honey," I said in a soothing voice, "You've had an unpleasant experience but tonight you're going to learn to trust again. Tiffany is a really nice girl but she has some problems she has to deal with. The house has told her she can't return until she kicks her drug habit. I'm so very sorry you went through this." I continued to stroke his hand as I talked to him. "Normally the gentleman chooses the party, but tonight I'm going to call the shots. We're going to have a gentle party with lots of communication. I'm going to tell you everything in advance that we will be doing and you can let me know if any part of it makes you uncomfortable. Agreed?"

He flashed a smile that showed relief. "Agreed," he replied.

I slowly helped him undress, did the physical check and then handed him a robe. "I'll take you to the Jacuzzi room and then get you a glass of wine," I instructed.

We talked while Wes drank his wine and relaxed as the warm water rolled over our bodies. I gently massaged his shoulders and felt him begin to relax. When the wine was gone, we put on our robes and returned to the room.

I lit scented candles and pulled out my massage oils. He stretched out and nearly fell asleep during the next half-hour. Our party was slow, tender and reassuring. Afterward, he held my hand as we walked down the hall toward the parlor. Then he stopped, pulled me to him and gave me a big hug.

"Thank you so much, Jessi," he said as he looked in my eyes. "I can't tell you how much this has helped." I squeezed his hand. He walked toward the office to say goodbye to Crunch. I returned to my room to freshen up.

A few minutes later I jumped as the intercom came on in my room. It was Crunch. "Amazing, Jessi. You handled that so well. I listened until you left for the Jacuzzi and you brought an entirely different man back to the parlor. A job very well done."

"Thanks Crunch," I replied as I pushed the return button. "Tiffany flat out mangled the poor guy."

"I know," the voice in the box said. "A bonus envelope will be waiting for you in the office at your convenience. It was a work of art."

"Goodnight Crunch," I replied. Compliments from staff were rare. I felt pleased. I was also happy to have helped Wes.

The following evening, the madam announced to the ladies that a gentleman would be arriving from the Midwest and would spend the next two days partying with every lady at the Ranch. He was due to get married in two weeks and this was his bachelor party for himself.

He arrived about 8:00 p.m. on a dead run and with a wide grin. A tall, skinny man with an immense nose, he looked like a crow. The ladies quickly nicknamed him "Birdman." He had a wonderful sense of humor, great respect for the ladies and was terrific fun. He had been saving for this adventure for a year and chose a different party for each lady.

Tanya and Jillian spent two hours in a *ménage a trois* and quickly told the other girls that Birdman was incredibly endowed and a great lay. He was definitely not a client for the faint-hearted. He was the one to choose the parties however.

I was petite and tight. Overly endowed men were a problem for me. Remembering Tanya and Jillian's words, I broke out in a sweat as Birdman walked toward me. Mercifully Birdman chose me for my breasts. Even though we would not be having intercourse, he had just partied with several other ladies and I didn't want him touching any part of me until I was satisfied he was prepared properly.

He had an outrageous sense of humor, which was fortunate because we both fell into spasms of laughter when his tree limb sized penis outgrew the "peter pan" as I washed it. Some clients were just plain fun but I said a silent prayer of thanks that he had picked me only for my breasts! I had seen a tremendous variety of joy toys in my tenure but none that matched Birdman's trophy.

He buried his face between my breasts and kept me laughing so much, I hated to see the half-hour end. At the end of his two day stay, Birdman went home with lifelong memories, the house made a lot of money and the ladies spent time with a fun human being.

Not all clients are gentlemen however. Most houses are surrounded by barbed wire fences with an entry gate that has a buzzer that must be pressed by an attendant to gain entry inside the house. Once a gentleman comes through the gate, he hears it slam behind him and knows he can't exit until he is buzzed out. Once inside the parlor, multiple pairs of female eyes greet him and he instinctively knows if he isn't on his best behavior, every single owner of those pairs of eyes will tear him to shreds. Seldom are bouncer's services needed. The rooms are equipped with emergency buzzers on or near the bed in case a gentleman does forget his manners. Most houses have also installed listening devises. Occasionally, however, a client will think he can get away with something.

Such was the case with Brooke. Half American Indian, she was street savvy despite her demure appearance. It was late; about 3:00 a.m. when she was chosen by the young, straggly haired man. After their party, she stepped into the adjourning bathroom before walking him back out to the parlor. She returned to the room just in time to see him pulling her half of his fee out from under her closet door.

At this Ranch, before partying, the client gives his lady the agreed upon fee and she takes it to the office where the cashier keeps half for the house and gives the lady her half. Each room has a closet with a padlock on the outside so no one can get in without a key. Brooke slid her money under the door but not far enough and her client was able to fish it out while she freshened her make-up.

He took off running down the hall with Brooke screaming after him. Any man returning to the parlor by himself was cause for alarm, not to mention one being chased by his date. Before the bouncer could figure out what was wrong, the man bounded out the front door and ran out the gate, which was being held open by new guests. The bouncer got his license plate and called the sheriff.

The sheriff relies heavily on the brothels for his paycheck. It took only two days for him to track down the driver and return him to the Ranch where he had to apologize to Brooke in front of an entire line-up, return her stolen fee, and was then banned from the Ranch for life. Occasionally, there was justice for the working girls!

* * *

"The phone's for you, Jessi," Jillian yelled from down the hall.

It was Yoshi, one of my regulars from San Francisco. He wanted to be sure I was working before he made the drive over the mountain that evening. He was one of my favorite clients and I always looked forward to his visits.

Yoshi was in his late 30s, average height but a muscular build. He worked out regularly in the gym and had an awesome physique. He was a stockbroker and worked inside all day. He loved his work but hated being inside, so he enjoyed every minute he could spend outdoors and it showed. He was always tan, even in winter. His face was handsome with kind eyes that crinkled when he laughed, which was often. He was raised in traditional Japanese culture and was always a perfect gentleman. That's why he came to the houses. To let down his hair and get wild. It certainly wasn't for lack of female company.

He always arrived impeccably dressed. Smart dress shirt, freshly starched. Dark business suit, conservative tie, black dress shoes. He never showed up empty handed either. Oriental culture has great respect for their courtesans. Going to the brothel always meant a shopping spree for Yoshi.

The first time he came to the house he had an armful of gifts. He spent two hours meticulously interviewing all the ladies before he decided to party with me. When our date was over, he placed all his parcels on my bed and explained it was his custom to honor feminine beauty. I thanked him but told him he didn't need to feel obligated to provide gifts. After all, he willingly paid top dollar for his party. He just smiled and showed up the next time with an even larger armful of gifts.

He always brought my favorite truffles found in only one particular fancy shop in San Francisco. Each small, individually wrapped truffle cost $2. Yoshi always brought two dozen. He loved the smell and look of fresh flowers and told me he routinely filled his office with dozens of bouquets. He did the same with my room. He took special pleasure in watching me open the brightly wrapped boxes. Each one was like Christmas. Sometimes they contained jewelry, lingerie, street wear, leather purses, even money. We were total opposites; I despise shopping: he shopped 'til he dropped.

He had a set routine that we observed on each date. He always booked three hours. Very traditional, he always brought a ceremonial robe for me. I would leave him in the parlor and go back to my room where I would put my hair up, apply heavy dramatic make-up, put on a g-string and pasties with the robe over them and then go back out to the parlor to get him.

Incense was already burning when he entered my room and we sat on the floor for our tea. The first half-hour was filled with ritual, including discussions about articles from the Japanese paper he always brought. We would go over it together and he would explain the background of certain issues. He always left the papers with me. After some time, I was able to recognize a few of the symbols.

After tea and conversation, the party began to relax. He loved the strip dances I did for him. The madam didn't know he quietly tucked money in my g-string as I danced around him, sitting on his lap or bending over his back to nibble on his ears. He loved the teasing and long drawn out disrobing. His as well as mine.

Next was the Jacuzzi with more teasing and laughing. Yoshi had a wonderful sense of humor that always made our dates a lot of fun. He also had an incredible physique that made our time together pleasing to the eye. The man was a work of art. And I was the lucky viewer.

The Jacuzzi was followed by a full body massage with scented oils and candles. Yoshi was a thoughtful lover and one of the very few gentlemen who took his partner's comfort and pleasure into consideration. In all my time as a bordello working girl, I can remember only a handful of clients who gave me a massage in return. I can't really blame the ones that didn't however. The parties were "no strings attached" which meant the gentlemen didn't have to worry about their partners in the first place and they paid big money for their dates and wanted to get every penny's worth for themselves. But it was a real treat when a client was also an attentive gentleman.

He would select a porno film from my collection and then the party started in earnest. Over a period of visits, he wanted to try nearly everything. He had the equipment and imagination to do it too.

One visit he requested a *ménage a trois*. I told him I was totally straight and didn't party with other girls. If he wanted to watch two women together, I would arrange for the "party girls" as they were referred to, to come to the room and he could choose the two he wanted. He didn't like the idea. He had spent a lot of time making his initial choice and wanted to remain "loyal" to me. He said he would be just as happy having two women just for him. I called several of the girls into the room and he chose Heather to join us.

Heather was a tall willowy girl with dark curly shoulder length hair, incredible eyes and a very sexy demeanor. Yoshi explained how he wanted this party to play out and the two of us went to work. At the end of the date, he weakly reached into his suit pocket for his wallet, fell back on the bed and threw money in the air.

"Take it all, ladies," he said with a huge grin. "You're worth every cent."

Heather said she understood now why there was always so much laughter coming out of my room when Yoshi visited. We just plain had a terrific time. He got pretty wild the last hour of each visit and the wilder he got, the louder he became. But when the date was over and I walked him back to the parlor, he always regained his regal demeanor and looked every inch the successful businessman. Bowing low, he kissed my hand and walked through the door and out to his Mercedes.

* * *

The madam's voice rang out, "Company ladies!" The Navy fly-boys quit hootin' and hollerin' when they saw the commander come through the door. The girls they were talking to quickly formed a line-up, hands behind their backs as required. The madam welcomed him but before the ladies could even complete their introduction, the commander impatiently pointed at me and said, "That one." I stepped forward while the rest of the ladies went back to what they were doing.

As we walked down the hall to my room, I made an attempt at small talk but he shot a look that caused me to walk the remaining distance in silence. He clearly was used to giving orders.

As soon as we stepped inside the room, he tossed two one-hundred dollar bills on the bed, told me he wasn't interested in conversation, was in a hurry, would tell me exactly what he wanted, how he wanted it and if he was satisfied at the end of the party, I would receive a nice tip.

"Oh boy," I thought to myself, "this one is a real charmer." As it turned out, he was a dream date. I wished they all could be so simple.

He demanded I lay out my heels and nylons. He chose the black stockings with the seam down the back and the four-inch spike heels with gold tips. He knew exactly what he wanted. I didn't have to exert the energy and time to pull his fantasy from him. He directed each move of the party, ending it ten minutes later when he slipped another hundred-dollar bill into my hand and marched out the door. Hurriedly I grabbed my robe, almost running to keep up with him. He paused briefly in the parlor, shook my hand, and was gone without a word to the young men in his command.

Sometimes there were sad cases. A beneficial service the houses offer society is to provide a place for men like Thomas where they feel accepted and are treated no differently from any other man.

Since he was a child, Thomas suffered a medical condition he didn't wish to discuss. It rendered him impotent. He was only in his late 20s and very depressed and frustrated. Medical science promised help soon for those in his situation but that was no comfort in the meantime. It kept him from maintaining a long term relationship and that's why he sought the acceptance of bordello ladies.

He usually visited twice a month, on payday. He liked to party with various girls but his routine was always the same. He wanted a cheerleader. The house kept a short pleated skirt, a high school letter sweater and pom-poms for his visits.

He brought his own bag. Any bag brought in by a client is searched by the madam or security for drugs or weapons. His bag contained neither. It had a pressure pump and something that smelled like ether. He sat on the bed with the pump over his penis, sniffing the god-awful stuff in the bottle and squeezing the hand bulb that operated the pump. It applied pressure to his penis, creating an artificial erection. At that point, he wanted a fully dressed cheerleader to lead him on to victory. It was the only way he could climax. When he did, the cheerleader had to do a full fledged cheerleading routine hailing the success of her team. That accomplished, Thomas packed his gear and split. None of the ladies ever had to touch him. They just had to have strong lungs and an enthusiastic routine.

Porno Pete was the nickname I gave a well-known public official that actually had the nerve – or stupidity – to visit the house in his official state vehicle on company time. It made one wonder if he paid for his party with taxpayer dollars. His antics were always in the paper. He lacked good judgment and was always getting in trouble but he had powerful friends who always got him out of his messes, so I don't think he worried much about the consequences of his actions.

He loved the houses. He loved getting rowdy even more. A few beers and he would be almost out of control. Add porn to that and he was in hog heaven!

Pete would fly through the gate with a grin and waltz into the parlor hugging everyone in sight. Everyone knew him. The bartender had his favorite beverage ready for him. The girls would crowd around him while he regaled them with hilarious stories. Then he would pick his flavor of the day and disappear into her room.

He grabbed my hand and headed for the hall. While he chose his favorite porn film, I went down to the supply room. Pete always partied on pillows on the floor. The maid and I returned to my room with armfuls of pillows. I threw them all over the floor and then tossed a sheet over the top. It was a warm day, so I opened the window and lit some scented candles. Pete was ready to go. He didn't bother with foreplay or conversation. He wanted to get right to it. He liked to recreate the scene he was watching on film, so we would role play what was showing on the TV monitor.

We were about half way through our party when we heard the most god-awful sound. It was in our room. We both jumped to our feet thinking it was a raid or some sort of disaster. Turning toward the window, we saw a big black and white face with huge eyes staring back at us. We both cracked up.

The Ranch really was a ranch. Cows roamed at will. My room was at the very back of the house and overlooked the pasture. This steer decided to see what all the commotion was about inside the house so he simply put his head inside the open window and said hello.

Pete fell back down on the pillows laughing so hard tears rolled down his cheeks. "Now I can honestly tell my buddies I screwed 'til the cows came home," he said.

The Ranch catered heavily to Oriental clientele from the Bay area. Ladies encountered an ongoing problem with a number of these clients that the hooker doctor finally solved.

Sasha came out to the office and asked if the doctor had left any finger condoms. Her date was so small, a regular condom wouldn't stay on. The office gave her several and told her to keep them in her room.

When faced with a similar situation, most ladies tried to talk the client into a blow job or some other form of sex play other than intercourse. They felt it was risky to have to hold onto the base of the condom the entire time to make sure it didn't slip off. They preferred to be able to see that everything was under control and a blow job was one way to do that. While most clients were willing to go along with suggestions from the ladies, they were always a challenge.

Regardless of the client's ethnicity, it became a silent joke among the girls that when a lady returned to the parlor with her date and held up her pinky finger for the girls to see, it meant "really small." Dates often wondered why everyone was chuckling.

The buzzer rang again. Short, stocky, disheveled and quiet, he dismissed the line-up saying he wanted to sit for awhile and enjoy his drink. Picking a seat beside Porché, he began telling her about his impending stay in the veteran's hospital the next morning. He expected to be there for a while and that's why he was visiting the house beforehand. Porché asked him if his health permitted a party and he matter-of-factly told her he would be checking into the psyche ward, not the medical wing. Porché knew she had to handle this one with kid gloves.

He asked her to take him on tour and when they reached Porché's room, they negotiated their party but he balked when she wanted to do the physical check on him.

"There's something I need to tell you," he said nervously. "I don't trust people so I keep a knife up my butt."

Certain she had heard wrong, she maintained her composure while explaining in a soothing tone that the party they planned to have would be more comfortable for him if he removed the knife. She offered to take it to the front office for him so they could keep it safe and then return it to him after their party was over. He said he rarely parted with his knife, as it was a safety measure he learned in Vietnam and he always kept it ready in case of emergency. He went on to explain that tonight was his party night, however, and he knew she was a friend so he would do as she suggested. Two tours in Vietnam had taken their toll.

He excused himself and went into the bathroom and returned with the knife. Porché held it between the tips of her thumb and index finger. Gingerly, she walked to the front office and laid it on the madam's desk.

The madam looked at Porché in amazement. "Don't even ask," was the reply.

Back in the room, she pulled out the peter pan and discreetly added disinfectant to the warm tap water.

"This one gets extra cleaning time and double condoms," she thought to herself as she began to wash his penis in the peter pan.

Clearly, an understanding of human nature and finely tuned inner radar are paramount attributes for any working girl.

***

Holier-than-thou do-gooders are quick to condemn what they view as the sinful nature of the work in the bordellos. They piously feel they are superior and in a position to judge others but their hypocrisy fails to allow them to realize that "there but for the grace of God go I." Many fine people are innocent victims of entrapment in a body that doesn't work the way it should. Human nature places too much value on superficial beauty while treating anyone who doesn't fit their mold, as inferior. It makes no difference whether they suffer from MS, cerebral palsy, are paralyzed, have erectile dysfunction or any myriad of other medical conditions. We are all human beings.

Contrary to what the self-appointed moralizers say, the brothels are a refuge for those whom society views as imperfect. Often, they are much better people than those that judge them. As a result, some have a finely developed sense of humor and compassion that helps them live their daily lives. Others become reclusive and lack self esteem because of one human being's cruelty toward another. Everyone needs human comfort, compassion and acceptance. Bordellos serve a valid social need in this arena that is sorely lacking in our society.

Used to being outcasts themselves, the ladies treat others who may appear imperfect to small-minded elitists no differently than they would treat any other human being. All of us had clients with special needs. Where would they go for social acceptance if the brothels were not available?

The houses make valuable contributions that will never be recognized by society but are treasured by grateful clients. Marla's client was just such an example.

Madam gathered the girls to discuss the phone call she had just received. A gentleman explained he was a paraplegic and was getting married in a few weeks. His condition prevented him from feeling anything from the chest down but he wanted to be able to sexually satisfy his new wife so he visited his doctor to discuss options. The medical choice he and his doctor decided upon was to administer an injection 10 minutes prior to intercourse that would properly prepare him to have sex. The doctor suggested he visit the brothel to determine how well the method would work. Madam asked if any of the ladies would be willing to assist him. Nearly all the hands went up.

When Trent arrived, he had his choice. Within minutes of visiting with the ladies, he felt accepted and began to relax. As he got to know their personalities, he decided he would be most comfortable with Marla. She was a woman with a warm smile, kind eyes and a mothering disposition who was quite capable of making even the most uneasy man relax. They adjourned to her room and when they returned to the parlor, Trent had a jubilant look on his face. Rejuvenated in the knowledge that he would be able to have normal relations and satisfy his new wife, he could now face his wedding day with confidence. Without the services available to him at the bordello, his special day might have been quite different.

While events at the houses are sometimes of a serious and healing nature, other circumstances took on humorous attributes even if they originally appeared disastrous. The proximity of the river was just such a situation. It was located close enough to the houses that flooding sometimes cut them off and prevented the ladies from reaching safety. Not long before I started work at the Ranch the area was hit with torrential rain and the resulting flood happened so quickly that the Ranch was virtually surrounded by water.

As the flood waters began to rise, staff borrowed a front loader from an aggregate pit near the Ranch and took the ladies across the bridge to safety in the scoop of the front loader. When that was no longer possible, Search and Rescue arrived with a boat. Frantic women in t-bars and bras, lingerie and other various degrees of undress clambered onboard a few at a time to make their way to safety. The helicopter hovered above much longer than needed and newspaper photographers spent most of their time covering only one area of the flood. One thing the bordellos never suffered from was boredom!

The Dark Side

I stood in my yard listening to the tour guide tell visitors in the tram about Julia Bulette and bristled. Hypocrisy was alive and well. It was obviously OK to make money off of tourists with tales of Virginia City's most exploited resident of the 1800s while shunning her modern contemporaries. Beginning with the gold rush, money seemed to be all that mattered in Nevada and things appeared to have not changed a bit in the ensuing 150 years.

Longtime residents of rural Nevada accept today's legal bordellos as part of the rebel history and independent tradition of this unique Wild West state. Brothels are simply another job choice in the rurals. I never felt I had to hide the fact I worked in them.

Despite northern Nevada's acceptance of the houses, history shows there is a dark side to both society and the bordellos. Human nature reveals its "real" face when dealing with prostitution.

The Nevada Historical Society records the age-old partnership between prostitution and law enforcement in the state, whether legal or illegal. Double standards are never more pronounced than when a police officer is personally involved with a prostitute, especially before the days of legal bordellos.

In 1906, Nye County Sheriff Tom Logan was a well-liked and respected family man with eight children. Newspapers reported he was shot to death at the Jewel House, a Manhatten brothel, while trying to stop two gamblers from proceeding with a pistol duel. It was, however, difficult to explain why the sheriff was dressed only in a blue nightshirt.

Accurate accounts later revealed the brothel's madam was a long-time mistress of the sheriff and he had spent the night with her that evening. A patron had slept off his drinking spree in her parlor and when she tried to rouse him early the next morning, the two wound up scuffling.

When the madam screamed, the sheriff burst out of the bedroom with his gun drawn. The patron didn't know Logan was the sheriff and pulled his own gun and fired. The two engaged in a gun battle as the patron ran out of the house but the sheriff was fatally injured.

The patron was subsequently found innocent since he acted in self-defense, not realizing he was fighting with a lawman. The outcome might have been different had Logan pinned his badge to his nightshirt.

Every occupation seems to attract a predominant personality trait in those working in a particular profession; i.e., cops with control issues. One trait that seems to be a common thread among the ladies is low self-esteem, although it's hard to say if this lack of self-esteem existed prior to employment in the brothel or came as a result of society's reaction to the prostitution label afterwards. Regardless, emotionally unstable women exist in all fields of work, as do stable ones.

Each woman who enters the sex industry brings her own unique history. The old tired myth that all women who choose to work in the sex industry are screwed up, molested, abused, drugged out, brainwashed, mentally ill or dependent on pimps is complete rubbish.

There is a common misconception that prostitution is legal throughout Nevada. That's not quite true. It is legal only in licensed brothels in certain rural counties. Bordello owners would have no business if it weren't for the ladies but because they have a monopoly on legalization, they know they have the power to call the shots. Many of their business practices are not only illegal, they are not in the best interest of the women who are making them rich. Ladies know they will be blacklisted from the houses if they don't abide by the wishes of the owners. They have no choice but to play by the owner's rules if they wish to continue working in a legal environment. Above all else, that issue needs to be addressed. Aside from the houses, additional alternative legal work environment options need to be explored.

The IRS has deemed brothel prostitutes to be independent contractors.

The minute ladies set foot in a brothel they are treated as employees, however, and must accept the rules of the house. These rules typically include long work hours, inability to turn down a date in some houses, payment to the house for "walking" (refusing) a client in others, restricted or forbidden use of the phone, confinement to the facility for the length of a lady's stay or hundreds of dollars in illegal fines for oversleeping or missing lineup. In some instances, ladies even deal with sexual harassment from an owner who thinks the house is his own personal playground. Just as infuriating, in a few instances ladies must also share a house with drug or porno activities as well.

Bordellos are a separate business from the ladies. Owners like the women's independent contractor status because it allows them to avoid paying benefits and providing worker's compensation insurance. The houses would not exist without the ladies, yet this lopsided tilt of power exists in too many houses. The degree depends on each owner.

Over time, ladies have gone to law enforcement with criminal complaints, only to be patronized, seldom with results. In some police departments, prostitute homicides are still listed as "NHI" (e.g. No Human Involved). Legal ladies have presented grievances to the National Labor Relations Board, only to have their concerns ignored and dismissed because of the nature of their work. Despite legal status, bordello working women virtually have no legal recourse and are clearly relegated to second-class citizen category.

Some time after I entered the profession, an attorney from Reno suggested a bill to prosecute rape cases in the general population differently from cases of prostitute rape. I was livid. Didn't our Constitution promise we were all created equal? That was the first time I "went public."

My sisters and I called the TV station, whose news crew came out to the house to give us the opportunity to present how the proposal would impact on us. Since I was always the outspoken one, the girls designated me as spokesperson. The evening news showed me in lingerie explaining how it felt as a human being to be told your life is not valued in the same manner as the woman standing next to you in line at the grocery store. That was the defining moment in which I made a decision to fight publicly for the rights of the ladies and the industry and try to change harmful attitudes.

While legalization far outweighs the negatives, there is no denying a dark side still exists in the industry and needs to be addressed by positive legislative reform.

Work cards are another gray area. Before a woman can work in a brothel, she must go to the doctor of contract who tests for sexually transmitted diseases and HIV. If she fails the physical, she will never see the inside of a bordello. If she passes, she goes directly to the county sheriff for a background check before starting work. If she clears that she is issued the required work card, which remains in the brothel office during her tenure. Law enforcement officers often make random checks of the houses to match cards with the girls on the floor.

The houses at Mustang Ranch had their own way of processing the girls. They all went to the doctor as required by law but were then told to report to work instead of the sheriff. The house immediately put them on the floor and told them the runner would take them to get their card when "the time was right." A certain number of girls – including me – never obtained work cards.

I always had my weekly physical and monthly HIV screen, but the house never sent me to the sheriff. I inquired about my work card several times and was always told not to worry about it; they would eventually get around to taking me. After a while, I quit asking.

Ladies paid daily room rates to the house which made them, from a legal point of view, renters. Before they buzzed the sheriff in, the manager would clear the parlor of any ladies who didn't have a work card on file. While the sheriff could bust the house for any girl found without a work card in a common area, management knew the cops would not invade the privacy of the girls' rented rooms. Since women who did not have work cards were not reported for tax purposes, it appeared they were pure gravy for the house. I could only conclude this was a profitable little scheme and the money they made from half the fee the ladies charged, plus room and board and fines, went directly into their undeclared cash box.

The Ranch's manager was an imposing and intimidating figure. His long dark hair was pulled back at the neck in a ponytail. He wore tinted dark glasses even in the darkness of the parlor. Well over six feet tall and muscular, he had an annoying and arrogant strut, the result of a major attitude due to the attention he received as a drummer in a casino rock band during his off-duty days. The fines he assessed the girls for being late for line-up or using the phone while on shift most likely went to his first love: a cherry red Corvette convertible. Or perhaps that was his second love as cocaine was undoubtedly his first.

Typical of some bully managers, Sheldon intimidated and used the women's weaknesses against them to control their actions. There was always heavy tension in the air when he was on duty.

Sheldon spent most of his time in the small office that served as the cashier's window and security gate control because he could watch activities throughout the house on the surveillance equipment.

Samantha had been on the floor 14 consecutive hours and was exhausted. He yelled at her to perk up and show enthusiasm because the Ranch was filled with Navy flyboys from the base an hour away. She gave him the international signal. He saw her flip him off in the surveillance camera and stormed into the room. As he grabbed her and pushed her down the hall into one of the rooms, several of the girls tried to intervene but Sheldon was too irate. After the yelling stopped, he pushed the security gate button and yanked Samantha out the door and through the parking lot.

An hour later Sheldon came back alone. Jillian asked where Samantha was. Sheldon told her Samantha was too much of a disturbance so he called a taxi and sent her home.

Rosa was her roommate. She had a bad feeling. When she was able to sneak back to the phone undetected, she called home. No one answered. She felt a chill go through her body.

The next day Samantha was found in the river that ran alongside the brothel. An autopsy showed a 0.22 blood alcohol level. Police determined she got drunk and must have wandered off while waiting for the taxi and drowned. Because she was a working girl, no particular effort was put into investigating her case. But, two things went through Rosa's mind as she packed Samantha's trunk: Sam didn't drink and there was always a taxi at one of the houses.

The underworld influence that existed in the early days has pretty much disappeared over time as the houses are now owned primarily by non-industry investors. Reasons people buy brothels are as varied as the owners, but one thing is certain: if they haven't worked in the brothel industry in some form, they don't have a clue how to run the business. It is not the average Fortune 500 business and takes a well-rounded knowledge of the profession – especially an understanding of the women and the emotional climate – to succeed.

A few become owners out of curiosity and for their own pleasure. Some envision a lucrative cash business or an opportunity for illegal activity such as drugs or pornography. Others are unsuccessful in previous employment and feel owning a house would be a "no-brainer."

Mustang Ranch constantly seemed to have trouble with its ownership. The Ranch again found itself in hot water in 1998 when key employees and some elected county officials were accused and/or indicted on a variety of charges including racketeering, conspiracy and money laundering. Storey County Sheriff Bob Del Carlo was listed as an unindicted co-conspirator in the case. He chose not to seek re-election after 28 years in office because the federal indictment said he was paid $3,000 a month by Conforte for more than four years while in office as part of a conspiracy to buy the Ranch back from IRS by setting up phony companies. Afterwards, AGE, the corporation that owned the Ranch, ironically made Del Carlo the president of the company and the manager who ran the brothel.

It is important to note that not all Nevada brothels are corrupt and insensitive. A few are truly professional operations which have a realistic view of the positive health and safety benefits involved in legal prostitution. Their business practices are above-board and their houses are run in a manner that is good for the ladies, management and society alike.

Sagebrush Ranch, in Lyon County just outside Carson City, is an example of this. The owner is a man that jokes with the ladies and keeps morale high while respecting them at the same time. He knows and understands the business and has the rare compassion and insight to view it from the eyes of the women who work in his house. He is a gentleman who runs his business as just that – a business. The ladies are treated as professional businesswomen with whom he has a business-only relationship and, in turn, they have high respect for the house. He is one of only a very few in the brothel industry who runs his business no differently from any other legal business and is an example for other owners to follow. If all the houses shared the good reputation Sagebrush Ranch enjoys, there would be few complaints in the industry and regulation of owners would be at a minimum.

The houses are regulated at the county level. The state mandates health requirements, but otherwise generally turns a blind eye to the industry. Government wants the revenue but prefers not to think about the houses any further than that (for example, the bordellos are officially classified in census documents as providing "miscellaneous services"). The very nature of the business makes consistency and improved working conditions among the houses all but impossible. Changes needed for all the houses to operate under the same rules would have to be made through the lawmaking process.

All of the ladies face some form of discrimination at one point or another. Incessant unjust treatment at the hands of society leaves scars and affects the women's self-esteem. Discrimination is a common complaint among ladies who work at the houses. Whether it's car loans, renting a house, child custody or applying for a credit card, they often find themselves denied the same rights as women in different occupations.

In the houses I worked in, even the doctor the ladies were required to visit each week treated them differently from their other patients. Ladies' files were kept separately from the rest of the patients; they were charged more and on a cash-only basis. I could only conclude someone was pocketing a lot of money.

Ladies are required to have HIV tests every month even though latex condoms are mandated by the state health department and used for every transaction. Bordello ladies are more proficient in safety and prevention than nearly any other segment of society. The law requires monthly HIV testing from no other profession, not even those in the medical community who deal directly with the virus itself every day (although many pornography producers mandate it on an industry-level basis). While regular testing in a business like this is of extreme importance, once a month is overkill; testing that often isn't necessary considering the other precautions taken in the houses. But it is a profitable cash cow for the doctors, so the women are forced to play by regulations for profit while being exploited once again.

The sound of cash registers also rings loud and clear for Nevada legislators. Most lawmakers recognize the significant revenue derived from liquor and room taxes, substantial quarterly license fees, property taxes and other fees assessed the brothel industry. Like undercover agents, they greedily hold out their hands to grab the bucks, looking over their shoulders to be sure no one sees where it comes from.

Officials who want to legislate morals unwittingly create crime as well as more danger for the women when they try to curry favor with their constituents by "cracking down on prostitution." For that reason, it would be wise to look at statewide legalization – and uniform regulation – rather than just concentrate on the few houses that now exist.

A particularly ambitious do-gooder state senator has gone after the escort services in Las Vegas through the legislature. This is a dangerous manipulation of lives that he clearly is incapable of, and unwilling, to understand. Prohibition should have taught us that when you declare a product illegal, it becomes even more desirable. It also pushes it underground where it can be exploited. A whole subculture of illegal activity can then surround an otherwise uncomplicated supply and demand business.

Only one member of the Legislature consistently had the courage and open mind to declare his support for the brothel industry. Assemblyman Bob Price is an exception among politicians who was always willing to discuss how changes might come about that would improve the industry and make working conditions more equitable for the ladies. A wise, low key, kindly man who has been a representative for a quarter century, his superior integrity is a glaring exception in a sea of self-serving associates who can never hope to walk in his shoes. He is outnumbered in the legislature, however, by those same co-workers and faces a wall of pious, do-gooder opposition whenever he alludes to positives changes through the lawmaking process.

From the beginning of time, prostitution has been a simple business arrangement. It will be around until the planet makes its last spin. We have only two choices: hide our heads in the sand and hope it will go away, which it won't, or deal with it realistically for everyone involved by legalizing and monitoring it. Statistics show Nevada enjoys the lowest sexual crime rate in the nation. The houses prove legalizing prostitution actually reduces crime.

I spent a great deal of time at the legislature talking to various representatives about changes to the industry. Most elected officials I spoke to were completely ignorant about how the industry operated and unaware of specific issues surrounding it. They just knew the state received a lot of revenue from the houses. Their concern ended there.

I visited with a senator I hoped would become an ally in my quest to make positive changes in the legal prostitution field. He listened as I spoke of a hypothetical police department with a $2 million a year prostitution abatement budget. I pointed out that trying to eliminate prostitution is a waste of time and taxpayer's money; a never ending revolving door whose activity will never cease.

Clearly, there is a demand for the service prostitutes offer and the supply won't simply disappear with the stroke of a legislative pen. Over 100 yellow pages are devoted to escort ads alone in the Las Vegas phone book. Hotels, escort services, massage parlors and the street scene certainly point out the need for putting aside moral hand wringing to address the issue in a manner that benefits everyone.

If prostitution were legalized outright, in addition to current legal brothels in Nevada, zoned areas of communities could be designated for the industry. Privately owned and licensed establishments where security would be mandatory could rent licensed prostitutes a workplace. Taking a lesson from Europe, these districts would not be near homes, schools or churches. Expanded legal options would offer those currently working in illegal avenues an alternative workplace.

A method is already in place for licensing and regulating legal prostitutes and could simply continue under a new expanded system. Concerns which would grant the women a more equal playing field could be negotiated during the lawmaking process. These could include such issues as less frequent testing for HIV, obtaining a sheriff's card that would be good for all legal establishments and remain with the working girl and an established arbitration board to hear grievances. No tax money is involved in current brothel operations and would not be involved with a zoned district either. Routine monitoring would ensure both the establishments and the women comply with the law.

Offering an alternative to present day illegal avenues would tremendously reduce the huge budget for prostitution stings leaving only a fraction that would still be needed to remove illegal prostitutes from the streets who test HIV positive and are ineligible to work in legal establishments. The substantial difference could be budgeted for constructive use such as gang prevention or providing shelters and services for the homeless. In addition, expanded legalization would add substantial revenue to local, county, state and federal coffers as opposed to costing the taxpayer in a futile abatement process.

"Interesting," was all the senator said before standing up, shaking my hand and departing. I never heard from his staff and no bills have ever been presented to the legislature that address the concerns we discussed.

I never understood the reasoning of those who continue to do something in the same manner when it's been shown it doesn't work or solve the problem. If it doesn't work, it would seem logical to try something different that might be successful. Obviously, government doesn't put much faith in logic.

Legislating morals keeps us from dealing with the business realistically. The harm that comes to women and their clients by pushing the industry underground should be considered by elected officials making decisions for us. But corruption, greed and climbing the political ladder are more important to most lawmakers in Nevada. It spotlights the lack of concern for women that moral elitists consider society's pond scum scapegoats.

Lawmakers' response – or lack thereof – is typical of so many throughout the nation who have jumped on the religious bandwagon that is the latest craze to seize the nation. Judgmental ostracizing of a segment of society only serves to perpetrate a witch hunt mentality and causes its victims tremendous emotional distress and fails to benefit society.

Depression is probably more prevalent in the sex industry simply because of the impact of society's treatment of working girls. I felt depressed at times too but it was always fleeting. "Sisters" from the gold rush up through modern times have a history of feeling this way. Constantly isolated, disrespected, ignored, and treated differently from other women, some of the ladies deal with rejection by drinking too much or taking drugs. Others turn off their feelings until they no longer are in touch with anything. A few remain grounded and are able to separate themselves from their work.

Those fortunate few are able to maintain a normal stable relationship with their families and themselves. I was one of those.

My blue moods resulted not so much from how I was treated by society as a sex provider but rather from treatment received in the political process. I entered the field of legal prostitution late in life and feel that made it easier for me to view it as simply my job and reserve my feelings and emotions for when I was off duty. It is harder for the younger girls to do that.

I care about others and it is not often returned. The emotional pain I experience stems from my sensitive nature. Although I do my best to form a hardened protective shield around myself, my inborn nature is to nurture. I found solace in the shared understanding of my professional sisters. Legal prostitution is an honest business. The ladies provide a desired service gentlemen pay to receive. It's a simple business transaction. You know exactly who is getting screwed and how much it will cost. That is not the case with politics. The only difference between prostitution and politics, I found, is that prostitutes are honest about what they do.

I often summarized it in interviews or in speeches when I said, "In the bordellos, I worked with professional business women who rented their bodies. In politics, I was surrounded by whores who sold their souls."

While the attitudes of lawmakers are frustrating, there are fringes of society that are downright frightening. Probably the most feared element of society in the brothels and for the women who work in them are religious fanatics.

Pious zealots usually fall into two categories: masquerading as benevolent watch dogs out to "save" prostitutes, or "protecting" society by getting rid of prostitutes to cleanse the world.

Some sincerely believe they have been given a mission from God; others have a misdirected sense of duty to society, a few can be as delusional and dangerous as abortion clinic killers. Those on the outer fringe of reality feel God has either given them a "mission" to save the women from Hell, or to kill them in order to rid the world of sin. With "God on their side," they are certain they have been singled out to pick up His protective shield and pursue a duty as His moral warrior. A Bible in one hand or a gun in the other, they stalk the brothels and society's "fallen angels" in the same vein as a serial killer.

Protection from this element of society is a main reason women work under a stage name, usually don't wear wedding rings, and never give anyone they don't know – especially clients – their address, personal phone numbers or information on their family. For their own safety, most working girls are intensely private. That probably also adds to the air of mystery surrounding them.

Brothel prostitutes go about their normal lives when they aren't working and are just as vulnerable outside the safety of the houses as street hookers or escort call girls. The women are more aware of their surroundings than most other females but everyone lets down their guard occasionally. It's too much of a strain to be paranoid all the time. Sometimes that can have tragic consequences.

A twisted mind may not always be evident at first. That certainly has been proven by the charmingly normal appearing Ted Bundys of the world. A brothel prostitute is safe within the confines of her workplace but sometimes a client will mistake partying with a particular girl as encouragement and develop an imaginary relationship with her. It can get out of hand; he may stalk her outside the house. Being too candid can give the wrong person information he needs to plan harm, or even a murder. Sometimes it is because of the obsession he has nurtured in his fantasy world and he wants her only for himself. Most often, however, he feels he must eliminate her "for the good of mankind." All prostitutes, legal or not, know of a sister that has met this end.

Magnolia came to the Ranch from Florida. A stout girl, she had no family and soon felt she had found one at the Ranch. She was young, bubbly and trusting. Most TOs are. She also liked cocaine. She said it helped her refrain from food and stay up late. She resented the brothel taking half her pay and made no secret about meeting clients at the house and then making arrangements to date them for money outside the brothel later. That's a dangerous thing to do. Brothel women work in the houses so they don't have the danger of the streets or hotels. It is also grounds for termination, but Magnolia wasn't one to learn the easy way.

Her shift was due to begin and she was no where in sight. When she failed to show up again a day later, management wasn't terribly concerned. Magnolia was flighty, often strung out and irresponsible. She may have decided to go back to Florida and didn't think it was necessary to let the house know she wouldn't be back.

The madam saw the sheriff park his car and buzzed him in. They walked to the office where he closed the door behind him. We saw madam get a concerned look on her face and then bury it in her hands. The sheriff opened the door and looked at all of us standing quietly in a huddle in the middle of the parlor. We knew his visit had something to do with one of our sisters and it wasn't good.

He looked at us, sincere compassion on his face. He tipped his hat before leaving and said, "Ladies, please be careful. We don't like bad things to happen to good people in our territory."

Madam composed herself and came out into the parlor. "Magnolia was found in two separate lawn bags in a field a few miles from here. She had business cards from the Ranch in her pocket."

We were shattered. That was the second killing of a prostitute in the area in the past six months. Both had been dismembered and put into separate bags. The girls all looked at each other silently.

Women in the sex industry most feared zealots they didn't know; the ones who were invisible and unknown. Most of the local anti-brothel activists are familiar to the women working in the houses and simply fall into the off-center "pain in the rear" category.

One of the better known activists is George. I don't like the man and detest his incessant efforts to ruin the houses. In a strange way, though, I admire his talent for writing and even understand his frustration with the Comstock.

I first learned of George during my research on gold rush prostitutes. He wrote an incredible book about one particular woman of the era named Rosa May. I read the book several times because it reached inside me and grabbed an emotional spot I thought was safely tucked away. If a person has not worked as a prostitute, it is impossible to understand the range of emotions a working girl feels and the toll the life takes on her. Somehow, George was able to get inside the head of this woman and put into words what prostitutes throughout the centuries have thought, felt and experienced.

He had a clear love affair with the history of the gold rush era and at one time or another had lived in several locales filled with knowledge of the era, including Virginia City. Just as many before him had done, he moved to town with a deep passion for the village, its people, and its history. He wrote moving chronicles of the Comstock and its characters but somewhere along the passage of time, the town turned on him, as it has done to so many others. The black cloud of evil that hangs over the historic district seems to have a jealous lining when it comes to anyone who finds any measure of success or happiness. Residents seem determined to chew them up and spit them out. Eventually, as so many before and after him, George moved on, burned out at trying to fit in and embittered by years of battling unfair treatment that I could certainly relate to.

I had to meet this man whose moving book reduced me to tears and who shared mutual experiences at the hands of former Comstock neighbors.

Nearly all the years I worked in the bordellos, George made the houses his unrelenting and very public target. He filed an avalanche of briefs with the courts in an attempt to put the houses out of business, tried to obtain names of credit card clients in an effort to determine if the lady they partied with insisted on using condoms, and unmercifully harassed the establishments, the women and some clients. The newspapers followed his bizarre antics and, despite house reassurance that their privacy would be protected, some clients began staying away.

George not only went after the houses in Lyon County whose owners fought back through the courts, he also went after Nye County brothels, which included the territory of the feared and powerful "brothel baron." He apparently was also afraid they might fight back in other ways, as he began to drop out of sight except for occasional stops at one of his favorite watering holes in Gold Hill. He was hard to track.

From what I could determine, around the time his book was published, he "found religion" and his outlook did a complete 180. Now blindly devoted to closing the brothels and freeing the world of prostitution, he wanted others to know the Lord's will as he perceived it.

It took a while but I finally tracked him down to a public establishment I had learned he frequented. He recognized me immediately from media stories and was clearly unnerved at our encounter.

"George, your book really touched me. Please let me buy you a cup of coffee back at one of the quiet tables where we can talk." I implored him. It took some doing but he finally agreed to give me a few minutes of his time.

He was skittish the whole time we talked and kept looking over his shoulder like he expected the ATF to barge through the door at any moment. During our brief conversation, I began to realize the author who understood the mind of the gold rush "soiled dove" so tenderly and sensitively no longer existed. Finally his discomfort compelled him to leave. After he left, I sat there digesting what had just taken place. Sadly, I understood that social abuse and religious overload had silenced his talent and ability to share in words the rich treasure of Comstock prostitution history.

Then one day, the huge cross George had in his yard disappeared. As abruptly as it began, his mission appeared to cease.

While George was persistent and more low key, Milo John Reese is flamboyant and outrageous. Reese worked with George in their mutual crusade to abolish the houses but he followed a more aggressive, bizarre, and annoying approach to closing the brothels than George did.

Reese admits he visited prostitutes in his younger days but now sees prostitution as morally wrong and offensive to his current Christian beliefs.

He was once arrested for chaining himself to the door of the building that contained the state Health Division. For years, he tried to find evidence that brothels spread AIDS and claimed the department hid results of positive HIV tests despite department records which showed no positive test results for the HIV virus among women already working in the bordellos since testing began in 1986.

On numerous occasions, he secretly taped conversations with prostitutes hoping they would incriminate themselves, which never happened. Nevertheless, he routinely turned the tapes over to the media.

He spent more than $1,500 of his own money to rent two billboards along the freeway leading to Mustang Ranch and Old Bridge Ranch which claimed brothels were not HIV-safe. When both Reese and the sign company were advised they would be sued for false information by the brothel association, the billboard company painted over the signs within a week.

His claim of wanting to open a gay brothel in Nye County was found to be only a story he made up to bolster attention to his campaign against the evils of prostitution.

Reese ran for state assembly on an anti-prostitution platform and lost miserably in a state where significant revenue from the brothels pad government coffers.

But his most scandalous stunt to date was a staged disappearance that cost him nearly $9,000 in reimbursement costs to law enforcement for expenses incurred in the search and investigation into his mysterious disappearance.

Authorities found his abandoned car near Old Bridge Ranch still running, with the keys in it, the driver's door open, the window smashed, and blood both inside and outside the car.

His wife said he told her he was going to the brothel for a meeting and would be back in half an hour. When he failed to return, she assumed he went on vacation, since he was known to disappear in the past.

Despite his wife's odd explanation, officials found Reese's disappearance suspicious and searched the river. They brought in a helicopter in an effort to determine how and why he vanished.

Several days later, video cameras in a California bank captured him withdrawing funds from his account. Shortly afterward, Reese called both his wife and authorities from Las Vegas, admitting he staged his disappearance to gain publicity. After investigators talked him into turning himself in, they paid for his flight back to Reno, which Reese must repay as part of his restitution.

Obviously, prostitution is not his only problem. I couldn't help wonder why anyone would go to such lengths to eliminate establishments he once frequented. Revenge came to mind. I imagined him buck naked in one of the houses with a hooker pointing at his cherished member while laughing hysterically. In reality, religion seems to be the more obvious answer.

The frightening thing about zealots or brothel patrons who become obsessed with particular ladies is that you never know when they will snap. People with a slipping grip on reality too often get so obsessed with their make believe world that they no longer are able to differentiate fact from fantasy.

I encountered similar religious zeal on TV shows I did but it was in a controlled environment so I didn't fear the messenger. By the time I had done a dozen shows, I was fed up with judgmental extremists and dished it right back.

I appeared on "The Jerry Springer Show" before his format changed into the now-infamous free-for-all riot zone with gutter-guests from hell. It was typical of the talk show format where my story was presented and the host and audience ask questions. I don't mind doing the shows because very few people outside Nevada understand the difference between legal bordellos and the illegal street and call girl arena. It gives me a chance to tell folks the truth about the industry, so I endure their often senseless, tasteless questions.

A large woman in a dress down to her ankles and her dark hair pulled up in a bun on her head, stood up. I hate the religious recitals. She went through the whole number though. From Mary Magdalene to her request that I turn my life over to God and get a "real" job.

"You're entitled to your opinion," I began, "but personally, I'm not concerned with my lifestyle or my chances of going to heaven because I don't think God is as narrow-minded as you are." She looked like I had slapped her and sat back down without another word.

In the hall after the show, we were walking out to the limousine when I spotted her up ahead. I ran up and extended my hand.

"Our lives are very different," I began, "but we are both human beings. I want to thank you for your view and I hope you will think about mine." We visited for a few minutes and the transformation in her attitude was worth every minute.

As we walked off toward the door, I heard her say to her companion, "Oh, I feel so terrible. She's really very sweet."

I smiled. Each person I can touch and every attitude I can change will be passed on to someone else.

One of the most severe reactions from a show came from the hostess herself on the now-cancelled "Rolanda Watts Show." Filmed on a freezing day in New York City, we were already tense from the weather. We became even more stressed when we faced a hostile audience who kept screaming at us that their mothers would work 10 jobs if necessary to feed their babies without turning to prostitution. Explaining that my particular job was not only a "real" job, but a legal one too, made absolutely no difference.

"Women in all walks of life have used sex to climb the business ladder," I explained. "My job just carries the label."

In a flash, Ms. Watts pulled herself up to full height and snarled righteously, "I'm a proud black woman and I'll have you know I got to the top on my feet, not on my back." Then she went to commercial and stomped off the stage. Hypocrisy knows no gender, race, age or barrier.

I had never intimated that my remark was directed at her. The tape showed it to be the general remark I meant it to be. Apparently a guilty conscience has thin skin. She was horrible to us the remainder of the show. We were glad to get back outside where the temperatures were warmer.

On the plane home after the show, I reflected on my efforts to do something positive for my community and the sadness I felt when my efforts were treated like dirt over and over again. It reminded me of Lottie Johl.

I've always had a fascination for western history of the 1800s, especially the gold rush mining camps. The minute I set foot in Virginia City, I knew I had lived there before. It felt so familiar. I knew I was home.

I've studied all the case histories I could research of gold rush era prostitutes. The most haunting for me personally was the true story of Lottie Johl. If one believes in reincarnation, they would be convinced Michael and I are this century's continuing love story of Eli and Lottie Johl.

Lottie and I were both born a century apart in Iowa and raised on a ranch. Country roots instill a solid sense of decency that no occupation can erase. Lottie's status in life was never in question to those who met her. She appeared to be a woman of class.

In reality, she was an unmarried woman working in the only profession that paid livable wages at the time – a high-class prostitute. Her spirit for life and caring for others set her apart from most of the other women and made her a favorite of clients.

The local butcher fell deeply in love with her and they married, despite her background which made her a total outcast of the town's "proper" society. Lottie's husband was her world and they lived a true love story.

Society was not about to let them forget she was not up to their standards, however. When she and Eli threw their first party, the "righteous" wife of Eli's business partner took it upon herself to "uninvite" the guests and no one showed up. Lottie's heart was broken. Eli hurt for her and was determined she would one day be accepted by the small minded town.

She was a good person and a devoted wife but was shunned by everyone except her husband. Eli adored her and did everything he could to ease her loneliness and depression.

He came up with a grand plan for the town to get to know and accept Lottie without realizing at first who she was. He purchased a most elaborate costume for Lottie to wear to the town's masquerade ball. Eli would stay home so her identity would remain secret. When she was declared winner of the best costume and her identity unveiled, they would finally accept her.

He was wrong. She did win but when guests realized who she was, they ripped away her dignity and let her know in no uncertain terms that she was not welcome at their ball. She left in tears.

Eli went wild. Lottie gave up and turned off her feelings. She knew then that no matter how good a person she was, society would never let her be one of them. Their special love pulled Eli and Lottie closer to comfort and care for each other.

When Lottie became ill, the doctor prescribed medication but she soon died. An autopsy showed the medicine had been poisoned. The final chapter of the witch hunt had been played out. Evil won. Eli never recovered from his grief and built a monument to his love that left many in the town in tears. Too late, the town realized Lottie and Eli had been real human beings after all.

Just as Eli knew Lottie would never be accepted by society when no one showed up for their party and Lottie herself finally came to that realization when she was evicted from the ball, Michael and I have had similar experiences and know the feeling all too well. Society continues to play the same sick games today.

"Company, Ladies!"

Company, ladies!" chimed the madam. Four men entered the room and looked around. Nervously, they headed for the bar. It was a busy night. Guys were lined up at the bar talking to the women. One by one, they drifted off to tour the facilities.

On weekends, nearly every specialty room was either occupied by potential clients on tour or booked. This Lyon County ranch was one of the most popular and easy to reach brothels since it was just over the county line from Carson City. I liked it because the ladies really did have control over their own business in this house. It had a relaxed comfortable atmosphere, and I could go home after my shift.

Ann-Marie was in the VIP room showing a tall, muscular man the massage table and Jacuzzi. This was one of the more popular rooms, especially for gentlemen who do manual labor and want to relax more than just their erotic muscles.

Ann-Marie and I were both skilled in massage. My specially built table stood in the corner. Hearts were cut into the wood on the sides—I was always the romantic. Soothing music, rain or waterfall sounds, scented candles and warming oils were always part of the full-body massages. The lighting featured blue, pink and green hues that were always kept dim to create an atmosphere of comfort and relaxation. A greenhouse roof with a sprinkler system allowed those enjoying the Jacuzzi to see the sky and trees above the room and the sprinkler system along two sides of the room kept the huge ferns that surrounded the Jacuzzi constantly moist and lush. An artistic placement of large boulders with water flowing over them into the Jacuzzi gave the illusion of an outdoor waterfall and soothed the ears with the soft sound of water splashing into the Jacuzzi. The four-poster bed at the end of the room stood as an invitation to the final phase of the VIP experience. Soft sheer drapes hung from the solid wood frame that formed the canopy around the top and pulled away at the middle to tie at the four posters. The down filled comforter and huge down pillows allowed occupants to romp in what felt like a cloud. Wine was always available on the antique night table beside the bed. An hour in this room was much too little.

At the other end of the spectrum was the dungeon room. While nearly every gentleman who visited the Ranch wanted to see it, few actually booked it and some even ran from it. The interior was all black and an intimidating stockade stood in the middle. Hang-hooks were secured into the back wall. Adorning the wall was an assortment of whips, feathers, hoods, masks, gloves, studded collars, leashes, handcuffs and leather attire. An ultra violet light was all that lit the room. Hard rock music blared when the room was in service. A window with a heavy removable black-out curtain faced the hallway for those who wanted their activities watched by passers-by. Only a few ladies were trained in S & M, dominance and obedience training and were the only ones at this Ranch that gentlemen could party with in the dungeon. These women had total control over their emotions and the house knew they would not get carried away with their activities. After all, gentlemen expected to leave with everything they arrived with – especially since they were paying for it!

The orgy room was comprised of wood paneled walls which showcased nude paintings and huge Italian framed mirrors. It was always booked. Massive pillows covered nearly every inch of the floor. Mirrors encased the entire ceiling. Gigantic ferns were everywhere to provide discreet privacy for those who wanted to wander off by themselves for a private encounter. Adult videos ran 24 hours, and sex toys were available in the credenza. A large bowl of variety condoms sat on the antique table just beside the bathroom door. There was a choice for everyone including glow-in-the-dark. The group sex room was always one of the most popular at the Ranch.

Each lady's room was an individually decorated private theme room and reflected the personality of the lady occupying it. Each lady put her room together when she began her shift and took it down when she left. That is one of the main reasons bordello working girls arrive and leave with huge steamer trunks. A gentleman may find himself spending time in a leopard infested jungle, a Victorian mansion, a biker's den complete with motorcycle, a movie star's sound stage, the nurse's quarters of a hospital, a wild west saloon, a school principal's office, a roaring 20s speakeasy, or any number of other fantasy retreats. The main appeal of the houses is that they are a virtual candy store of fantasy with no strings attached.

The buzzer rang and the ladies began filtering into the parlor. Two men in business suits entered. The taller man immediately chose a tall, sophisticated looking girl named Priscilla and went directly to her room. The shorter man went to the bar. Music blared, conversation overlapped and every so often the bartender reminded gentlemen not to touch the "merchandise."

Composure begins to wear thin after about the 10th hour on the floor. Each lady has her own way of dealing with exhaustion. Cassandra had a wicked sense of humor that kept the girls laughing and was usually upbeat and vivacious. She had been on the floor 12 hours, however, and was really tired.

A clean scrubbed athletic girl, her shiny long black hair hung down to her waist and her big eyes always had a hint of mischief in them. Unlike the other girls, she usually wore fringed "Daisy Duke" shorts with a crop top and combat boots. She looked like she was ready to go hiking instead of a romp in a bordello.

Jose took one look at her and right out in the middle of the parlor pulled some crumpled bills from his pocket. "I want to get fucked for $50," he announced loudly. Cassandra told him money was never discussed outside the rooms and stomped off.

"Fifty dollars, now!" Jose insisted.

Many Hispanics who visited the ranch were used to Tijuana prostitutes and spending no more than $10. Consequently, they felt they were being generous to American women by offering $50. You'd think the ladies' sarcastic sneers and an empty parlor time after time would be a clear clue but they continued to make the same old insulting offer.

"The house minimum is $100," Cassandra informed him. "Nothing happens under $50 except drinks at the bar."

"No," Jose insisted. "I want to get fucked for $50." He kept repeating the offer, getting more and more insistent and irritating as he looked Cassandra up and down, drool curling out the corners of his mouth.

Not a woman to mince words, Cassandra finally had it with his disrespectful whining. She smiled sweetly at Jose and batted her eyes. "OK, sugar, give me your $50."

Jose got a wide grin on his face, puffed out his chest in macho triumph for his buddies and handed Cassandra the money.

Still smiling but spitting out the words between clenched teeth as she tucked the $50 into her bra, she said, "Why thank you, darlin'. Now you're fucked!"

Stifling a laugh, I turned to the madam who also was trying to keep a straight face. She asked me to come to the office. She motioned for me to close the door and then began to explain the phone call. A high level political VIP called inquiring about an out-date for the evening.

While most officials seeking services from the houses are from Nevada, they weren't the only political leaders with whom the girls spent time. It wasn't unusual for high level political figures from all over the nation to visit or request out-dates from the brothels when they visited Nevada. Those in public office knew their identity would not be revealed and ladies would show no sign of recognition should their paths cross in public later. The houses provided anonymity that gave these guests peace of mind.

The guest described by madam was no stranger to prostitutes. He went to great lengths to project a spotless public persona since he was now one of the most powerful men in politics but he had not always been so discreet. In years past, his affinity was known and utilized by those seeking favors and became public knowledge even as he tried to keep his trysts low key.

Mr. VIP described the date he wanted as a petite woman with a classy appearance, preferably a redhead, upbeat personality and able to converse on a wide variety of subjects. The madam assured him she had the perfect companion for him.

Pulling my hair up and putting on a sequined gown, I was ready when his car arrived at the appointed time. The chauffeur paid the madam and then drove me to an elegant hotel where he escorted me to Mr. VIP's room. When he answered the door, his eyes registered approval. I instantly recognized him. Extending my hand, I introduced myself. He took it, quietly closing the door behind us.

While he poured a drink, I looked around the room. The table was set with a tablecloth, china, lighted candles and soft music, clearly awaiting my arrival. He handed me a glass and motioned to the couch. He picked up the phone and announced he was ready for room service and then we visited while waiting for dinner to arrive.

An average sized man, he looked every bit the part of the important political figure he was. He had on a dark business suit and conservative tie. "Your madam was right," he said. "I'm not disappointed. You look lovely."

"Thank you," I replied, reflecting on the picture I had seen of him and his wife in yesterday's newspaper. I appeared to be a more flamboyant version of her.

We were afforded a pleasant amount of time to relax and visit before the knock on the door. Dinner had arrived. After the elegant meal and interesting conversation, Mr. VIP suggested we relax in the in-room Jacuzzi and enjoy another glass of wine while he told me about his fantasy.

He had already described his fantasy to the madam so I would be prepared when I arrived. As he talked, I got a clear idea of the role reversal Mr. VIP had in mind. Burdened with making decisions of major impact, he wanted absolutely no responsibility during the party and wanted me to take over with obedience training and dominate him.

It was quite a sight to see Mr. VIP on his hands and knees, buck naked except for his black spike studded neck collar whose attached leash was held by Miss Jessi – now a woman in control in black studded leather with cat tails, spiked heels and a take-charge look. Leash in one hand, whip in the other – he was at my command.

The session was great fun. I took special pleasure in making him massage my feet and thank me for the honor. Here I was, a bordello call girl, telling one of the most powerful men in politics when he could speak and when he could move. And when he was a bad boy – I whipped or spanked him.

As his final command of the role play session, I turned to Mr. VIP and demanded he plant a big kiss on my firm behind. I chuckled silently as he did as he was told. What a great evening. It's not every day you get to tell a powerful public official to kiss your ass and get paid for it.

The next morning I returned to the house but slept in until afternoon. After a leisurely shower, I asked the maid to make up my room while I went to the kitchen to see what Betty had prepared. Then I put on my war paint, a flowing kelly green see through robe with a t-bar and bra underneath and joined the other girls in the parlor.

Every house has local clients that visit on a regular basis. This Ranch is located in the country just outside Nevada's capital, Carson City. Agriculture and ranching are an important industry in the area.

In most regions of the state, as soon as one leaves the city limits the terrain becomes brown and covered with sagebrush as far as the eye can see. Here however, as one descends the hill just a few miles from the Ranch, a treat awaits their eyes.

Lush green pasture land covers the rolling hills as far as the eye can see. A windmill turns lazily in the breeze creating water for the well where the cattle and sheep drink. The river runs behind the barn situated at the back of a ranch. It supplies the water necessary for the luxuriant crop of trees and bushes that line both sides and provide shade for the animals that graze along its banks. Cattle munch on alfalfa at one end of the property while the landscape is dotted with sheep at the other.

Clients enjoy themselves at the bordellos in widely differing ways. A case in point is "Marilyn." She was probably the ugliest woman to have ever donned lingerie and perched on a couch in a brothel parlor. That probably was due to the fact "she" was actually a "he."

In reality, Marilyn was really Tater, a huge construction worker who was a regular at the Ranch. His co-workers nicknamed him Tater long ago due to his love of French fries. Over time, the fries had all accumulated around his belly. Tater was 6'3", 280 pounds of solid construction muscle except for his stomach, in his 40s, balding and sported a full, bushy, salt and pepper beard. Hardly the petite, demure little hooker he pretended to be.

Nevertheless, Tater was one of our favorite clients. Any day Tater came to visit was a day filled with fun and laughter. He brought his own suitcase filled with make-up, wigs, cheap jewelry, perfume, high heels, mesh nylons and hooker clothing. He always came in after work and booked three hours so he could shock unsuspecting gentlemen who visited in the evenings. It would be safe to say he never failed to accomplish that goal.

His truck was loud and could be heard before we saw him ring the bell. He'd lumber up the walk and madam would buzz him in. Looking around the room, he'd break into a wide grin.

"Hey sisters," he'd say, putting his hand on his hip and sashaying around the room, "the queen is here! Eat your hearts out. I'm going to make all the money tonight."

The ladies laughed. We were always glad to see Tater. He always booked four girls for a "slumber party." Nearly an hour was spent doing his make-up, combing his wig just right, and arranging his clothing to hide obvious "flaws." There was absolutely nothing any of us could do about his beard, however. After the giggling and primping was done, Tater would join the rest of the girls at the dinner table. He was now "Marilyn."

Dinner finished, "Marilyn" joined the other ladies in the parlor. For the next hour it was hysterical to watch the faces of potential clients as they entered the parlor. In disbelief, they looked at "Marilyn" as if they had taken a wrong turn and wound up in a loony bin instead of a brothel. Some turned tail and ran. Others played along and bought him drinks and sat on his lap. Everyone had a good time. Tater always brightened the day.

Not long after Tater left, I saw Kat lugging her big trunk up to the gate. She rang twice. Two rings meant no line-up or parlor gathering was necessary because it was either a repeat customer or one of the girls. Madam opened the gate and then the entry door for her and Kat gave her a hug.

"You're in room 14 this shift, honey," the madam informed her. That was Kat's favorite room. She always got the suite because she booked so well. Lots of ambiance, closet space and close to the Jacuzzi.

Kat's name fit her. Almost all her outfits were leopard skin and her room was decorated like a jungle. A tall girl with honey colored hair, big liquid eyes and boobs the size of punch bowls, she didn't walk – she slinked like a she-cat on the prowl. She drove men wild.

The other girls hated to work on Kat's shifts. She was always high booker and morale suffered. The worst part was that Kat was a sweetheart and it was damn near impossible for the girls to dislike her!

"What a bummer. Kat makes all the money and is still liked by her sisters," pouted Renee.

Kat decided to take her shower first, grab something to eat and then decorate her room. Pushing her trunk into the closet, she pulled out her robe, got towels from the maid and disappeared into the bathroom.

As Kat opened the bathroom door to leave, Amber was just walking her gentleman back to the parlor. He spotted Kat. She had a towel wrapped around her head, no make-up and wore her comfy old robe and floppy slippers.

"Helllllooo, Sugar," he bellowed, dropping Amber's hand. "How about I dry your back?"

"That's extra," she laughed as she glanced at Amber and rolled her eyes upward.

"I just know it would be worth every dime," he answered as Amber rounded the corner to tell the madam her date was over and he was now talking to Kat.

"My room's not ready and neither am I, sugar," she explained to lover-boy.

"Who cares," he shot back. "I am and I'm the one with the money."

Realizing he wasn't bluffing, Kat looked back over her shoulder and shot him one of her killer looks. "Then follow me big boy." It was going to be a good shift.

Who could figure? For every man who walked through the front door, there was a different fantasy in each one's head. One wanted an innocent school girl, another wanted a femme fatale in a long slinky gown, while still another wanted shorts and combat boots. This one wanted a substitute for his wife – complete with bathrobe and no make-up. Men . . . ya gotta love 'em but don't even try to figure 'em out.

The interesting thing about the Ranch was its proximity to Carson City and Lake Tahoe. The door was opened to many well known political figures who sought diversion from the hum-drum grind of bureaucracy. The madam greeted famous celebrities whose vacation homes were located just up the hill among the pine trees of the lake.

Usually, recognizable public figures call for an "out-date." Rather than come to the house, they prefer companionship in the privacy of their own territory.

They either come to the house and pick the lady they want to take out or they describe the date they want to the madam and she picks the ladies that most closely match a gentleman's description and then have him talk to them and make his own choice. The date is arranged and the lady of choice goes to the client.

Others prefer the unique excitement of a "house of ill repute." The houses provide anonymity so most gentlemen are not uncomfortable about visiting. Many like the naughtiness of making love in a bordello instead of their home or a hotel and prefer the houses where the atmosphere is unlike anywhere else. There is always excitement in the air, constant activity, an on-going spark of fun and a continual tingle of commotion not found anywhere else. A good many recognizable people were not a bit shy about spending time at the houses. They knew their privacy and secrets would be protected.

As I walked down the hall toward the parlor, I heard his voice. It was distinctive, loud and recognizable. The girls were laughing hysterically. Only one person I knew sounded like that and had the ability to put people in stitches instantly by just looking at the crazy expressions on his face. But that person was back in Hollywood at the studios. I had worked with Shane at Warner Brothers. His famous comedy roles in film had endeared him to millions. What was he doing in a brothel in Nevada? I peeked around the corner. There he stood, surrounded by women in t-bars.

I walked into the room and put both hands on my hips and waited for him to look in my direction. When he finally did, he threw his head back and laughed uproariously.

"I heard you were here, Jessi," he said as he broke loose from the throng of female attention and walked over to hug me. "Only you would have the balls to do honestly what everyone else does under false pretense."

We talked about old times for a few minutes and I asked him about various people we had both worked with on the sets.

"I knew you were seeing a few actors on the sets you worked on," he commented.

"We were just friends then because I was involved with someone at the time. I'm not involved any more and I'd like to be added to the notches on your bedpost now!" he laughed as he grabbed my hand and headed down the hall.

He booked two hours. We spent part of the first hour reminiscing. Making movies is not all fun and glamour. It's hard work, long hours and tremendous stress – for those behind the scenes as well as talent. On some sets, cast and crew did very little mixing. On others, everyone was one big family working toward the same goal. Shane's set fell into the latter category and the bizarre approach to humor we both shared made us instant friends.

Shane was fascinated with my cowgirl lifestyle. During filming breaks at the studio he had me teach him the two-step, cotton eyed Joe and the cowboy waltz. He'd never been to a country western club and wanted to go dancing. His girlfriend was back east, and since we were just friends he felt comfortable going with me. I loved country dancing and often went to a club in Glendale, not far from the studios, where there was an exceptional live band.

It was a funny sight. His limo pulled up outside my house and neighbors peered out their windows expecting some important, impeccably dressed yuppie to step out. Instead, a cowboy dressed to the hilt in western style, hat pulled low so he wouldn't be recognized, rang my doorbell. I cracked up. It was not his style and he must have picked up the costume right out of studio wardrobe. He even had on chaps. He was having trouble walking with all the fringe flapping around his legs and was quite relieved to learn real cowboys don't wear chaps to go dancing. He quickly took them off, threw them in the air and headed for the car.

The club was big and friendly. As soon as the music started, no one could sit still. It had a huge dance floor and it was quite a sight to see all those hats moving in a graceful circle to the beat of the music. We had a great time. Folks recognized him and said hello but left him alone. He liked that best. Toward the end of the evening, he had enough beers that his feet were no longer doing what he wanted them to do, so we decided to call it an evening. Then he got a bright idea.

He had never ridden a city bus before. I pointed out that a recognizable star would have a problem being faceless on a bus and would draw a crowd. He didn't care. It was two in the morning. Who would be riding a bus at that time anyway? He was determined and when Shane decided he was going to do something, it would be easier to move New York City to London than change his mind. He told his driver to go home and we began walking to the bus stop.

We walked a few blocks away from the business district into a residential area and headed for the main boulevard to catch the bus. It was dark and deserted and I wasn't having as much fun anymore. The liquor made Shane oblivious to anything except the great time he was having just being a regular person.

"I have to take a leak," he said out of the blue.

"Great," I shot back, "We're in a section of town filled with houses instead of businesses with restrooms, it's the middle of the night and you have to go to the bathroom. You can't just go up and knock on someone's door and ask to use their restroom," I explained logically. "Just hold it, Shane."

It was dark and I wanted to get to the lighted boulevard as fast as we could. I walked a little faster. Then I became aware of the fact I was walking alone. I looked back just in time to see Shane haul someone's recycle crate over to the mailbox, pull down the lid and solve his problem. Smiling, he caught up with me. I couldn't take him anywhere!

He finally got to ride a bus. But the one we got on was filled with young gang members. They kept eyeing us. Really scared, I told him I wanted off the bus and for him to call his driver and get us to our respective homes in one piece. Now.

The group of about ten young men dressed all in black looked angry and intimidating. Then they began to point. I was terrified when they all started coming back to where we were sitting.

The leader stopped and sat down in the seat in front of us. "Hey man," he said to Shane, "aren't you the crazy dude in the movies?"

Shane went into a full routine. He had them all laughing. By the time the group reached their stop, they were best buds with Shane and each gave him a high five as they left the bus. We both let out a big sigh of relief and got off at the next stop and called his driver. I never took him dancing again!

And now, here he was. I was really glad to see him. He had a house at the lake and came up twice a year — once in the summer to enjoy the water and in the winter to ski. We had never been anything but buddies and it was always a bit more difficult to party with someone you knew prior to the house. A "business" feeling is harder to maintain when there is already some form of history between client and working girl. Partying with Shane could have been a bit awkward if he had had a different personality. He made everything relaxed and comfortable, however, and we had a great time.

* * *

Entertainment and sports industry people who had vacation houses in the Lake Tahoe area and partied at the bordellos were almost
always fun. Political figures who worked just a few miles down the
road in Carson City were another story. They were almost always full
of themselves, stuffy, uptight, tightwads and extremely spoiled and
picky. The girls hated to see them come through the doors.

Penny had a regular bureaucrat client that worked in a legal field
for the state. He didn't just walk through the gate, he strutted. He fit
the mold perfectly. Penny could get along with anyone. "Mr. I'm So
Fine" was one of her biggest challenges. He was a flat out jerk. He
never tipped and he always tried to get reduced prices with vague
promises of legal assistance should she ever need it. He was a lot of
work and not much fun.

An exception to the political rule was Eddie. The houses were a
candy store to him and he became a kid every time he walked through
the doors. His open, happy nature and genuine love of people made
him different from other legislators. Small in stature, he was large in
personality. He liked spending time with a woman who made no
demands and didn't stake a claim to him after one date. He loved the
ladies and treated them like gold. He became a willing ally later when
I spent time at legislative sessions on behalf of brothel issues.

Many elected and appointed pillars of the community spent time
within the walls of the houses. The usual joke was that they were
doing "research" so they could better decide how to vote or make
decisions on brothel related issues. Right! We made sure their potential votes or decisions would be positive!

Sometimes clients fall in love with the ladies. More accurately,
they fall in love with a fantasy, but it still is one of the most difficult
and delicate situations a working girl faces.

The majority of clients who visit the houses are looking for something in addition to, or in conjunction with, sex. The houses often
provide a service to the spirit as well as the body. In a hostile world
where people are treated like a number, in a cold indifferent manner
that rules out human warmth, gentlemen often visit the houses for
conversation, companionship, validation, a warm accepting female
touch, or simply to be able to joke around and relax with a woman

without fear of a sexual harassment suit being filed against them. This was the case with Joel.

I first saw him sitting in the parlor with some of his buddies. He was the kind of guy that always caught my eye. Big, rugged, earthy. His friends were partying but Joel was sitting by himself. I couldn't understand why he wasn't partying.

He was a big man; 6'5", 220 pounds of solid muscle, neatly trimmed beard, sandy colored hair, kind mischievous eyes, well dressed in clean crisp western attire, early 40s and good looking. He was sitting on the couch entertaining the ladies with funny stories and jokes. He had good manners too. Since he wasn't going to party but had the pleasure of a free fashion show, he bought all the ladies a round of drinks explaining he was the designated driver and would not be participating.

Knowing that, most of the ladies wandered off realizing their time would be better spent on another guest. I remained. I love a sense of humor. It was nice to spend a few minutes just talking to a pleasant person and sharing a few laughs. The more we talked, the more we enjoyed each other's company.

Impulsively, he turned to me and said, "Hey Red, how about taking me on one of those infamous tours?"

Newly divorced and clearly missing female company, he said he changed his mind and wanted to know if I would spend time with him in the Jacuzzi, give him a full body massage and just talk and cuddle with him. I was delighted. He booked an hour-and-a-half which went by in a flash. He was an extremely sensitive, tender person and big as he was, he was a teddy bear who loved being snuggled and rocked while we talked. Simple human comfort was what caused him to confuse compassion with love.

The following day, a dozen roses arrived at the house for me. They were from Joel. Later in the afternoon, I got a phone call. After that, Joel visited me on a regular basis.

Once a week, he would make the several hundred mile drive from northern California, over the mountains to the house to spend two or three hours together. I knew he was not a man of wealth but rather a rugged man who lived alone in a log cabin in the mountains. I was not the kind of person to take advantage of another human being and was concerned that he was becoming too emotionally involved.

I resolved to talk to Joel during his next visit and let him know that this was a business to me. He had already begun to express how important I was to him; how he would like me to spend time with him at his ranch. I could see the direction this was going. I had to put a stop to it before he got hurt.

It wasn't that easy or that simple. Sitting in the Jacuzzi, I explained to Joel that this was a business where the lines of fantasy and reality often become blurred and confused. Mine was a business in which clients always saw their ladies in a dream state and all their fantasies were fulfilled – just the way they wanted them to be. Clients didn't see the wild mane of hair pulled severely back into a simple ponytail, the face without make-up, the curves covered by a baggy sweatshirt, over sized jeans and clompy tennis shoes, or perfectly manicured nails dirty with soil from the garden that had just been tended. In the world of bordellos, ladies were forever perfect in the eyes of their gentlemen. When seen outside the walls of the houses, they topple from their pedestals and become mere human beings – faults and all.

While most of the ladies genuinely liked and enjoyed many of their clients and often became friends with them, those friendships still fell within business perimeters. Emotional involvement was reserved for home.

I tenderly put a hand on each side of his face and looked right into his eyes. "I have a life outside this house," I said gently. "I have a lifetime commitment to the man in my life. I'm very happy to fulfill the fantasies you have, Joel, and to be the woman in your life for a two-hour love affair when you visit the house but when you walk back out that door, you have to understand the fantasy is over and you have to return to your normal every day life and reality."

I told him I was flattered to receive his roses but encouraged him to not spend his hard earned money on me outside the house. I thought he understood. The following day; however, another dozen roses arrived and I knew he didn't understand after all.

Over the next few weeks, I did my best to continue talking to him and help him understand that his fantasy could never be reality. I hated to give him up as one of my regular clients because he was one of the warmest, dearest people to come through the doors of the brothel.

He had already professed his love and asked me to end the relationship I was currently in and marry him. I knew the time had come to make it clear that he had to move on without me.

The next time he called to make an appointment, I told him as gently as I could that he needed to start visiting other ladies. I told him he would always be a dear friend and remembered fondly but he should not plan on partying with me again. As delicate as I was with explaining my decision not to see him any more, he was equally incapable of accepting it.

I talked to the madam and the next time Joel walked in the door, the madam greeted him warmly and explained I would not be available but there were plenty of other ladies he could get to know. He stared sadly at the madam for a minute and then turned and left. His truck would never come up the driveway again.

I hurt for Joel and was really bummed, so I was glad Mondays were usually slow. It gave me time to work through my blue mood.

* * *

Several girls were in the parlor with me talking about tricks of the trade. One of the oldest tricks in the book, and one of the most pleasurable for gentlemen clients, is the "Alka-Seltzer Fizz." It was also a prank the seasoned ladies often played on TOs, especially ones with an attitude. Faith was such a case.

The same fizzling little bubbles that calm a stomach also enhance intercourse. When a lady inserts half a tablet before partying, the bubbles tickle, massage and grab a client's "magnificent animal" – even with a condom – and drives him wild at just the right moment. It is pleasurable for the female partner too ... as long as it's only *half* a tablet.

* * *

Faith was a pain from the minute she walked through the door. A tall, extremely thin girl in her late 20s, there was no disputing she was sexy. She had a pretty face and long auburn hair that she usually wore up in a wild bird's nest style because she always did a strip tease dance in her room for her clients. Letting her hair fall loose into the client's face during the dance number was part of her routine. She came from the strip clubs in St. Louis and was used to enticing clients with dirty dancing.

Some brothels, such as Villa Joy in Winnemucca, now feature strippers in their café area who are not prostitutes. Others, like Sagebrush, have installed a pole in the parlor for working girls to tease clients. At this particular time, however, "dirty hustling" was not allowed in the parlor because it gave some girls an unfair advantage that caused the others to be in foul moods and therefore ruined the atmosphere. When caught, the madam would send a dirty hustler to her room for several hours, depriving her of potential business. Faith just didn't get it, however.

Time and again, she would stand at the back of the room near the bar and do a modified version of her bump and grind routine within direct eye view of a potential client but out of sight of the madam and where most of her sisters had their backs to her. It usually worked. The girls were fed up.

As "mom," I tried talking to Faith on several occasions, each heart-to-heart becoming stronger than the last. She had spent time in her room when caught and even that didn't make an impact. It was clear she didn't care about the other girls and simply wanted things her way. The only option now was "hooker revenge."

The next couple of warnings were extremely explicit and stern. They were also ineffective. The next step was the Fizz. During slow times in between client rushes, ladies normally sat in the parlor and talked. We agreed to "educate" Faith about Alka-Seltzer.

"Have you tried the biggest turn-on of all yet, Faith?" Shawnee asked her innocently.

"What's that?" Faith inquired, taking the bait.

"Alka-Seltzer," came the reply.

"What are you talking about?" asked Faith.

The girls did their best to keep a straight face as Shawnee began explaining this miracle sexual mystery.

"If you insert *three* Alka Seltzer tablets just before partying, it will drive your client wild and they leave so happy they tip you BIG time!" Shawnee said in all seriousness.

"No kidding," Faith replied. Greedy as she was, we knew it wouldn't be long before we saw – or heard – the outcome of her little experiment.

Sure enough. An hour later, a smiling client left Faith's room. She followed shortly after holding her stomach. Plopping down on the couch she complained that the bubbles were making her feel really uncomfortable instead of sexy. Some of the women had to leave the room, hands over their mouths to stifle uncontrollable laugher.

Within minutes, Faith was truly miserable. As she stood up to go to her room, a large and very loud escape of air filled the room. Embarrassed, she headed for the bathroom. For nearly 24 hours, every time she got up from a sitting position, loud gas sounds followed her. She couldn't work. She stayed in her room mad as a hornet, determined to hustle even harder to get back at her sisters. Not a wise decision.

Outright discipline by fellow sisters was something all ladies wanted to avoid at all costs. Life hath no wrath like a pissed hooker's revenge! Over a period of weeks, Faith pushed it to the limit and finally crossed over the line.

Almost never do ladies take revenge on a fellow sister. But when they do, intervention by management is not necessary. The women take care of hard core cases themselves, in the middle of the night.

Faith had been counseled, warned and even been the recipient of mild discipline by her fellow sisters. All to no avail. I had one last talk with her and warned that any further dirty hustling would result in action she would regret. I described the seriousness of my warning but she was too impressed with what she envisioned as her superior sexual attraction to discontinue her dirty dancing antics in the back of the parlor.

It was about 3 a.m., a usually quiet time in the houses. No parties were going on and only the madam was on duty. She was in the office napping between buzzes at the gate. Faith's room was near the back of the hall, a long way from the office.

The girls silently opened Faith's door and tiptoed over to her bed. As the girls jumped on her, Amber slapped duct tape over her mouth and eyes and bound her wrists and ankles. Throwing a blanket over her, they quickly carried her to the end of the hall into the Jacuzzi room and closed the door.

While Savannah stood guard, scissors chopped away at Faith's prized long hair. Razor blades shaved her bald. In extreme cases, super glue would be used to literally shut a girl's business "doors," leading to an emergency room visit, but no one wanted to touch Faith's "business" area. She was nasty.

Back in Faith's room, two girls cut her condoms in half, destroyed her makeup and ripped up her lingerie. Her room looked like a bomb hit it.

Told not to breathe a word to management or super glue would be the next step, Faith was returned to her room.

Within minutes, leaving all her belongings behind, a bewildered madam saw an obviously hysterical bald hooker run through the parlor and get into a taxi, never to return. Madam walked up and down the hall looking into each room. All the ladies were asleep. What happened, she wondered? She had a feeling she knew but she would never ask and she knew she would never really know the answer.

* * *

The next day, it was business as usual. No one even inquired about Faith's whereabouts. Mercedes and Tawny were doing each others nails. The bell rang and the girls could see several cowboys head for the front door. China wandered off to her room; she hated cowboys.

The madam greeted them and directed them to a comfortable sofa while she checked the ID of one especially young-looking cowboy. Satisfied, she asked if any of them wanted a drink while they visited with the ladies. Each of the tongue-tied young men nodded as they politely held their hats in their laps. There were four of them, not counting the older one. "Dad" explained he was just the driver. This was the first visit to a bordello for his two sons and their friends and Dad came along to keep tabs on them and drive them home safely.

Having grown up on a ranch, this type of rough-around-the-edges family closeness and concern brought back fond memories as I listened to Dad talk. Most of the men that came through the brothel doors were pretty average looking. This man was drop-dead gorgeous.

Fairly tall and slender, ranch work obviously kept him in shape. He had wide shoulders, tight back muscles, a trim stomach that tapered down to slim hips and the cutest little tush a pair of jeans could contain. He was wearing a new pair of jeans with a belt that had his name engraved on the back and a large rodeo belt buckle in the front, ostrich boots, a charcoal gray blazer, crisp Wrangler shirt and a smoke gray colored George Strait hat. A heartstopping vision of the elegant Western gentleman rancher.

A cross between Robert Redford's good looks and the he-man, raw, yet politely humble nature of Montgomery Clift – he took my breath away. He smelled of Old Spice, an aroma that always kicked my hormones into high gear. What really got me though, was his protective manner toward his terrified young bucks. I watched him as long as I could stand it and then decided it was my mission to change his mind about partying!!

The girls had already spirited the young cowhands off on a tour. Amber took a couple steps toward Dad. I cleared my throat and she glanced at me. The look I gave her clearly spelled out, "Leave him the hell alone. He's MINE." All the girls knew cowboys were my specialty. Most of the girls were happy to turn them over to me. Cowboys were a strange breed to city girls.

Amber announced she was going to the kitchen and the parlor cleared out. I went over and sat next to Dad. He had Paul Newman eyes and I couldn't quit looking at them. I was making him nervous.

"Come on, Dad, your brood is touring the house. You may as well see it too." I urged.

"No, ma'am," he reiterated, "I'm just the driver. I'm not participating."

"You don't have to." I cooed. "But the boys will be busy for awhile, so why not walk around the house and visit with me while you wait?" I stood up and reached for his hand.

"OK ... I reckon ... as long as you remember I'm just the driver," he said tentatively. I smiled as I tucked my arm in his.

When we reached my room, I guided him inside. He looked around in awe. The lights were low and gave off a soft reddish glow. I had created a pink canopy with draped material above and surrounding the bed. The bedspread, rugs, turn-of-the-century antique bedstands with their pitcher and bowl and other old fashioned decorations created a Victorian motif that was comfortable and inviting. Sexy lingerie hung on padded hangers all over the room. Dad looked at the photos of me with Geraldo Rivera, Jerry Springer, and Leeza

Gibbons, as well as cast members from *Entertainment Tonight*, *Inside Edition*, and many other TV shows on which I had appeared. I could see he felt intimidated.

Standing there with his hat in his hands, I could see it tremble slightly. I sat down on the bed and motioned for him to sit down beside me. Nervously, he perched on the edge of the bed. Over the next few minutes, he began to relax and we joked and talked and enjoyed each other's company.

His eyes and sweet innocent nature were driving me crazy. I stood up and moved in front of him. Gently, I pushed him down on the bed, holding his wrists above his head with my hands as I sat on his chest.

"OK, cowboy, you may as well just empty your pockets because you're not leaving. I asked your mama if you could come out and play and she said you could," I purred as I planted soft kisses on his neck and nibbled on his ear. Sweat started pouring down his temples. He was in a true panic now.

Suddenly a voice came over the intercom. "Jessi dear, this is *not* recess. You and your gentleman have been in your room quite some time now. Please don't forget to finish up the details surrounding the party you want to have, so you can get started."

Dad jumped to his feet, knocking me on the floor. Helping me up, he exclaimed, "What the hell was that?"

"The voice of God." I said sarcastically. "The rooms have intercoms and the madam listens to negotiations to be sure the girls turn in all the money they negotiate. She's telling us we've been in here too long and need to make up our minds or return to the parlor."

"You knew I wasn't going to party." Dad said looking embarrassed.

"It's not your fault, sweet thing." I cooed. "You're so yummy, you can't blame a girl for trying. You know how in some countries it's a tradition to burp after a meal to show your host you enjoyed their cooking?" I asked. "In the houses, its kind of a tradition to party before leaving. You know the madam you have to walk past to leave the house?" I continued. "Her feelings get hurt if you leave without partying. She feels her girls let you down. You don't want that on your conscience do you, darlin'?"

Dad looked at me for a long minute, broke out in laughter, grabbed my hand and headed for the hall. When we reached the parlor, he turned and took both my hands in his and said, "Ma'am, you're about as tempting a woman as I've ever seen so I think it's best, for my own reasons, that I mosey on down the trail now."

His boys were already in the parlor waiting for him and as they all stood to go, Dad stopped at the door as the madam held it for him and turned. He locked eyes with me and stood silent for a moment, a clear message of "another time; another place" in the look he gave me.

Then, in true Western gentlemanly fashion, he tipped his hat and disappeared into the night, leaving me standing forlornly in the middle of the parlor.

Mirror, Mirror

Mercedes came into the parlor and plopped down on the couch with a dejected look on her face. "What's the matter with you?" China asked.

"I rented a really nice apartment," began Mercedes, "and my landlord found out that the corporation I listed as my employer was the holding company for the Ranch. She said she didn't want a working girl conducting business out of an apartment she owned and told me I'd have to find another place to live," Mercedes explained sadly. "Like I'd even want to work when I'm off duty. Pleeeese."

Each time I heard a similar story from one lady or another, my frustration level rose. The business is legal and the houses are a significant source of tax revenue, yet the ladies are still treated as second class citizens.

I was put on a pedestal and treated like a queen in the bordellos. Many clients became good friends and regular customers. Once outside the doors of the brothels, however, it is an entirely different situation. Discrimination is common among the women whether it pertains to renting, child custody, applying for a credit card, trying to obtain a loan, or just being accepted by neighbors and the community. Every one of us has been subjected to double standards and narrow minded hypocrisy at one time or another.

I contemplated doing something that would demonstrate bordello working girls are no different from women anywhere; that we have all the strengths, faults, dreams, fears, feelings and emotions of any other human being.

Only another working girl knows what we experience at the hands of others and that's why we are so protective of each other. I was able to "go public" and decided the best way to improve acceptance

120

for the ladies was to do something very public that would present a visual example of class and dignity. I decided to push the envelope if no one would listen.

I saw an ad in the paper inviting women to compete in the Mrs. Nevada, International beauty pageant. Perfect. I entered and was chosen Mrs. Virginia City. Who better to represent the history and tradition of my community than a person who has lived the history of the town's past? I never expected the community-wide turmoil that would result, however.

I figured the pageant would be a perfect opportunity to publicly demonstrate legal "ladies of the evening" are no different from ladies anywhere. I planned to compete without fanfare and be judged no differently from the other contestants. When the contest was over, *then* I would tell them I was a legal "red light lady." That would make a strong statement as well as alter some outdated misconceptions. The resulting publicity would force those in a position of authority to listen to the concerns of Nevada's working ladies who, up until now, had been ignored.

A scraggly, sour, aging hippie, the editor of the small local paper used his publication more as a high school gossip rag in which to inflict his views. When it was announced I would represent Virginia City in the state pageant, he took it upon himself to inform readers of my profession. The Associated Press picked up his story and all hell broke loose. Media from all over the world wanted the story. The Chamber of Commerce wanted me to disappear.

The Virginia City Chamber of Commerce contains some real pieces of work. Although the chamber pays plenty of lip service to it, little is done to promote the Old West heritage for which the town has become known. They are too busy with their primary objective: enhancing their cash registers. The town's shady reputation doesn't stop these snobs from imposing their own system of values upon newcomers who naïvely believe the chamber actually wants their assistance.

Representing Virginia City in a state beauty pageant opened a Pandora's box for which the town was not about to forgive me – especially the chamber. I thought bringing attention to the true nature of the town's history would increase tourism and help the area thrive. They thought differently.

The chamber summoned me to appear before them. Two dozen somber faces stared back at me. They informed me they liked the tourist money my notoriety brought to merchant cash registers but they didn't like what I stood for and wanted me to drop out of the pageant. They made it clear they would be even happier if I left town. I found it hypocritical to ostracize me as a current day working girl when the town was founded by miners and prostitutes. It was my first experience with attempts to run me out of town on a rail. I didn't take kindly to it.

Made up mostly of town fathers and newcomers, the chamber had decided to change Virginia City into a "family destination" instead of the Wild West town it had always been. Despite cashing in on tales of famous silver and gold rush prostitutes in Virginia City and the presence of a "red light museum" located on Main Street, the chamber felt I didn't fit in. After enduring what felt like an eternity of self-righteous indignation, I called them hypocrites, proclaimed the community to be a small-minded, evil Harper Valley PTA type gossip town, told them to go to hell and walked out. Their attitude and disrespect remained unchanged as long as we lived there. We came to realize public faces are often deceiving.

Decent folks do live in town even though they are outnumbered by their nasty neighbors. My daughter seems to bring out the guardian angels who distance themselves from local shenanigans and quietly help others. Cindy, a local deputy sheriff, treats Becky with friendship, takes her shopping and offers a helping hand when needed. Joe and Ellie Curtis own the bookstore and quietly see to it that Becky's life is enhanced by caring friends and that she receives necessities her budget will not allow. Carol, who owns the ice cream parlor, keeps a motherly eye on her and strengthens her self-confidence. Regardless of the community, there are always good, decent, caring people to whom we are grateful and who help smooth the rough edges of a town's flaws.

After the story broke, tourists came to town looking for me, yet the chamber office always told them they had never heard of me. Those tourists spent money with the same Main Street merchants who, in all their sanctimonious virtue, proclaimed I sent the "wrong message."

Evidently the red light museum on Main Street that was dedicated to the memory of Julia Bulette, Virginia City's most famous 19th Century "soiled dove," doesn't fall into the "wrong message" category. This little tourist town makes money retelling Julia's story, but city fathers are in no mood to accept the real thing in modern times.

The local paper refused to print anything about me from then on and treated me as if I didn't exist. Unless of course, they wanted to print something nasty or disrespectful. Years later, that childish attitude continues.

Little support was received from those in my hometown, continuing the tradition of stigma toward prostitutes that has existed since the beginning of time.

Once worried about embarrassing the town, I now relished the thought. It was time for the town to realize the job is legal and should be treated the same as any other profession. The ladies deserved to be treated better as well. I had nothing to be ashamed of by choosing this legal form of employment just because some people didn't approve of it. Why should they care? I paid taxes, paid my own bills, was not on welfare and was not a burden to society. The industry provided substantial revenue to government coffers as well.

The hypocrisy didn't escape me as I laughed remembering all the local parades with the town females dressed as wannabe saloon girls.

"Get real," I thought to myself. "I may wear the label but who are the real hookers? Prostitution is my job. For others, it's a way of getting what they want. The only difference is the degree of honesty," I reasoned.

I picked up the phone and called Vic. He was a wonderful dressmaker and I knew he would make a 19th Century gown that would accurately represent the history of Virginia City and wow the pageant audience. A smile began to cross my lips.

"Yes indeed," I mused, "This town of double standards WILL be represented!"

People who live out-of-state tend to believe the only part of Nevada is Las Vegas with its artificial meccas where everything is smoke and mirrors and gaudy neon lights. Little is known about the breathtaking natural beauty and significant contribution to history that is found in northern and rural Nevada. Despite reprehensible treatment by locals, I felt honored to have the opportunity to reveal to those attending the pageant, the contribution this distinctive town made to the history of the Battle Born State of Nevada.

A hooker in a predominately Mormon beauty pageant changed the peaceful pattern of anonymous life in town. Media from all over the world descended on the area. You couldn't turn on the TV without seeing my face, hearing interviews on radio or reading the story in tabloids and newspapers. I couldn't even go to the grocery store in peace. My hometown, meanwhile, had become judge and jury.

CNBC arrived with their cameras. Jim was the field producer. A young man, he nevertheless knew what he was doing and was quite fascinated with the small town wild west atmosphere which was vastly different from the New York pace he had just left.

Janice was the on-air host. Efficient, personable, and a younger version of Barbara Walters, she was all business, yet warm and sincere.

Both found residents of this historical hamlet to be as memorable as the town itself. Some looked like Festus, right out of a Miss Kitty TV show. They were eccentric loners, alcoholics happy to find a town with so many saloons yet small enough that they could walk – or crawl – home, those on the wrong side of the law who could blend in and hide out, and corrupt officials who had long been "on the take" since the infamous inception of the Mustang Ranch.

Carl was an old cowboy who knew where all the bodies were buried. He was the town's unofficial historian and a dear little man who stood barely five feet tall and nearly as wide. He was more tolerant than most residents and a lot more candid. When the town beat up on me, it was Carl who defended me in the paper.

The town has parades at the drop of a hat and there are always a bevy of wannabe saloon girls and obvious hooker types who get hoots, hollers and approval from the crowds. The real thing got trashed. Carl was always quick to call them on it too. He would remind the town that if they checked their family tree, they would more than likely find a "colorful" grandma or great-grandma in there someplace. He was always the first to point out that working girls are, after all, human and have feelings like any other person. He was a dear little man whom I called the "dearly cantankerous conscience of Virginia City." He just chuckled at his title.

It was windy as usual the day CNBC taped. Residents stopped to watch as I strolled down the boardwalk in a 19th Century gown, reciting a history of the contribution of soiled doves. We wound up at the Julia Bulette red light museum. Carl gave the cameras a tour of prostitution paraphernalia of the era displayed in the downstairs museum and told the history of Julia herself.

Carl was pleased as punch that he had been featured in a tape that would be seen nationwide. The Mrs. Nevada Pageant was coming up soon and so he outfitted Michael with a 19th Century "formal" cowboy hat to wear during his duties as escort on stage for Mrs. Virginia City. It quickly became Michael's favorite hat.

Carl started having chest pains. We drove him to his doctor appointments because he felt he was too old to drive safely any longer. He was told his main heart artery was blocked and he needed surgery. Tired of being short of breath, he wanted to take care of it as soon as possible. A week later, he went into the hospital for surgery and never woke up again.

Michael built a six foot cross, painted it white and engraved it with Carl's name and birth date and a message from the Winchesters. We planned to climb the hill to the "V" overlooking Virginia City where we would place the cross. A local historian asked to accompany us so he could film the event for his archives. Carl was always the overseer of the town and it was the perfect place for him to keep an eye on everything that went on below.

The site just above the "V" was a thousand-foot climb and the four of us were out of breath by the time Michael hauled the cross that far. He planted it firmly in a hole he dug by a bush near the middle at the top of the "V." We placed a single rose on the cross and just as the sun came up, the church bells began to toll. All four of us bowed our heads and said good-bye to a loyal friend. Just before descending the hill, I told Carl I would dedicate my participation in the Mrs. Nevada Pageant to him.

Coming down the hill, we encountered the sheriff's car on the narrow dirt road. Both doors were open and a deputy was standing by each door with their hands on their hips. We laughed. They looked just like Boss Hogg's minions on the *Dukes of Hazzard*. But the deputies weren't smiling.

When they realized it was not vandals but the Winchesters they were confronting, they relaxed a bit but were still very stern. Deputy Will had known us for a long time and we had joked around on many occasions. He normally had excellent people skills. Today, however, he told me to hike back up the hill and take down Carl's cross because it was on county property. I refused. I reasoned Carl had a right to be remembered where he was. Will said I would go to jail if I didn't do what I was told. I told him he'd better cuff me right then because I wasn't taking Carl's cross down. I told Michael to call the media and tell them Mrs. Virginia City was being arrested for honoring her friend in a manner that defied the dictates of cold-hearted authorities.

As I stomped down the hill yelling at Will that I was going straight to the sheriff's office to be booked, he ran after me frantically saying we could "work it out." I told him to go to hell for not giving a damn about a longtime resident who carefully cataloged the history of the town and for having no compassion for dedication to friends. He told me to go home. It was a long time before we spoke again.

In time, Will retired and we ran into him again when I was campaigning in Austin, Nevada. We rekindled our friendship and talked about Carl's memorial. Will explained he had explicit instructions from the county sheriff at the time and had to follow orders even though he didn't agree with them. Nevertheless, under orders, his actions that day came to represent an attitude that was becoming more and more prevalent in this Harper Valley PTA type town.

The white speck that is Carl's cross can still be seen from Main Street to this day, a reminder that the town used to have a few residents that cared about each other and a petite redhead feisty enough to fight for what's right.

Everyone knows everyone else in this unique little village and all seem to have a secret life. Intensely private, residents speculate about everyone else's lives but don't invade their neighbor's privacy or probe into their reason for hiding out in the mountain. It is a town where you can go to Fly's, the saloon the locals inhabit, to drink with friends, have a good time, and know you don't have to account for your life history. The town is filled with loners who like it that way.

They were quick to turn on a fellow resident, however—especially the women. Being under the microscope of public scrutiny was still new to me so a "witch hunt" mentality at the hands of jealous, pious, self-righteous local women – neighbors in my own hometown – was hurtful. Attacking another makes their own pathetic lives more tolerable. They are the modern continuation of the women "red light ladies" faced in the late 1800s when the gold rush miners began to bring their "proper" women west. Clearly, these type of women are still with us today.

* * *

Numerous national television talk shows like *The Leeza Show* focused on a legal brothel working girl in a predominately Mormon beauty pageant. Leeza flew me to Hollywood and delivered me to their stage at Paramount Studios by limousine where I was escorted into make-up and then to the VIP waiting room for brunch with Debbie Reynolds' son, Todd, and Katie Couric, who were shooting a later segment of the show. It was always fun to do the shows but the resulting notoriety created backlash from pageant officials and participants by the time the affair rolled around.

The pageant was predictably tense and uncomfortable but I went through with it. All hell broke loose when pageant officials learned they had a legal hooker in the contest. The organizer did her best to find a loophole in the rule book that would allow her to disqualify me. My job was legal and, therefore, I was just as eligible as the pristine Mormon girls with whom I was to compete. Media from around the world closed in.

We quit answering the phone at home. Whenever we had to go anywhere, Michael pulled the truck up as close to the front door as possible so I could scramble into it, slouching down so no one could get my picture. I instructed family and friends not to come to the house so they wouldn't be subjected to reporters. My son did our grocery shopping because the media even invaded my privacy in the stores. I felt like a caged animal.

All I wanted to do was send a message to the world that ladies in my profession have class, dignity and education that is no different from any other woman competing in a pageant. I had no clue it would forever change my life.

In northern Nevada, my colorful background endeared me to longtime residents who tenaciously hang on to remnants of disappearing history and rebel spirit that make Nevada one of the last bastions of the Wild West. My outspoken nature and feisty fighting spirit formed the basis for a wide ranging legion of supporters. Some in my own hometown may not have wanted to claim me but the remainder of northern and rural Nevada saw me as a symbol of Nevada's unique and dauntless past and hope for refreshing and forthright transformations in the state's future.

Each year the *Reno Gazette-Journal* holds an informal survey of readers to determine their opinions and interests. Readers fill out the survey in the paper and results are printed in a special section. I was surprised and honored to be voted one of the people readers most wanted to hear about.

Many residents of Las Vegas, on the other hand, live in their own money oriented world. Their philosophy is that if it doesn't happen in Las Vegas or benefit Clark County, it isn't worth caring about. Unlike Northern Nevada, it is evident that this city which demolishes its fascinating antiquity to build adult Disneylands in the desert, has absolutely no reverence for something as inconvenient as history. None of the other contestants dressed according to the credentials of their town's history.

When we arrived in Las Vegas for the pageant, one of the first people I spotted was the Carson City newspaper reporter who hounded my every move. We had become friends. He wanted to follow me as I prepared for the show and promised to portray a human side as opposed to the sensationalism being written all over the world. I trusted him and granted his request.

The days of preparation and rehearsal were miserable as expected. It was as if I had suddenly developed a contagious case of TB and no one wanted to be near me for fear I would cough. No one talked to me. The organizer was frosty. The other contestants avoided me. I was included but blatantly ignored.

While others avoided eye contact, one of the girls, Ruthann, always smiled when we ran into each other. Finally, she took me into a side room and explained that contestants had been instructed to pretend I wasn't there and were told to not even speak to me. The Mormons were sticking together and doing as they were told but she wasn't part of that clique. Their actions made her so mad she decided to tell me what was going on.

At the Bordello Ball

Artist John Hunt admires his "Soiled Dove" painting of Jessi

Jessi with Jerry Springer — prior to his "Gutter Guests from hell" format

Relaxing after one of Jessi's guest appearances on the Geraldo Rivera Show

*Reno Headquarters for the 1998 Republican race
for lieutenant governor*

One of many parades

*Nevada G.O.P. State Chair John Mason,
Jessi, and about-to-be governor Kenny Guinn
at the 1998 Republican State Convention*

*Congressman Jim Gibbons,
Jessi and Assemblywoman Dawn Gibbons
at one of an endless procession of
political events*

Her revelation and kindness made the pageant more bearable and we remained friends long after the show.

The show was held in the large theater arts auditorium of the fancy new library with the futuristic architectural style in an upscale part of town. The grounds surrounding the library were as stark as the lines of the building. A low maintenance landscape, only a few cacti and plants popped up to greet visitors. At that moment I felt as lonely as the cactus.

Michael cleared a path through the cameras and satellite equipment in order to enter the building. While the other women presented in flashy sequined gowns, I honored the annals of my town's past by doing the entire show in 1800s attire and hairstyle. I wore a long cream colored gown with a lace parasol. The crush of media surrounding me made it difficult even to move.

The auditorium was packed. Spectators overflowed into the lobby. I inched my way through TV cameras and escaped into the dressing room. On the news that evening and in the following day's paper, the winner was inundated with questions about "the hooker." She tried to avoid answering but reporters were relentless. I was incensed to see her put on a benevolent face and give a heartfelt rendition of how she purposely went out of her way to talk to me and how she found me to be "a really nice lady." We had never exchanged a single word but the media dutifully captured her stellar performance.

Even though the pageant went to great lengths to disrespect me, I was gratified my participation gained worldwide attention and allowed me to put a human face on the women who work in a much misunderstood profession.

Attitude Adjustment

Double standards that permeated the pageant made it obvious there was a lot of work to do if society was to see the brothel industry the way it is instead of the way people envision it in their minds. It just whetted my appetite to make changes that would be good for my professional sisters, both inside and outside the houses.

When I worked in Hollywood, I learned how publicity stories were created and developed and how they shaped the way the public felt about certain stars. Facts could be presented in various ways, each of which would have a different result. I came to realize how damage control was addressed by political spinmeisters, how products were sold by commercial endeavors, how public opinion could be inspired to view something in an entirely biased fashion.

Remembering those lessons, I decided to invite the public into the lives of the women who work in the bordellos by marketing a product that would present a slant different from that normally envisioned. After talking to girls in several houses, I decided to produce a calendar featuring real working girls. It would be sexy but classy, so there would be no problem with displaying it in department stores and other family establishments. In fact, the girls actually wore more clothing than women in many other pinup calendars. Nevertheless, I was about to learn a disheartening and expensive lesson about real life in business and hypocritical double standards in marketing.

Despite legal status, many of the women could not "go public" because of the stigma that surrounds the sex industry in their hometowns. Most of the women came from other states where the legal sex industry is not part of the local scenery as it is in Nevada. As a result, people in other states tend to envision prostitution as the drug-crazed, crime-infested, illegal street scene they see on TV. They don't realize there is a caste system in prostitution that includes many tiers of sex providers, including legal bordellos. The families of many women didn't know how their loved ones earned their salary and the girls didn't want to take the chance of embarrassing their families. I hoped to be able to help dispel that attitude.

Fliers were distributed to the houses inviting ladies willing to go public to submit a snapshot and brief bio of themselves from which a panel would decide on 12 finalists for the shoot. I hired a photographer I knew from my studio days who has an artistic camera eye and is used to beautiful women as his subject matter. He put the ladies at ease without hustling them. A professional make-up artist was excited about doing the project. I contracted with a publishing firm to do the art and print work and hired a public relations expert to promote and distribute it.

The shoot took two days. Two incredible days. These women, who are too often viewed as cold-hearted gold diggers, looked a whole lot more like happy, excited schoolgirls getting ready for their first dance. Free of pressure and without a single person expecting anything of them, they reminded me of my high school years and slumber parties with my classmates. I stood back and watched. Even if we didn't sell a single calendar, the magic that was happening before my eyes with the elevated self-esteem of my sisters would be forever worth it. With each brush stroke of the cosmetologist and each coaxing word of encouragement from the photographer, they were like flower petals that unfurled, showing a full bloom of exquisite beauty. They simply glowed and it showed in the final product.

There was only one small hitch. The original Miss December backed out the day before the shoot under pressure from her boyfriend, so reluctantly I took her place. Everyone came out looking fantastic. The calendar also includes a history of prostitution in the West from the gold rush days to present-day bordellos. The back cover is a tribute to the ladies and features several more photos of them.

It is a terrific product and a memory maker for all the women involved. Sales were set up to be divided among the women so they could hopefully enroll in college, pursue vocational training, buy a car, put a down payment on a house, or whatever dream each woman had that would help make her life easier.

I hadn't counted on the business world being so narrow-minded. Everything went extremely well until it came to distribution. My representative was unable to get the calendar on shelves anywhere in the nation because of the subject matter. It seemed it was all right for famous models, lingerie stores, sports and male-oriented publications to put out calendars of women wearing much less than my girls. The hypocrisy of three little words, "Red Light Ladies" and the fact the women were true working girls and not models, kept the calendar off the shelves.

It also kept the ladies from reaping financial rewards that would enhance their lives. There was a huge demand for the calendar and the business world's refusal to treat it the same as others is only one example of second-class citizenship brothel women endure.

We quickly ran out of time and options. By this time I had a full media schedule. The calendar would be featured on all the nationally syndicated daytime television talk shows and television magazine shows. I started tapings in just a few short days. Radio stations all over the nation had booked me for interviews. Print media had already begun their focus on our calendar. The only problem was that no one could buy it.

The only option left was an 800 order number connected to an answering service willing to take orders, fill them and keep current on inventory status. Most were not willing to go beyond the phone service.

We narrowed it down to the only service which would meet our criteria. It was located in Carson City and we met with the owner, a Mr. Jenkins. He was a take-charge businessman who did most of the talking and not much listening. His confidence in his staff and service made me relax but I got the uneasy feeling he understood all too well that our backs were to the wall and he was in a position to call the shots.

When asked, he indicated he had no problem with the subject matter but in the next breath he told us his father was an elder in the Mormon church. After my experience with the pageant, I freaked. He assured us this was a pragmatic business decision and not a moral judgment. He indicated our account would be handled no differently from his other clients. We were faced with either trusting him and continuing on or walking out the door with absolutely no other option. We negotiated the terms and asked him to put it in writing, a request that was never carried out.

We told him Black Magic – Miss March – and I would be featuring the calendar on *The Geraldo Rivera Show* in just a few days and asked if his operation was large enough to handle the thousands of calls expected to flood his lines within minutes after showing the calendar on-air. He convinced us that was no problem and took us on a tour of his facilities to explain his extensive phone capabilities. He said if we would let him know ahead of time whenever we did a show, he would simply hire extra operators for a few days. We left feeling he truly understood the magnitude of calls that would result and was equipped to deal with the avalanche.

We returned from New York to find frantic messages from Mr. Jenkins on our answering machine. After promising to hire additional operators the day of the show, he instead decided to wait to see if they would really be needed. They were, but too late. He clearly hadn't understood our conversation after all.

Instead, he complained about obscene calls and said, as a good Mormon, he was offended. He explained that orders were bombarding his operators and that some customers were using offensive language, asking for a description of clothing worn by each "whore" and so on. He said he had a problem with a product that elicits that kind of response so *he simply disconnected our 800 line and quit taking orders*. We couldn't believe our ears.

We reminded him of our first conversation when he emphatically stated he had no moral problem with our subject matter. He backed down and said he would reconnect the line in a few days when the pace slowed down and his operators could handle it. We'll never know how many orders he cost us. We could either shut it down and gain nothing or continue for another week or so and see what happened. We instructed him to immediately start doing what he was contracted to do: take and fill orders.

It became apparent very quickly that even though this was our only option, it nevertheless was a mistake. Despite repeated requests for a written agreement, we never received one. Every time we got a bill, we had to go into his office to clarify mistakes. He just blustered and got irritated with us.

Worst of all, he arbitrarily kept changing the terms of our agreement and when we objected, he would simply say, "No problem. I'll take you downstairs to the shipping room and you can remove the remaining inventory."

I was sick of threats, extortion and intimidation after all my years of dealing with brothel management. He had us by the short hairs and he knew it.

Our fax number was on the back of the calendar and we were starting to get angry faxes from customers who ordered the calendar but never received it. After obtaining no help from the 800 line, many were calling *The Geraldo Rivera Show* to get a contact number for the calendar. I personally got in touch with each complainant and apologized for Jenkins' "oversight" and then mailed a complimentary copy of the calendar and included my working menu as a bonus. The man was costing us instead of helping us. To our dismay, we had to face the fact it also appeared to be intentional.

After only one short month, we fired him. I was really tired of being victimized and just wanted to rip his balls off for taking advantage of us. But I was too weary and depressed to fight any more. We worked so hard to produce a product that customers would enjoy, that would help elevate the perception of the industry and would financially assist my sisters and the business world just wanted to rip us off. I'd been beat up too much. I just wanted him to go away and leave us alone. He knew that.

In the end, the calendar was featured in *Playboy* and various other places. It proved to be hugely popular; folks simply didn't know how to get one after awhile thanks to hypocrisy and the fact that the Internet had not yet entered virtually every household. Ironically, it became a favorite door prize at political functions in northern Nevada. A one-of-a-kind collector's item, requests continue to come in years after its publication as a result of still being shown on my web site.

The fiasco surrounding distribution of the calendar only served to point out society's view of women in the sex industry as abnormal. Psychologists are often among the worst at promoting such fallacies. Some theorize the majority of women who work in the sex industry do so because they suffer from lack of self-esteem as a result of being sexually molested as a child. They point to this pet theory as the primary reason for a woman's decision to become a prostitute, which perpetrates a myth that is destructive, twisted and just plain not true. Additionally, bleeding-heart liberal views expressed by those in the psychology and social service fields that women in the sex industry harbor deep-seated anger toward men as a result of abuse at their hands, is equally without merit. Reasons for working in the industry are as varied as the women themselves.

Women in other occupations experience life traumas too, yet they make different career choices. Contrary to misguided conclusions by shrinks and social workers, more than a few working girls have perfectly normal childhoods. I certainly did. Common sense would seem to make it apparent the percentage of troubled childhoods in the legal prostitution field is neither more nor less than that of any other female dominated profession such as waitress, nurse, secretary or teacher.

Assumptions like those were exactly why I had to continue. Not one to give up, I decided on a different angle that would put the public in direct contact with the ladies in a comfortable setting. Being able to actually mingle and talk to the women could make a difference.

Out of that, the decision to begin a tradition of holding an annual Bordello Ball was born. It would raise funds for charity so folks would have a "reputable" excuse to point to in order to justify their attendance. Each year would benefit a different charity which would always remain local so folks knew where their contributions went.

I decided it would be fun to feature a different period of history each year. A chance to dress up and live another era in time for an evening appealed to nearly everyone.

In the hope of putting a human face on the industry and of my hometown finally accepting me, I decided to hold the first Ball at Cabin in the Sky just outside Virginia City. Isolated and small as it is, the town is not close-knit. Everyone seems to have some secret that prevents residents from uniting and working together in the best interest of the community. Double standards and hypocrisy are just as prevalent in Virginia City as anywhere else. I had certainly experienced that as the victim of the chamber of commerce witch hunt. I knew first hand how cruel some of my neighbors could be.

Most working girls have found through experience that those who point a finger and yell the loudest are usually the ones who have the most to hide. That is certainly true of residents of Virginia City. Many feel they have the right to judge my decision to work in a legal occupation in Nevada and make me feel like an unwanted outcast in my own hometown. Few see me as a human being with feelings. I felt the Bordello Ball could begin to bring the town together.

Cabin in the Sky was owned by AGE Enterprises, the holding company for Mustang Ranch, and was managed by Jim, who took his orders from AGE Enterprises. He was one of the few folks in town that was openly supportive of me. He also was part owner of the Washoe Club where the artist who painted the tasteful nude portrait of me socialized on a regular basis. Michael and I presented a large print of John's painting to the Washoe Club and the Silver Dollar Saloon as a token of friendship. I asked Jim if the Ball could be held at Cabin in the Sky. After checking with the owners, he said it could.

An AIDS organization was chosen to benefit from the Ball. Its representative promised volunteers and assistance in exchange for the funds raised during the evening. A promise he would not keep.

Cabin in the Sky was decorated in early bordello style. Red flocked wallpaper, garish accessories, massive bar. Perfect for the Bordello Ball. I asked the AIDS representative to provide Hollywood klieg lights to give the event glamour and provide guidance to Cabin in the Sky's remote location. He said his organization knew of a great group of female impersonators that would be willing to put on a mini-floor show and a band that would also volunteer to play. My assistant Kristin and I would invite working girls and brothel owners throughout the state to attend as honored guests and present an elegant "red light ladies promenade." It would be such fun.

Michael and I were in Las Vegas campaigning the week before the Ball. I always hate it when the phone rings in the middle of the night. It usually means bad news and proved to be true three days prior to the Ball. Jim was on the other end in a state of total panic. After fortifying himself with a bit of "liquid courage," he decided he'd better call Mustang Ranch representatives and tell them about the female impersonators. According to Jim, they said the Ball would be canceled if the revue performed, as Mustang Ranch was renowned for authentic female sex image and they weren't about to have a "fag" inside any of their establishments. The AIDS representative told us the review had appeared on television and in clubs with their sensational impersonations of Barbara Streisand, Cher, Madonna, Whitney Houston and others. No amount of discussion with Jim or Mustang's representatives could convince them the review was simply a tasteful, as well as entertaining, impersonation of women. The bottom line was Cabin in the Sky would be shut down immediately if the revue appeared.

Absolute turmoil prevailed during the final few days before the Ball. The AIDS representative said the revue was insulted and both they and the band would not appear. AGE demanded the regular duo that entertained at Cabin in the Sky play during the evening. They again threatened to shut down the club if their duo didn't appear. They also told the working girls at Mustang that they would be fired if they appeared in the "red light ladies promenade." Their bully control tactics demonstrated a typical "pimp" mentality too often seen in the industry. The Ball appeared ruined by last minute strong arm intimidation.

I had underestimated the town's passionate desire to party. To my surprise and delight, the community appeared to pull together. Incensed at Mustang Ranch tactics, a local band and gunslinger reenactment group volunteered the day before the Ball to perform. I scheduled the duo required by Mustang reps for the last hour of the Ball when everyone would begin leaving.

The evening of the Ball, the AIDS representative smelled money and showed up to collect. He didn't provide the klieg lights as promised, nor did any of his professed volunteers show up to help decorate or assist during the evening. He simply helped himself to all the money and left.

Mustang's henchmen roamed the room while Jim paced nervously. He knew there would be trouble if the Mustang people disliked anything that went on inside the establishment. He also knew I was furious with him for creating the problem in the first place. I was barely civil toward him. The henchmen glared at him. He was in the middle. The bar was his safe haven and he was beginning to feel no pain.

I intended to remove the copy of the painting from Jim's Washoe Club as soon as the Ball was over. I was a woman of my word and I had presented the print to Jim in good faith but he crossed over the line and betrayed me. He no longer deserved the tourist attraction print and I would see to it that the message to him was loud and clear.

My loyal co-workers showed up for the "red light ladies promenade." The owners and ladies of Salt Wells Villa, a brothel outside Fallon, arrived by limousine in incredible costumes. They brought a replica model of their ranch to be auctioned off during the evening. One of their ladies was chosen Queen of the Ball by the guests.

The promenade began with each lady entering the room on the arm of an escort, followed by a spot light to a latticed flower covered arch where she was presented roses and guests could take pictures. After each lady was introduced, they were presented as a group and brothel owners were recognized. Then they mingled with guests and a wonderful evening was enjoyed by all. The band and shoot-out were huge hits. Everyone present had a great time despite broken promises and a complete change of plans.

A few days after the Ball, I called the AIDS organization to be sure they received the money. Not only did I not receive so much as a thank you, the chairperson curtly informed me that their representative claimed one of my volunteers pilfered most of the money. The AIDS representative only turned in $500 of the nearly $5,000 taken in during the evening.

The entire experience had been a nightmare but I learned a valuable lesson to be in control of every aspect when my name was at stake. The Ball would become an annual event but it would *never* be held in Virginia City again. Never again would I lift a finger to bring publicity to the tourist town I then called home.

At the Washoe Club, the print of my painting was propped up against the mirror along the back of the bar. At three feet by five feet, it was the first thing you saw when you entered.

John Hunt had been trying to convince me to pose for it ever since the pageant. He is a wonderfully gifted artist who is famous for his collection of over sized portraits of notorious old west gunslingers. He paints in the "Saturday Night Art" style, one of only two artists in the nation to paint in that romantic, long-forgotten manner. A realist, he has an uncanny knack for capturing a subject's features and personality. He is so skillful at portraying his subject that his work almost looks like a snapshot.

He told me he had always wanted to paint an infamous courtesan, placing her in the elegance and romance of the Gold Rush era.

"Paintings of 19th Century courtesans were almost always nude, John," I observed.

"That's right," he replied.

I gulped. "Where would it be displayed?" I asked.

A man of few words, he simply said, "That's up to you, ma'am."

He said he wanted to portray me reclining on an ornate velvet 1800s divan with appropriate wallpaper of the time. I told him I had researched prostitution in the 1800s extensively and he might want to include a poodle because elegant gowns and expensive pets were a symbol of prostitution affluence. "Proper" women wouldn't be caught dead with the same breed of dog as a prostitute. John said he would put a poodle in the painting. I had seen and admired his work and his reputation was above reproach. I told him I would do it.

When he was nearly finished, he asked me to come to the studio to see if I felt he had captured my likeness to my satisfaction while he could still alter it. I climbed the stairs to the loft and nearly fell back down them when I saw the painting. Expecting a normal sized portrait, I was speechless to see a canvas that nearly covered his wall. The painting was larger than life. It was magnificent and perfect in every detail. It was as if the man had studied every curve of my body for a century.

The velvet sitting couch dominates the painting. The rich wood trim and ornate design almost makes you want to touch it to see if it is real. A fern hangs to one side. The poodle sits at my feet waiting to be petted. I recline against a blue-green pillow with my right arm stretched out along the back of the couch. Long red hair falling down my shoulder toward my breast, it was me alright. There is only a gauzy wisp of a cloth draped across my lap. There is no doubt who the model is. I can truly say I have "nothing to hide" now. I am in awe of John's talent. We titled it "Soiled Dove."

Michael and I quickly decided we'd better buy it ourselves rather than have my nakedness roaming around the country. As it was, a wealthy rancher from eastern Nevada who is familiar with John's work and was a client of mine, heard about it and offered an incredible sum for the painting, sight unseen.

Because the painting is so big, the custom frame is a foot in width.

The original "Soiled Dove" has been displayed only once. The calendar ladies made one appearance to autograph calendars for the public and the painting was unveiled at the same event. Since then it has found a safe and secure home, awaiting the time I finally own a Victorian home and it can hang in the parlor.

A few folks in Virginia City felt it would be a tourist draw if Mrs. Virginia City's infamous portrait could be viewed by visitors who come to town wanting to know more. Both Jim and Fly had been supportive when others hadn't, so we had two 3' x 5' replica prints made and presented one to each saloon owner.

The print was presented to each man with the understanding it would be framed and hung with respect high enough where drinks and dirty hands couldn't soil it. Fly kept his print locked safely away in the back room of his Silver Dollar Saloon until it was framed and ready to hang. Then he gave it a place of honor high up on the brick wall opposite the bar.

Jim's print had been propped up behind the bar at the Washoe Club for months. Word spread and his business increased. Dust settled on it and t-shirts for sale were hanging all over it. After the Ball, I went into the club, marched behind the bar, removed the print and walked out, leaving everyone present speechless.

Hazel, the artist's wife, is an intellectual hippie who spends a great deal of time at the Washoe Club. She was furious that the print was gone and didn't mind giving me a piece of her mind. She had no idea what had transpired to nearly ruin the Ball because of Jim's actions. She simply wanted the glory of telling tourists her husband painted the famous "Soiled Dove."

Hazel angrily told me she would have John paint someone else to replace me. I told her I didn't care; the decision was theirs but a new subject would not have the history or notoriety. Virginia City's pettiness no longer mattered to me. Fly's Silver Dollar Saloon is now the only place anywhere to have a print and that's just fine with me.

The following year I took full charge of the Ball. I was determined this event would not a repeat of the previous year's disaster. I was businesswoman enough to see it to successful completion.

The legislature was in session, so the vintage Ormsby House hotel/casino across the street from the Capitol in Carson City was booked with an eye toward making this a largely political function. A talented and trustworthy committee was assembled to begin planning the event months ahead. They made sure contributions were fully accounted for before turning them over to the benefiting organization.

The Ball was attended by congressmen, state legislators, mayors, county commissioners and the general public. Some came to be seen, others to see the promenade of real "red light ladies" from Nevada brothels. Everyone had fun. It was a huge success.

It was broadcast live on KOH radio. Ross, their on-air host, was the emcee for one of the floor shows, a hilarious dance revue. We finally got our female impersonators! Called the "Carson Creampuffs," they were dignitaries from all walks of life in northern Nevada. Somehow, I was actually able to talk these big hairy macho pillars of society into dressing as women in can-can outfits to do a dance routine for our 1800s Ball. After a few bottles of "liquid courage" backstage, they finally found the nerve to make their grand entrance after Ross announced them.

The first year they appeared, the audience expected women. What a riot to watch the faces of the audience as the Creampuffs appeared. Delighted expectation turned to bewilderment and you could almost hear them thinking, "Those are some of the ugliest women I've ever seen."

Bewilderment gave way to disbelief as 500 guests began to realize these weren't women after all. Then laughter drowned out the music and everyone was on their feet stompin', hootin' and hollerin'. The Carson Creampuffs were the hit of the evening and returned each year by popular demand in attire appropriate to the theme of the year.

An honored king was always chosen prior to the event by the organizing committee to reign over each year's Ball. The queen was chosen by popular vote of attending guests during the evening.

The year the Ball was predominately political, Assemblyman Bob Price was a natural choice as honored king. He is well known in political and social circles in Nevada for his compassion and tolerance toward others. People's differences are a study in human nature to him. He learns from everyone and gives them his full attention, never rushing them. He truly enjoys finding out what they feel and why. He finds all human beings fascinating. Nevada's working girls are extended the same degree of respect as the wives of his legislative co-workers. The ladies were really glad he was chosen king.

Assemblyman Harry Mortenson's wife, Helen, was chosen queen by the attending crowd.

The media was not such a pleasure, however. Over time, I had carefully developed a good rapport with the press. Few granted me the respect I had earned as a candidate who researched issues, had a good pulse of what the public wanted and who went directly to the people instead of feeding them 60-second sound bites on television and radio. Others preferred to sensationalize my work in the bordellos and continued to portray me as a bimbo joke running for office.

I trusted the *Reno Gazette-Journal* reporter who was stationed out of the Carson City office, as he had done several articles on me. They were serious pieces and granted me dignity. He followed my story since before the pageant and we had become friends. I was one of the first to call him with congratulations when his first child was born. I was shocked to see a nasty side after all this time.

He wanted to attend the Ball with a photographer and roam freely invading the privacy of guests for a story in the next day's paper. I explained that guests were recognizable and deserved to be left alone for an evening. Since it was a private party, I would not allow it. If he wanted to ask the guests before taking pictures or mentioning their names, I would work with him but he indignantly informed me the press always had free reign.

"Not at my party they don't," I snapped. "I protect the privacy of my guests. Security guards have been hired to ensure privacy is respected, so please don't place me in the uncomfortable position of having the guards eject you if you show up uninvited." He was furious. We would never again have a civil conversation.

I was in the hotel suite getting ready when the phone rang. It was a different *Reno-Gazette-Journal* reporter. I knew Susan from previous stories. She sounded distressed.

"Jessi, I respect you and want nothing to do with dirty tricks. I'm calling because my supervising reporter has instructed me and a female photographer to buy an entry ticket to the Ball, take pictures, gather names and then create a scene where the guards eject us so we will have a great story for the paper tomorrow," she lamented. "You've been the target of enough abuse and we don't want to do this. Can the three of us put our heads together and come up with something that will save our jobs and grant your guests privacy at the same time?"

I couldn't believe my ears. Did it ever end? I told Susan to have the guard come and get me when they arrived and we would figure out a plan. In the end, the two women promised not to interview or photograph anyone unwilling if I would walk them through the room and let them get enough for a story. The women kept their word, were invited to stay and watch the floor shows, were invited back the next year and left without incident. The next day's coverage was perfect. No tricks. No sensationalism. How I would have loved to have been a fly on the wall in that newspaper office!

Another year, my friend Meyer Lansky II was selected to reign over the Roaring 20s theme, and Sue Polen, one of the ball's main organizers, was chosen queen. Everyone had a chance to get involved with activities during the evening and always had a lot of fun.

Each year the balls were better than the year before and soon became an event looked forward to in northern Nevada. They changed attitudes and opened doors that had been firmly locked to working girls before.

I began working with members of the legislature and explored options to unionize the working ladies. The particular circumstances of the brothel industry and reluctance on the part of the ladies brought to light the exploitation and intimidation that still remains within the industry and resulted in an early death of the union issue.

There are only around three dozen establishments in Nevada where prostitution is legal. The owners know they have a monopoly. If ladies want to work legally, they are at the mercy of the owners to "allow" them to work in their houses as well as to remain working. It tilts the balance of power in favor of the houses. The ladies know if they walk out to force the formation of a union, they will be blackballed from all the other houses and thus denied work in the legal arena.

For many ladies, prostitution is their only option, so the majority declined to participate. Owners knew that would be the case. Without the women's cooperation, any effort toward uniting failed.

The balls produced major achievements in altering attitudes and for that reason alone, they were well worth the effort but I could see

I would have to make regulation changes through the law making process instead.

I had reached a crossroads. To pursue my efforts with any chance of success, I would have to travel down an unfamiliar path. Little did I know it would test me nearly to the breaking point.

PART TWO

Land Mines

Second-class status is bestowed upon the brothel industry despite its legal standing and considerable source of revenues. The system fails this industry miserably.

Officials don't mind grabbing brothel bucks in the form of sizeable taxes, licensing and fees but they deny the business the right to advertise. Escort services and strip clubs can advertise, but brothels are not allowed to. That is a direct violation of a legal establishment's First Amendment right to free speech under the Constitution of the United States. Owners need to unite and demand their prerogative as business owners who are being discriminated against. They don't want to rock the boat, however, because they fear the legislature will outlaw prostitution if they are verbal about demanding their rights under the law. Still, remaining silent only allows the industry to be further exploited. Representation on behalf of owners has been ineffectual over the years as nothing new or helpful has transpired for the industry.

Prostitutes have gone to authorities with valid issues and received no help from the system even though they have the same rights as any other woman. Clearly, the industry is completely ignored until it's time to rake in the bucks.

Advocating on their behalf was proving to be a losing battle. Pursuing changes through the legislature differently than has been done in the past might level the playing field and force fair treatment of this business.

I had already begun to seek out allies within the lawmaking ranks and spent a lot of time researching how to introduce bills into the legislative process. The brothels are a hot button lawmakers are not willing to tackle. Privately, a number of policymakers admit revenue received from the industry makes closing the houses an unattractive

147

option but publicly, few are willing to take a stand on their behalf. It was beginning to look like I would have to run for office myself if I expected any honesty or action.

Assemblyman Bob Price is a powerful senior Democrat in the Nevada Legislature and one lawmaker who is not afraid to let others know of his support. He is also a fellow union member of Michael's and a cherished family friend.

Bob is not a typical politician. He cares about his fellow human beings. He acknowledges the financial support the brothel industry contributes to government coffers and realizes that as long as the industry is legal and monitored, opportunities to exploit it are reduced. His compassion and decency put others to shame and his style as a caring representative of the people sets a high example and is an inspiring model to follow. He is always an invaluable source of research assistance and legislative information.

It was 1996. Congresswoman Barbara Vucanovich, the longtime Republican incumbent for my district, announced she would not seek re-election, making the race an open contest.

Assemblyman Price suggested I run for the seat. I laughed. Surely he was kidding. I was shocked when he assured me he was serious. Before my story broke, no one in authority would even listen to a "ho" – let alone encourage one to run for office! I listened in amazement.

"Your international notoriety has changed how the world views bordellos and the women who work in them," he insisted. "Use it to your advantage. People see you as an intelligent woman who knows the issues and can represent them. Women look to you to make important changes for them. The legal avenues available to you as an elected official can help make important changes for women in all fields. You already have a million-dollars in name recognition alone."

I pondered his comments over the next few months while I continued to observe the legislature. Bob often included me beside him in his seat on the Assembly floor, introduced me to shakers and movers and opened doors that had previously been off limits to someone of my standing. He soon became my political mentor.

After much thought, I decided I could make a difference – not only for my professional sisters – but in particular for the every day working man and woman. I decided to seek the open House seat.

The Democratic Party had more of a reputation as the party of the blue collar and I felt they might be more tolerant and inclusive of my particular and unique background. How could I have known I could be so wrong! Nevertheless, that's the ticket I chose to run on.

The rural West is often overlooked on the national level. Before reapportionment after the 2000 census, the states of Nevada, Idaho, Utah, Montana and Wyoming combined sent only nine people to the House of Representatives (compared to 52 from California alone). Nevada's political landscape is particularly strange. The First Congressional District is completely within Las Vegas; over 99 percent of the state's land is encompassed by the Second Congressional District, making a race there – for all practical purposes – statewide.

A high profile statewide race would provide the exposure I needed to get past my label as prostitute. I knew all hell would break loose again with the media and that I would have to endure the endless bimbo jokes but I felt strong enough to do it.

A press release was sent out announcing my candidacy. The official announcement reception was held in an upscale restaurant in Virginia City. I was overwhelmed with the press and TV coverage, as well as with the voters that came out to show their support. It was an evening that empowered and energized me to be strong and vocal for the working man and woman. Seeing myself commit to being a candidate on the evening news made it somehow tangible and very official.

The media was tipped off that the hooker was officially signing up with the secretary of state for the House of Representatives. The press corps is headquartered only doors from the election office in the basement of the Capitol. Seconds after arriving, I was besieged with flashbulbs and questions. I did my best to respond while completing the legal documents necessary to make my candidacy official. As I turned to leave, my exit was blocked by a throng of reporters with note pads, cassette tapes and cameras.

One reporter in particular badgered me incessantly about whether I would take contributions from the brothels and if my candidacy revolved solely around the legal prostitution issue. I assured him no donations would be accepted from the houses and that while legal prostitution was not my platform, the industry and the ladies who worked in it would receive as much representation as any other legal business. As if he could force a different answer from me by continuing to ask the same question, he insistently drowned out the other inquiries. I ignored him but finally, in exasperation, I announced there would be no other questions and left the room.

The next day's paper revealed a scathing and disrespectful critique of my perceived ability as a candidate by that reporter. Every article he wrote after that referred to me as "former prostitute" and never mentioned my other former occupations or even that I worked in the legal arena of the sex industry.

While others were kinder and more willing to wait and see what my reception into politics and abilities to represent would be, it became crystal clear it would take a lot of work to cross over the line from hooker to candidate. Just as clear was the fact the media had the power to make or break a candidate and were paramount in forming public opinion.

As soon as my story was picked up by the AP, my life was no longer my own. News of my candidacy soon went national – even global. Accounts of my campaign appeared all over the Internet. An intensely private person, I went into the political arena with my eyes wide open but still agonized at the amount of intrusion into my private life.

Even Jay Leno had a field day for weeks on the Tonight Show with "Jessi Jokes." His most often quoted joke was, "Jessi has a new campaign slogan: vote for me or I'll tell your wife."

I learned to take the expected ribbing in stride and hoped the tide would change as voters began to realize there was much more to this colorful candidate than the media was willing to reveal.

Packing away my lingerie, I replaced them with smart, conservative business suits. My wild mane of red hair pulled up on my head and make-up toned down, I was ready to make my entry into the stuffy and perilous world of politics.

Bob was a dear about guiding me along the confusing political path and keeping me informed as to meetings and events I should attend. He advised I had little chance of winning an election without being the party's anointed choice but he felt a high profile race would allow the public to see the real side of me instead of the one portrayed by the media. It would establish that running for office was not a publicity stunt and I was capable of being an excellent representative. It would also pave the way for a future race if I didn't win this one.

Knees knocking, I linked arms with Michael as we put on a confident face and walked into our first public Democratic political event. The Virginia Roast is a fundraising dinner in honor of two Democratic women, – both named Virginia – who had contributed a great deal of time and money to the party. Michael and I were seated at a table with several high-ranking elected officials. Although instantly recognized, I was snubbed the entire evening.

Michael spotted the top state official of AFL-CIO whom he had known as a union leader for many years. We went over to shake his hand and say hello. He glared at both of us, refused to shake hands and walked away. He would repeat his boorish treatment toward us on other occasions in the future.

The evening was a stressful event and we were glad to have it over. It was clear I would have to develop very thick skin. Alligators filled the waters, and they were biting.

Given the response I received at the Virginia Roast, I realized I should expect the cold shoulder from certain elements for the remainder of my campaign. Some people in political circles considered me a joke – a "ho" running for a respectable public position. Others felt this was nothing more than a publicity stunt, a way for me to thumb my nose at society. Others felt they were too elite and so much better than I, or feared I might reveal their secret fantasies and the time we spent together. Remember, certain politicians are known to be customers of the bordellos on the sly. However, being a convincing actress is part of the working girl's job description; I would pretend I was meeting each public official for the very first time regardless of whether I really was or not.

I began attending political functions to become acquainted with elected officials and important shakers and movers, to be seen by political observers and get a better feel for public opinion on issues. One thing I knew for sure: I would be a voice for the average citizen, not the pompous elite.

Assemblyman Price gave me an itinerary of events and meetings I should attend in order to be taken seriously by the party. One upcoming event was the Democratic precinct meeting in Storey County, then my home base. Despite that, the county chairman would not give me any information or take my calls. After several attempts to reach the county chair, his wife curtly told me, "Quit calling for information. My husband doesn't want to talk to you." They certainly went out of their way to make me feel less than human.

I tried to develop the proverbial thick skin but some things just plain hurt. I called a female friend who was a political activist and didn't like the way the party shunned me. Under the condition of anonymity, she found out where and when the meeting would be held and was kind enough to pass the information along. I would hold my head high and attend.

The party chair was certainly stunned to see Michael and me enter the room and sit down. The local state legislators in attendance ignored us. As an official candidate for office, however, the chairman was forced to allow me three minutes to address the gathering. Begrudgingly, he introduced me.

I swallowed hard and wiped my sweaty palms. Forcing any animosity out of my voice and pretending there was nowhere else I would rather be, I gave my first official political address. The words came out perfectly and I said all the right things which reaped genuine applause from the audience.

In the hall afterwards, the elected officials still pretended not to see us but the wife of the party chair fell all over herself apologizing and trying to make things right after so blatantly shunning me. I left feeling most folks in politics were pompous phony bastards that had taken leave of their senses.

The precinct meeting in nearby Washoe County was held a few days later in Reno. It was a chance to meet many of the other shakers and movers in northern Nevada's largest city, as well as the man the party had chosen to be their congressional candidate and who would be my primary opponent.

A *Time* magazine reporter and cameraman doing a story on me accompanied me to the meeting. They snapped away when David Ward, my opponent, came over to introduce himself. He was a really nice man who looked like he had just stepped out of the pages of GQ magazine. The party picked a perfect pretty boy but I liked him. At a later function, the two of us made a pact to avoid personal attacks and stick to the issues. True to his word, David remained a gentleman throughout the entire race and we remained friends long after the election was over.

However, Harry Reid and Richard Bryan, Nevada's US Senators and the state's two most powerful Democrats, were another matter altogether. They provided the first clue that not only would the party not support me, it would go out of its way to disrespect me.

Both senators avoided me. Whenever I made an attempt to say hello to either one of them, they would both head in the opposite direction. Determined they were not going to snub me, I walked right over to one of them when I spotted him standing alone. Before he realized who was standing directly in front of him, I extended my hand.

A look of trapped panic washed over his face. His beady eyes darted wildly around the room. Acutely aware of my bordello background, he didn't want any photographer taking his picture with a hooker. Wouldn't they love that in Washington? The *Time* photographer was still with me, and every time he positioned himself for a picture the senator turned his back. He was clearly distressed and not listening to a word I said. Finally, when it became clear to him the photographer was determined to get a picture, the senator abandoned all attempt at civility and simply ran away from me mid-sentence. At that moment, I had no idea his intense fear of what I knew would result in the demise of my campaign.

Party headquarters announced several elected officials would be available to mentor novice candidates. I thought that was a great idea and called. I was told the senator who ran from me was the main mentor and would recommend others as needed. The voice at the other end of the line asked who was calling. When I gave my name, there was a long silence at the other end, only to be told the list had been "depleted" and there were no more mentors available.

"Uh-huh, right," I thought as I dialed Bob's number. He verified what I suspected. I was on my own except for his help. I was beginning to understand what the pundits meant when they said a candidate won't get to first base in Nevada unless they are the anointed choice.

Each of Nevada's 17 counties holds a major fundraiser in February called the Jefferson-Jackson Banquet in honor of Thomas Jefferson and Andrew Jackson. Michael and I attended nearly every one. Candidates for top offices were given the opportunity to address attendees in each county and they were an excellent way to get to know party notables in each district.

The Elko County Jefferson-Jackson dinner featured political columnist Jon Ralston, then with the Las Vegas Review-Journal, as its keynote speaker. A pompous man, he was very impressed with himself and had an annoying habit of using big words no one could understand without a dictionary. He was the big city boy who was going to show the rural hicks what sophistication and superior intelligence was all about.

The central committee president, Dorothy North, sat beside me on the dais. She was short and stocky and had a no-nonsense attitude. She didn't hesitate to make not so quiet retorts to comments Ralston made that particularly agitated her. And nearly everything he said had that impact.

Ralston was extolling the virtues of David Ward because he was the anointed choice. He continued to disrespect me and trash my chances. Dorothy pushed her plate back and looked at Ralston. "What a piece of work," she grunted disgustedly.

Party officials and central committees are supposed to remain neutral throughout the primary election in order to equally support all candidates in their party who might be running for the same office. Only after the primary election is over and the field is narrowed to only one choice per party, should the organization get behind their candidate. But that's not how they did it; the Democrats were making no effort whatsoever to remain neutral. Dorothy was getting riled.

Then-Governor Bob Miller sent a letter that was read to the guests urging them to vote for Ward. Dorothy was mortified. When she invited these VIPs, she certainly did not expect them to make a mockery of the event. She had just about reached the end of her rope.

Senator Reid sent a videotape. He explained how important it was for attendees to choose the right person for each office and then came right out in blatant support of Ward.

That was the final straw for Dorothy. "To hell with staying neutral," she snorted. "This is a disgrace!"

She pulled out her checkbook and in front of the entire room wrote out a check and stomped up to the podium.

"I guess our exalted leaders and media have set an example this evening," she spit out, "to pay no attention to the directive of our party that mandates remaining neutral until after the primary election."

Walking over to my seat, she handed me the check she had just written and sat back down. Turning to me in feisty defiance she announced, "I've put my money where my mouth is. I'm also offering my services as your campaign manager if you would like."

I had met my match. Stepping up to the microphone, I told the guests how much the rurals meant to me since I too lived there and understood their unique concerns. I spoke of my desire to be a strong voice for areas of the state that are too often ignored in favor of Las Vegas and its pervasive gambling influence. I thanked attendees for being warm and receptive and then said, "I'm very pleased to tell you that my campaign manager is from your hometown!" Guests broke into applause and Dorothy smiled for the first time in nearly two hours.

My appearance schedule filled up quickly. I enjoyed meeting residents one-on-one. The state is filled with old-timers with fascinating, firsthand accounts of local history. I looked forward to events throughout the state.

Parades are a favorite and frequent event in Nevada. Despite the shoddy manner in which my hometown treated me, it was still my home so I decided to participate in the St. Patrick's Day parade. Its fabled mines long since played out, Virginia City today depends on tourism. Over the years the local St. Patrick's Day event has become so well-known for its outrageous celebration that folks from all over come to town to join in.

Inside Edition was there to follow my activities for the day. They asked spectators along the parade route how they felt about a former working girl running for high public office. Nearly every person replied that the job was legal as well as part of Nevada's history and tradition. As long as I could represent them well, they didn't care what my former profession had been. Producers had to leave Nevada and go to Los Angeles to find a minister who would say I was a menace to society.

The next few months were a blur of speeches, meetings, events, walking picket lines and traveling up and down the state to meet voters. Still a novelty that was not yet taken seriously, I received many requests to talk about brothel life as well as political issues when I addressed organizations early in the campaign.

Then, as I am now, I was very open about my past employment and always granted their requests. Fascinated, guests always asked many questions about the bordellos during the question and answer period following my addresses. But as the campaign wore on, I noticed something; it began to dawn on me that clubs and organizations which invited me to speak, became less and less interested in that part of my life. Towards the end of the primary campaign, almost no one asked questions about the bordellos any longer. As voters got to know me, they began to view me as another of Nevada's interesting and colorful characters, but also as someone who was capable of representing them. I was making the transition to credible candidate.

Unfortunately, none of this made any impact on Democratic Party insiders. They tried their very best to make sure I was not told about any meetings or functions and was completely left out of the process. Party officials, activists and even rank-and-file organizations and clubs went out of their way to shun me. During the entire campaign, not one group with the party asked me to address them.

It wasn't surprising then, that when the state convention came up an agenda was not provided to me. In theory, all candidates were to be given an opportunity to address the convention, which ran for three days in Las Vegas. Because of commitments elsewhere, I only wanted to attend for the day in which I was scheduled to speak.

I called Jan Jenkins, then party head in Las Vegas. The voice at the other end of the line was extremely frosty. "I'm a very busy woman and haven't had time to put together an agenda," she snapped.

I expressed surprise at her answer, since the convention was only a week away. She coldly repeated what she had just said and then indicated my background was an embarrassment to the party and that I should do everyone a favor by not attending. Beginning to get riled, I advised her that I was as entitled as any other person to run for office and to be heard at the convention. I had just had it with hypocrisy and abuse. I was certain an agenda had already been sent to everyone else, so I told her I expected mine right away.

Not surprisingly, the agenda never arrived. I called Assemblyman Price. A couple of days before the convention, he faxed me a copy. Written in longhand at the very bottom of the last page was my name. Bob had evidently persuaded Jenkins into adding my name but she scheduled it at a time when no one would be present. The final day was not only the wind-down day when all the speeches were over and nothing of note was going on, it was also Mother's Day. Not a soul would be present.

I called the offices of Nevada's top Democrats. They had played enough games and I was not going to be manipulated any longer. I related my encounter with Jenkins and asked that they ensure I be granted an appropriate time slot along with the other candidates. I told them I was certain their mama's had taught them better manners than to play games with people's lives. I expected to be treated the same as anyone else at the convention. In addition, I told them in no uncertain terms that if this biased treatment continued, I would take on the issue of party "games" in front of the entire convention.

The "good ole' boy" system ignored and disrespected me from the time I announced my entry into the race. I would be shocked if they actually did as I asked. However, it would be a major mistake on their part to underestimate me. I fully intended to keep my word and nail them in front of the convention audience if they continued the games. I had nothing to lose. It was time to expose who was responsible for behind-the-scenes manipulation that determines the outcome of political races.

Bob met me at party headquarters before going over to the convention. He had asked Jenkins to meet us there to try to reach a workable resolution to the animosity she harbored toward me. She didn't show. In addition, the dozens of brochures I had put out alongside the other candidate's on the table the day before were gone. All indication of my involvement in the race had been removed.

Bob and I went on over to the convention and met Dorothy at the door. She handed me an agenda and I saw nothing had changed. It was the main day of the convention and David Ward was scheduled to speak in an hour. The remaining candidates were also scheduled.

One of Michael's union friends presided over the convention. I went up to Charlie before the speeches began and talked for awhile about his family and union activity. I told him since the next day was Mother's Day, that I needed to fly home and spend it with my aged mother. I also told him it would only be fair for me to speak the same day as my opponent and inquired as to whether that would be possible.

"They're playing games with you aren't they?" he asked, cutting right through to the real issue.

"Yes. All the time," I answered relieved.

"I can't promise anything, Jessi, but I'll really try." Charlie said with a pat on my shoulder and a kind look in his eyes. I believed him.

Senator Bryan was talking to delegates and waved to Bob to join him. Bob pulled Dorothy, Michael and me into the conversation, which irritated the senator. Spotting a sticker for my opponent on the floor, the senator began pushing it with his toe while he made a deliberate point about what a fine man my opponent was and what a good representative he would make.

I looked him right in the eye and sarcastically purred, "Why Senator, I was under the mistaken impression you had high class manners. How rude of you to pull such a trick in front of another candidate in your own party. It will be my pleasure to follow your example when I address the convention." I smiled at him sweetly as he shot me a cold stare.

Speeches during the morning session were filled with the same old pious rhetoric and tired promises we've all heard countless times before. The audience responded with polite applause and moved around restlessly. Jan Jones, then-mayor of Las Vegas, was scheduled to speak right after lunch, but 20 minutes after her scheduled start time she was nowhere to be found. Charlie then announced that the mayor had evidently been delayed and in order to continue with the convention, they would hear my speech now instead of Sunday – before the mayor. I couldn't believe my ears; someone actually did what they said they would do! I grabbed my notes and almost ran to the stage.

Charlie extended his hand to help me up the steps and whispered, "Go get 'em, tiger!" I squeezed his hand in gratitude.

"Each election year, candidates tell you how they will magically change the world and give you the perfect American dream," I began. "After the election the reality is we're left with the same old thing and back to trying to find solutions to problems we all face every day. The truth is your life is not going to magically change by electing me – or any other candidate for that matter – but at least you'll have an honest person in office if I'm your choice."

People stopped talking amongst themselves and began to listen. "I intend to be a different kind of representative but before I explain my platform, solutions and background, I want to talk about hypocrisy and the good ole' boy network in Nevada," I said slowly as I turned to face the top leaders. They squirmed and the audience got very silent. It was payback time.

For the next 20 minutes, I kept my promise to those who continued to play games and who denied me an equal chance to compete with "anointed" choices. You could have heard a pin drop.

Although Bob has a reputation as a non-conformist himself, he still plays by the book for the most part. This was all a bit much even for him. He just put his head in his hands. Playing by the book didn't work for me and I knew the "boys" were going to thwart my chances anyway, so I had nothing to lose.

Predictably, some party loyalists walked out, but slowly a murmur swept through the room and when I finished, the crowd registered its approval with healthy applause. Afterwards, many congratulated me on having the courage to stand up publicly to those who had an iron grip on the political process and for telling it like it is.

The only mention in the paper the next day was that a hooker had preempted Mayor Jones. She arrived just as I was finishing and declined to stay.

Donkeys and Jackasses

The AFL-CIO endorsement convention was the party's *coup de grace* that sealed my political fate and doomed my ability to run equally with my opponents. Not yet used to high-level behind-the-scenes manipulation, I didn't even see it coming. Republicans pull dirty tricks right to your face while Democrats stab you in the back.

I presented an outstanding speech that included a cost effective school-to-work proposal for a program that would incorporate union apprenticeship training, targeting high school students who would not be going on to college.

My husband is a 30-year union member which, by the very rules of AFL-CIO, was supposed to accord me an edge over candidates without union ties. Delegates from various unions pledged their votes. I had an excellent chance of winning the endorsement over Ward who had no ties to collective bargaining. It would have been a major boost in both funding and support that could lead to winning the primary election.

The AFL-CIO convention was held on the same day as the filing deadline for public office. Shortly before the secretary of state's office closed for the day at 5 p.m., we had every reason to believe the current slate of candidates would be the final, official list. But there would be one more addition. The announcement shocked everyone. The convention president moved the microphone closer and repeated his statement: the delegates would not be voting. Attendees were told that the governor's wife had just called the AFL-CIO state president to inform the convention that former state senator Thomas "Spike" Wilson had just signed with the secretary of state for the congressional seat Ward and I had been campaigning so hard for all these months. That changed everything.

The next morning's paper triumphantly proclaimed Wilson's entry. Exhibiting total insensitivity towards the hard work both David Ward and I had put in on behalf of the party, Jan Jenkins was quoted as saying, "Now *that's* doable."

Wilson made no appearance before the labor endorsement committee as other candidates had. No one knew his platform or where he stood on issues. He was an attorney who had no direct connection to the unions. Nevertheless it was clear he would get the endorsement; the matter was shelved and sent back to the AFL-CIO Executive Committee for "further action." It was also clear it was no coincidence. I was devastated.

Wilson hated campaigning and lacked the charisma and people skills necessary for one-on-one contact. He felt his "anointed" status and past political standing would carry him to victory. He was a short-tempered, pampered man who wanted to avoid the public contact and hard work of early vote gathering. Instead, he intended to enter the race at the last minute after the party manipulated someone else, namely Ward, into doing all the early footwork. The party then dumped the early candidates in favor of Wilson, who would mainly rely on paid advertisements from that point on while doing as little in-person campaigning as possible.

Additionally, one of my campaign staffers learned that certain party officials didn't want a "whore" elected and would do whatever it took to derail my campaign. On top of that, our polls showed I was gaining fast on Ward. The intent was obvious: Wilson's entry was engineered to give the party a candidate they felt could beat me if I refused to withdraw, while at the same time driving Ward out of the race completely. That's exactly what happened.

A tremendous amount of time, sacrifice and effort had been extended by both Ward and myself. I promised voters I was in the race for the long haul and announced I intended to honor that commitment. Ward's withdrawal from the race was reported in the next day's paper. He was understandably furious with party tricks and betrayal and vented his anger to the press.

Two days later Ward gave a more subdued interview. He called me and urged me to also "withdraw for the good of the party." I told him

I fully understood why he dropped out but I was mad as hell and was seeing it through to the end.

The AFL-CIO and top Democrats successfully executed a back-room deal and intentionally pulled a dirty trick to manipulate the outcome of the election. I knew who was behind it – and why. I also knew I would not lower my standards to theirs by revealing names from my little black book. But I would be a thorn in their side and make them publicly sorry.

The AFL-CIO convention featured more dirty closed-door dealings than I could cope with. How could a hooker, whose business it is to deal with human nature, have been naïve enough to think politics would be as straight forward and upfront as bordello prostitution? Clearly prostitution was the more honorable of the two professions. I was ready to go home.

On any given day, Las Vegas' McCarran International Airport is crowded with people waiting to leave this artificial Mecca in the desert. Some sit dejected, pondering how they are going to recoup their losses at the tables. Others stare out the windows at all the neon and fantasy. It is an evil town full of selfish, greedy, power-hungry people and I am always glad to leave it.

We checked in and spotted Jim Gibbons, one of my Republican opponents, waiting for the same plane. A lady sat next to him and they were laughing, oblivious to the crowd of people waiting around them. Hooker instinct kicked in. The woman was clearly not his wife and the situation smacked of non-business fraternization. I grabbed my pocket camera and snapped a picture of them.

The ticket agent made the boarding announcement for our flight to Reno. Michael and I found two seats near the rear of the plane. After settling in, I looked behind our seats and saw Gibbons and the unknown lady sitting behind us in the back row huddled together giggling and completely engrossed in each other's company.

It was strange to see an opponent in this light. He was always pleasant but aloof, giving the impression he felt he was just a bit too good for the common folk he sought to charm. He always held himself ramrod straight, perfectly attired, a perpetual smile, and politically correct words always flowing from his mouth. Continually gracious, there still was something that just felt not quite genuine about him.

I had a window seat and kept looking out because it reflected the two of them behind us. I was certain they were not business associates. She clearly was not his campaign manager or a relative. I vaguely recalled seeing her at political functions for his campaign. Was she was a volunteer? Hooker instinct made me curious about the nature of his association with Ms. Unknown. Especially since she was pregnant.

Everyone was struggling to get their luggage out of the overhead bins when they reached Reno, so Michael and I waited, making ourselves as invisible as possible. Gibbons hurried to retrieve his bag and was one of the first to dash off the plane.

Ms. Unknown stayed and chatted with the flight attendant until everyone else had departed except Michael and me. I was sure I had it figured out now! We walked down the aisle toward the exit. I glanced back just before leaving the plane and saw Gibbon's friend was still stalling.

A few minutes later on the ground floor of the airport, we saw Ms. Unknown turn right into baggage claim. Walking toward the opposite end of the terminal, we saw Gibbon's wife wave to him as he strode toward their Suburban.

"Interesting what you observe traveling," I thought to myself as my suspicious nature turned to thoughts of DNA tests.

Predictions and polls showed Gibbons had every chance of being elected to Congress. Considering the ongoing investigation of Bill Clinton's antics at the time, Gibbons might even be called upon at some future date to help determine the president's future. Depending on what one might have in their own closet, that could be a daunting – not to mention, hypocritical – task.

I remembered Dawn Gibbons' kindness just a couple of months earlier at a candidate dinner when Gibbons, one of his Republican opponents, Patti Cafferata, and I debated each other after dinner. Now an elected official in her own right, holding her husband's old seat in the Nevada Legislature, Dawn is the perfect Southern belle. Pretty, smart, charming and ambitious, she comes off as Little Miss Innocent. I spent my summers growing up on my grandparent's ranch in southern Tennessee so I recognized that brand of charm. Cunning as a cobra. All Southern belles are taught to catch flies with honey and Dawn has it mastered.

She came up to me with a thousand-watt smile and laid it on thick. Even though my hooker instinct told me to watch out, I was taken in by Dawn's magnetism.

She treated me like I was her newest best friend and it worked. I was so used to being ignored or disrespected that I was grateful for any show of kindness at this point. She not only made it appear effortless, she made it seem genuine as well. She gushed about how brave I was to take on the establishment and how much she admired my determination to fight the "good ole boys" to make a difference in a system that had been mired down too long in the status quo. She asked me to autograph her copy of my calendar, gave me her cell phone number and asked me to have lunch one day soon.

I unwisely let down my guard and decided I liked this woman with the warm nature. Later, I would learn Dawn was her husband's most effective campaign collaborator. I hoped both of them were sincere in their desire to get to know me but I had been betrayed by so many political figures already, I no longer trusted what I saw. I liked them both however, and hoped they would turn out to be what they appeared. Only time would tell.

The land issue debate was civil between Gibbons and myself. It's not my style to initiate personal attacks and Lord knows Cafferata was making enough of them for two people anyway. Not that it mattered. Gibbons had firm rebuttals to Cafferata's snide remarks.

I sat between Gibbons and Cafferata. Tension between the two was heavy. When an audience member asked what I thought about an issue, I decided to lighten the air by referring to the fact that I was caught between two lawyers and perhaps it would be in my best interest to plead the fifth. The audience laughed but neither Cafferata nor Gibbons appeared to be in the mood for humor.

Gibbons had presented incomplete information regarding the issue about which the audience member had inquired. The subject matter was of special interest to me so I quietly and calmly presented the correct information. Gibbons appeared embarrassed and irritated.

Putting his hand over the microphone and turning toward me, he softly snapped, "May I remind you, I am also a geologist and probably more aware of land issues than you are?"

I was really surprised. "Ten-four, Red Rider," I retorted with a mock salute which irritated him even more.

That would be the only fit of temper I would see from Gibbons during the entire campaign but it was enough to know this was a man used to having his own way and determined to get it.

Dawn wanted her husband to run against me in the general election because they both felt I would be easier to beat than Wilson. That logic prompted them to assist me over some rough spots in order to help make that happen. Regardless of her motivations, Dawn did prove to be extremely helpful on at least one occasion.

I was attending a candidate's event in Ely, a small, dusty town five hours north of Las Vegas. My cell phone rang. I reached for the light and looked at the clock on the motel bedstand. It was midnight. Dawn was on the other end.

"Jessi, they're playing tricks on you again. I know your word is your honor and you have a speech in Hawthorne tomorrow night but you have to get on a plane and go to Vegas instead," she said excitedly.

"What are you talking about Dawn?" I asked, trying to figure out what was going on.

"Remember when Wilson refused to debate you on cable TV and you did the show alone?" she asked. "His ratings suffered after the media tore into him for his ungentlemanly treatment of you. They conspired to neutralize that bad publicity by having another debate in which you don't show up. It's tomorrow night in Boulder City."

"Damn, Dawn, that's the date they asked me about and I told them it was the only date I absolutely could not clear for them," I lamented as their plan became apparent to me. "Jerks. I've already committed to Hawthorne."

"Girlfriend, you're solid in Hawthorne. You've been there a lot and they know you're in their corner. Call them and send Michael in your place and get down to Vegas," Dawn pleaded. "I really hate what they're doing to you."

"Thanks, Dawn," I said wearily. "I owe you."

I hung up and rolled over. Putting my arm around Michael, I purred, "Honey …" Then I called Bob Price and the party representative in Hawthorne.

The next day Michael worked a full day and then drove two and a half hours to Hawthorne to give the speech in my place. He was well-received. I knew he would be because Hawthorne is one of my favorite towns with special residents who were very open about their support.

I boarded a plane and Bob picked me up at the airport and drove me to Boulder City, a town 25 miles outside of Las Vegas in the heart of Clark County's burgeoning desert suburbia. Arriving a few minutes before the debate started, we waited in the car until the last second. Then we marched down the hall and into the room just as the TV cameras began to roll. The look on Wilson's face was priceless. The moderator added another chair. Wilson was in a foul mood the remainder of the evening.

Only one more debate remained before the primary election. It was scheduled for the following day in Carson City. I hopped another plane and flew back north, tired but in time for the event. Wilson didn't show.

The final week before the primary election was a blur of activity. There were parades and events all over the state because of the Labor Day weekend. Candidates went from town to town as a group in the rurals.

Saturday started with a pancake breakfast in Fallon, an agricultural community over an hour east of Reno, which allowed residents to meet and visit with candidates before the parade. This was always a big event for locals. Most were ranchers or small business owners who took their politics and civic responsibility seriously. They wanted to talk face-to-face with the candidates.

We lined up along the sidewalk leading into the breakfast area to greet voters. Wilson and I were next to each other. He didn't like campaigning so Senator Bryan accompanied him to make sure Spike attended all events and to do PR work for the sour but influential man the party had picked as their choice. Every so often, the senator would jump in front of me and extend his hand to a resident and pull them past me to meet Spike. Obviously votes were more important than manners to him.

The parade is a big event in this part of the rurals. The community is a small, close-knit unit. Residents are hard working, no-nonsense country folks who jump at the chance to enjoy themselves.

The parade theme that year was World War II, so the cars designated for the candidates were from that time period. I had been promised a wonderful old car. As I walked toward it, the driver informed me the governor had called asking that the car be assigned to Wilson instead.

"Which car did Spike originally have?" I asked, knowing it would do no good to protest. It was only a parade after all. I would swap cars and ride in the vehicle Wilson was originally assigned to.

"There weren't enough cars to go around so the governor asked that Wilson be given your car," the driver told me.

"I see," I replied. "I'm so pleased to see the party refrains from favoritism." I walked the length of the parade, content to shake people's hands and talk to them.

Everyone congregated at the fairgrounds afterward. Senator Bryan donned a Wilson button and was greeting voters while Wilson wandered off to get a beverage and never returned. As the senator walked past us, Michael confronted him about wearing only Wilson's button.

"Party rules state you are supposed to remain neutral, senator," snarled Michael. "You need to add Jessi's button to your jacket too."

"I don't think so," retorted the senator as he glared at Michael. Bryan was clearly used to calling the shots, but Michael is not intimidated by arrogant swaggering and is not a man to back down on principle.

The argument became more heated and both continued to take steps toward each other. When it looked like it might come to blows, Bryan's aide rushed up and guided him off.

That evening, all the candidates, regardless of party affiliation, attended the traditional final party Dorothy North always put on in Elko just before the primary election. It was always lighthearted fun and a chance to relax from the hectic pace we had all been keeping. Even Senator Bryan and his reluctant charge were there.

I put one of my bright red stickers in the palm of my hand and walked over to the senator. I came up behind him, slapped him on the back and greeted him.

"No sense in harboring bad feelings, senator. Glad you're here," I said as I walked off.

Glancing back, I felt a big wave of satisfaction as I looked at my sticker on the back of his jacket. It took nearly a half-hour before anyone had the nerve to tell him. There were times when campaigning was just plain fun.

All the months of hard work were over. Dorothy told me not to go down to party headquarters as they had already taken all my posters and literature out well before the count started coming in. I was getting used to being disrespected.

The votes were in. Not surprisingly, Wilson won the Democratic primary hands down (61%) with full assistance of the party power machine. I placed second (21%) in the field of three without help of any kind. As expected, Gibbons scored a plurality win of 42% in the crowded Republican primary, leaving the remaining seven hopefuls to divide the balance.

The Democrats would have their hands full with running a reluctant candidate in a Republican-leaning district who didn't want to go out and mingle with the people. I would take a breather.

But not just yet.

With the primary election over, the Democrats demanded I pledge my vote count and support to Wilson for the general election. I told them to go to hell.

The day after the election, Michael was fired from his job. Despite being a good employee, his boss was mad because I refused to support Spike Wilson in the general election and indicated I would encourage voters to cast their ballots for Jim Gibbons instead. As a union shop, the AFL-CIO had instructed all affiliates that Wilson was their boy and told them the Republican I now supported was anti-union. I figured AFL-CIO "forgot" Wilson was an attorney and not a union member. Michael was disgusted that his fellow union members refused to think for themselves.

My showing in the primary took the party by surprise as I received the same vote percentage as seasoned politicians Patty Cafferata and Cheryl Lau, who both lost to Gibbons in the Republican primary. Cafferata is the daughter of then-Congresswoman Barbara Vucanovich, whose House seat she was seeking. In the 1980s, Cafferata served a single term in the Nevada State Assembly and then was elected state treasurer. She later served as district attorney in Lander County. Lau is a former secretary of state and was a staff member for Newt Gingrich when he was speaker of the House. Garnering a quarter of the state vote with absolutely no budget or any of the mailings or ads enjoyed by my veteran opponents made me feel pleased to do as well as I did.

Republican organizations inundated me with requests to speak at their meetings. I was booked solid through Thanksgiving. My phone rang off the hook from well-wishers within the Republican ranks. When I appeared at Republican functions, people shook my hand and were genuinely gracious.

"What a breath of fresh air," I thought. I decided to change parties as soon as my work during the general election was done. Until then,

I resolved to assist Gibbons in defeating Wilson with a one-woman guerrilla campaign. I knew Wilson was an elitist with a nasty temper. I also knew how to push his buttons.

With a large sign that read "Democrats for Gibbons," I traveled all over Nevada attending every event and debate in which the two men appeared. I went to union meetings, to the union halls in the early mornings when the men were picking up their job assignments, to job sites and any other place union rank-and-file assembled and told them why choosing Wilson was not in their best interest despite the endorsement of AFL-CIO and why Gibbons would better represent them. My endeavors were so successful, the AFL-CIO was forced to do a rebuttal campaign against my efforts to neutralize the damage I was causing. By the time of the general election, we had secured around 20 percent of union rank-and-file vote for Gibbons. Given the Democrats' dependence on the union vote, that alone was probably enough to seal Wilson's fate.

At a debate between Wilson and Gibbons that was broadcast live on KOH, a Reno-based talk radio station heard statewide, Wilson saw his chance to get back at me for constantly being a thorn in his side at all the events he was scheduled to attend. He told the audience that, as a lawyer, he would take a strong stand against crime.

"For instance," he said as he looked directly at me, " I prosecuted Joe Conforte and cleaned up the mess he was creating with his brothel. We need our communities to be free of undesirable elements and I'm proud to have been a part of making that happen."

What a slime. During the question and answer period after the debate, I stood up and said, "This question is for Spike Wilson."

"Mr. Wilson," I began, trying not to show a telltale smile of revenge, "I was raised on a ranch where country folks were taught good manners. You claim to have spent time on ranches so I'm amazed you don't have better manners. I'd like to know why you agreed to appear at this evening's debate with Mr. Gibbons but were ungentlemanly about refusing to debate me on the public service channel during the primary election."

Without missing a beat, Wilson lied through his teeth. "I debated you elsewhere and there was another debate you missed," he snarled.

The radio station didn't want a heated argument to erupt so they quickly moved away but the host came up to me afterward and told me they were well aware of all the debates and it was blatantly clear Wilson was not forthcoming with the facts. They asked me to do a show with them.

During the program, I was able to establish the true facts, and one show led to many. Even when I was not guesting on their show, they continued to replay the part of my interview where I referred to Wilson as "pathetic." The station roasted Wilson, and listeners saw a dark side of dishonor to one congressional candidate.

I got a lot of hate calls from those in the Democratic Party who had a vested interest in Wilson's election. I also received congratulatory calls from others, including a woman who told me she was proud a female was the one to be open and honest about political deceit.

Taking a controversial stand proved to have a frightening side too. Virginia City is nestled at the 6,200-foot elevation in the mountains, 15 miles up a treacherous road from Carson City. The road is windy, with hairpin turns and only two narrow lanes. During the winter, it is an icy and dangerous drive.

Shortly after I began guesting on the radio show to clarify Wilson's debate statements, I was driving down the mountain to Carson City. It was fall and a soft rain made the road slick. I am an experienced mountain driver but it always makes me a bit nervous to negotiate the mountain road during inclement weather because there is no where to go except down if an emergency situation arises.

The big car coming toward me turned on its lights, laid on the horn, crossed the line into my lane and came straight at me. Panic stricken, I fought to keep my truck on the road while pulling over as far as I could. The car jerked back into its own lane just seconds before hitting me head-on. It was so close, I didn't see how he missed sideswiping me at the very least. I caught a glimpse of the driver. He was laughing.

That evening the phone rang. "Did you enjoy our little meeting earlier today?" the voice on the other end smirked. "I drive your road often. Perhaps we'll meet again."

I called the police but the car and driver were never found.

Everything in Virginia City is built on a hill. Not long after the attempt to run me off the road, I began to notice a white van sitting on the hill above our home. It never appeared on a regular basis and the driver always seemed to know when I had spotted him and called the sheriff. I frequently saw a man with binoculars standing outside the van looking my way. It continued for several weeks and then, as suddenly as it began, it stopped and I never saw the van again. A basically trusting person, at the time I found it disturbing to think my little village, tucked away from the world, could be touched by anything sinister.

Michael and I are proficient with firearms and participate in gun shoots with various clubs. I am not a fragile little female. I refuse to relinquish my independence simply because some bullies are trying to intimidate me. If they planned to set traps for me, I would have a surprise ready for them. Besides, there was still work to be done and I wasn't about to be sidetracked by scare tactics.

I did a speech for postal workers with Dawn. I owed her after the Boulder City coup. Many of the postal workers were volunteers on my campaign and knew they could trust what I said. I told the union members that AFL-CIO had backed a candidate that was a lawyer and not connected to a union. They were appalled and mad to discover Wilson not only could care less about their concerns as everyday working men and women, he also did not share or understand their union mindset.

Dawn charmed them and told them funny anecdotes she experienced campaigning for her husband. She had the crowd in the palm of her hand.

Wilson arrived for his speech. Dawn left but not me. I sat down in the chair in the front row directly in front of Wilson. I pulled out a cassette tape recorder and turned it on. He became visibly irritated. Union members began to ask him very specific questions. He glared at me, knowing I was behind this. I just smiled.

He blew up at one of the union members who insisted he answer a question directly instead of dancing around the issue. Nearly half the audience walked out. While Wilson regained his composure and tried to do damage control, I slipped out the door and went home.

Despite accusations to the contrary, Gibbons himself had nothing to do with my little plan. Wilson couldn't believe I would travel all over the state just to sit in front of him with my sign. He was at the end of his rope. He must have been glad when the last debate before the general election in Ely rolled around. At that event, he turned his chair so he wouldn't have to look at me.

After it was over, one of his volunteers called him over to the literature table. For weeks, I had been passing out a flier with a red circle at the top with a line through it, the words "NO RATS" inside the circle. Below, it detailed Wilson's lack of union ties and even mentioned that Jim Gibbons belongs to an airline pilots association and was therefore more sympathetic to union members. I had purposely kept these away from Wilson. But that night I put them on the table. I knew it would be the final straw.

Sure enough. Wilson flipped. Two days later the newspaper called me for my reaction to the story that appeared in that day's paper. Wilson made accusations that I worked for Gibbons and "Democrats for Gibbons" was an undeclared and illegal organization. He pitched a fit and came unglued in his interview. I loved it. I never involved the Gibbons campaign directly with what I was doing, so Gibbons could truthfully tell the press that he knew nothing about it. I didn't work for him and was a private citizen now, he said. I was free to support whomever I wanted, in whatever manner I wished.

I said the same thing and added that I had no organization; my sign was my own and I simply took it with me whenever I attended functions. I had no idea what Wilson's problem was.

It couldn't have been more perfect. Wilson had a very public temper tantrum only two days before the general election. Gibbons trounced him at the polls. He lost by 22 percentage points.

The hooker got the last laugh. Barely able to contain my glee, I sent Jan Jenkins a fax that simply said, "Gibbons – 58%; Wilson – 36%. Now *that's* doable!!!"

The next day I changed my voter registration to Republican.

Soon after, Gibbons was interviewed on KOH and asked about names of his potential staff. Recognizing I had contributed to his victory, the host asked if I was on his list for consideration. Gibbons said I was. I never received the call.

The Weeble and
the Devious Duchess

Early in 1998, Nevada's Republican lieutenant governor, Lonnie Hammargren, announced he would not run for re-election, instead opting to run for governor. That left his seat open and I immediately decided to run for it, since one important duty of the office involves working with Hollywood and the film commission, a natural match for me with my movie industry background.

There was little time between the congressional and lieutenant governor's campaigns to reclaim normalcy in our lives. When a campaign is frugally funded and the contender is not assisted by their party, emphasis is placed on grassroots efforts, volunteer involvement and a whole lot of traveling up and down the state to personally meet voters. An 18-month minimum of hard work is required for those who campaign the old fashioned way as opposed to party choices who rely mainly on paid advertisements in the final weeks to "buy" them the election.

Experience taught me my involvement would take longer than my opponents since I could expect to be excluded from the normal avenues of the political process. I spent the majority of my congressional race outside Las Vegas and had therefore established an ongoing rapport with voters in that portion of the state. While the main headquarters for the lieutenant gubernatorial campaign was located in Reno and although I would cover the state frequently, we felt it prudent to concentrate a great deal of effort on the city this time.

Each month, approximately 4,000 new residents move into Las Vegas while about 2,000 leave, making it one of the nation's fastest growing cities. With so many new faces, this huge influx and turnover has a significant impact on campaigns. Most newcomers don't have a clue about those running for public office in Nevada. A large concentration of voters is located within the state's major city, however, so office seekers must focus heavily on the metropolis six months prior to any election.

For six short months after the congressional campaign, we spent time at home living a normal life and reestablishing the tight family bonds that are so important to us. Then Michael accepted a union assignment to work on Sheldon Adelson's huge Venetian hotel/casino project on the Strip for the duration of the campaign. We moved our operation base to Las Vegas; a temporary move I dreaded and hated but knew was necessary. Since the campaign was statewide, I had the reassurance of being able to travel frequently to my beloved north and rurals, a thought that sustained me throughout the race.

For the next 18 months, I was certain I had wandered into an alien nation filled with strange inhabitants. Nearly every Las Vegas event, a great many of the residents – and especially those running for office this time around – made me wonder what the hell I was doing here.

One character in particular was uniquely colorful.

When my children were little one of their favorite toys was a group of roly-poly miniature people called Weebles. When tapped, they would teeter back and forth but never fall over.

Aaron Russo reminds me of a Weeble. He is nearly as wide as he is tall and has a wardrobe that would be the envy of any used car salesman: shiny suits, scuffed shoes, frayed shirts with no tie. His hair at the time was long, greasy and naturally wavy. His face was scrunched up into overlapping layers of blubber that puffed out his cheeks and made him look like a wrinkled shar-pei dog. He always had a snarl on his face like he was ready to tear someone's head off. Promoting him as an ideal candidate for governor is a clear stretch of the imagination but nonetheless that's exactly what he tried to do.

During his Republican gubernatorial campaign, Russo's clear intent was to take control of the party to ensure his election – and he almost accomplished it.

Russo's primary goal was to get his own choice, Dr. Fuller Royal, elected head of the Nevada Republican Party to replace John Mason, who was up for re-election during the state convention. That way,

Russo could create a better-than-even chance of getting himself elected. To accomplish this, Russo saturated the Clark County Central Committee with his own supporters who in turn nominated Russo delegates to the state convention where the state party chairmanship was to be decided.

At the Clark County convention, Russo was challenged by supporters of Kenny Guinn, a former UNLV president, the establishment's choice for governor and a man who had been actively campaigning for the 1998 election since early 1996, thanks in no small part to contributions from gaming interests. There were accusations that Guinn illegally paid people to show up and vote his allies in as delegates to the state convention. During the county convention, Russo publicly challenged Guinn and tried to have Guinn's delegates declared invalid. A brouhaha ensued, the police were called, and the final result was that both camps wound up with about the same number of delegates for the state convention.

Mason retained his chairmanship and Guinn kept the upper hand within the party. That tactic having failed, Russo tried instead to stack the major statewide races with his own people, who in turn solicited support for him as they campaigned for their own offices. Royal was his choice to run for lieutenant governor and as a result got a lot of votes from independent, renegade Republicans, particularly in Clark County. These were votes that in all probability I would have received had he not been in the race.

A Californian by way of New York, Russo was a carpetbagger in Nevada who created total chaos during the 1998 primaries. A public relations nightmare, he made statements early on that he searched for a state where voters were unsophisticated and he could "buy" an office. As a former movie producer, he certainly had the money to try but he didn't understand the first thing about Nevada mentality. He didn't have much appeal either.

He did, however, have strong opinions and made it clear his were the only ones that mattered. He had a mouth to match his convictions and he put both into high gear like an out-of-control bulldozer plowing down everything in its path. He surrounded himself with wannabe gangster types that scared off mainstream voters.

While disruptive, he does shake things up and make people think about freedom issues, which is a good thing. His campaign was definitely not about the incessant rhetoric we were all sick of hearing. He told the public exactly how their rights were being violated and their freedoms were being stripped. He verbalized the reality of what people need to know. Some of his views were innovative and good for the general population; others were off the wall. Much of his message was vital, but the wrong messenger delivered it.

I first met him at a Carson City Republican Women's Club meeting. He was accompanied by a perennial fringe candidate, who ostensibly was there to point out who was who and give Russo the background he needed to appear knowledgeable about the state and its people.

Russo's salt-and-pepper hair flowed around his shoulders. He wore earrings, a tacky outfit that belied the fact he had money, baggy pants down around his hips, a shirt that still retained part of his lunch, and no tie. His eyes were cold as steel. He was about 40 pounds overweight and the elevation made him wheeze. Sweat poured down his brow.

Russo and his assistant were handing out a videotape outlining his message titled, "Aaron Russo's Mad As Hell." The tape, which Russo had marketed through infomercials among other things, is complete with dramatics that include his own hands clutched around his neck and him falling down on the stage. Despite his marketing efforts, no one had ever heard of him. Few paid attention to him. Even fewer took the tape he offered. Most wondered why he was there.

Russo was a legitimate player in Hollywood, producing such films as *The Rose* and *Trading Places*. He played a big role in Bette Midler's success. We had the movie industry in common but that wasn't what held his interest. I had already run a statewide race. He hadn't. He wanted to have lunch and learn about my experiences as a novice candidate and an outsider.

I met him in a crowded dining room in the Las Vegas Hilton. His assistant was with him. Neither bothered standing when I approached their table. I wasn't surprised. I sat down across from them.

Russo monopolized the conversation with tales of his excellence. All the time he talked, he also ate. Lowering his mouth to near table level, he simply shoveled the food inside and continued talking. It was difficult for me to finish my lunch as I watched the food fall out of his mouth as he spoke. I listened quietly for an eternity and then explained I needed to leave, as I had political meetings of my own to attend.

"You can't go yet!" he said in surprise. "I need to hear your experiences so I'll know how to avoid the same treatment."

"I only have another five minutes, Aaron," I replied. "Either ask your top priority questions or we'll have to make it another time."

He didn't like a woman telling him what to do. He glared at me and then said he would reschedule but he wanted to ask a couple of strategy questions before I left.

The particular strategy he intended to employ would have alienated voters. While his concept was good, the approach was not. Nevertheless, he insisted he was right. I told him to go ahead and do it his way and see how far he got.

Suddenly he was on his feet, knocking his chair over backwards. "You stupid little bimbo!" he shrieked in an embarrassingly loud tone. "Who the hell do you think you are?"

I was mortified. The room got suddenly quiet. Everyone was staring. The restaurant manager was headed our way.

"You sir, are an ignorant pig," I said as I got up to leave.

When I got back to the office, his assistant called to apologize. I extended my sympathy that he had to put up with Russo's abuse but made it clear I wouldn't, especially when Russo didn't have the balls to call himself.

Our paths didn't cross again until the Pahrump Harvest Festival Parade in Nye County. Michael's uncle Bill owns a restaurant in town and is an active member of the local chamber of commerce. He organized the parade. He and his wife, Ellen, are very active in the Republican Party. A retired full colonel, he is a whirlwind even in his 70s. Trim physique, full head of white hair, eyes alive with involvement in life, and a dapper figure in his military uniform, he took control of the parade and made it a huge success.

I was scheduled to ride in the first convertible. Russo wanted to be first. He was told he would be behind my car, at which time he stomped back to his vehicle and pouted. His goons came up and tried to talk us into switching. We reminded them that rules were rules.

Eventually Russo came over and began visiting like we were old buddies. When he returned to his car, I'm sure he thought he had charmed me enough that the Hilton misadventure was forgotten.

After the parade, candidates mixed with the public in the event's area. The local cable TV channel was interviewing political attendees so candidates were gathered at their booth to wait their turn.

It was clear Uncle Bill was an important community figure just by looking at him, so Russo ambled on over. He put his arm around Uncle Bill's shoulder and looked at the nametag on his uniform. Addressing him by name, Russo began to shoot the bull.

Uncle Bill's assignment in the military had been as an advisor and consultant to the film industry to ensure military details were depicted accurately. He became close friends with John Wayne's family and knew many of the people Russo said he worked with in the movie industry. Michael and I walked over. Russo extended his hand to Michael and gave me a peck on the cheek. Then he introduced Uncle Bill to us and began to tell us how he and Uncle Bill were old buddies because of their shared connection to the film industry. We looked at Uncle Bill who had a mischievous twinkle in his eye. Russo continued for several minutes to impress us with his relationship with Uncle Bill.

Finally, after Russo had dug a hole big enough to satisfy Uncle Bill, he turned to him and said, "Michael and Jessi are my nephew and niece. They already know who my friends are."

Russo turned beet red and muttered something we didn't quite hear as he walked over to the TV booth. Mr. Important wasn't quite as blustery any more. He inquired about his interview, stating he wanted to be next. After all, he was running for governor. The host referred him to Uncle Bill. Without a word of protest, he walked away and waited his turn.

Aside from people skill problems, Russo was also having problems with residency. It appeared he had not been a resident of the state for the required period of time to file for office. He claimed he bought a house in an area of northern Nevada not far from where I lived, interestingly in an area locally known for militia activity.

Russo apparently felt his assistant had sufficiently smoothed over the Hilton fiasco enough that we were able to be cordial during the Pahrump festivities. He felt comfortable leaving a message on my machine asking to reschedule a meeting to discuss my experiences with the party. When I returned his call at his headquarters, I was advised he had gone home for a few days. At our first meeting, his assistant had given me Russo's home phone number, so I called it. His assistant answered. Russo wasn't there. It turned out to be his assistant's home, not Russo's. He was in California at his ex-wife's house. Home in Nevada was apparently a room at the Las Vegas Hilton or his campaign headquarters across from UNLV, although he was somehow able to work around the legal technicalities when it came time to declare his candidacy.

I knocked on the hotel room door several days later. We had an agreement that there would be no repeat of the spectacle that had occurred downstairs weeks before. He wanted to pick my brain and knew I would simply leave if he could not control his temper. We were alone so I walked over to the door and propped it open. I never received good vibes from Russo.

The meeting went well. He was civil, although I got the distinct impression everything I said was a waste of time and he would do everything his own way. It didn't matter. I extended a courtesy meeting to a fellow candidate as he requested. It was up to him.

Russo didn't have a chance at elected office in Nevada. But he was a crafty scrapper who shook up the status quo and forced real people to give serious thought to freedom issues. He also caused more than a few arrogant party controllers to reach for the aspirin bottle. In that respect, I found him somewhat entertaining.

He finished with 26 percent of the vote in the primary, a distant second to Kenny Guinn (Lonnie Hammargren's gubernatorial campaign, incidentally, never took off; he finished third almost as an afterthought and eventually became chairman of the Clark County Central Committee). In July 1999, publicly claiming he "kisses no one's ass," in his inimitable style Russo angrily bolted from the Republican Party and became a Libertarian. Rumors have been floating he may run a third-party candidacy for Congress or again for governor. It is likely Nevada has not seen the last of Aaron Russo.

* * *

In my own race for lieutenant governor, I knew I would have my hands full with Lorraine Hunt, a Clark County commissioner of questionable ethics who was clearly in cahoots with the Kenny Guinn crowd. I didn't know if I had the stomach, strength, or desire to fight it any longer. I had been beat up unrelentingly ever since I entered the Mrs. Nevada pageant and I was drained.

It would take all my energy to cope with the power elite. Without a doubt, there is a power elite in Nevada in general and Las Vegas in particular. The "good ole' boy" system has an iron grip on how business is run in the Silver State. Gaming dominates the political process almost to the exclusion of everything else. Raw political power silences already elected officials who want to keep their jobs.

The same small clique makes up campaign teams whose job it is to see that only people in their corner get elected. They don't even try to be covert anymore; it was so obvious Kenny Guinn was the choice to be the next governor that one Las Vegas political columnist dubbed him "the anointed one" months before the election. The public knows all this goes on but feels helpless to do anything about it, so they remain silent. By going along with it, the real culprits are not the power mongers, they are the silent public.

Hunt was for all practical purposes Guinn's running mate from day one. I didn't stand a chance. It was an amazing thing to watch this woman evade justice and, instead, slip haughtily into the second highest office in the state. Too bad it was a story of tarnish instead of inspiration.

A snobbish woman with incredibly bad wigs, a perpetual conceited look and sanctimonious behavior, Hunt reminds me of a combination of Leona Helmsley and Norma Desmond. She has the matronly padding of later years and always looks the same. I never saw her in anything other than a business suit and a jet-black wig that looks like a lethargic black widow spider camped on top of her head. Her official campaign photograph was airbrushed to conceal the telltale signs of unwelcome aging. Her favorite expression is the wide-eyed innocent look, which she has down pat. To go along with the look, she is adept at laying on the "I'm just an innocent little victim" act, one folks saw in abundance during her ethics violation hearings.

An aging cabaret singer, she still fancies herself a star, not unlike the character of Norma Desmond in *Sunset Boulevard*, who was a pitiful woman clinging on for dear life to a vision of how things used to be. Dying to always be the center of attention and bring the spotlight to herself, Hunt is known to break into song at any occasion despite a painfully antiquated repertoire.

Known for exorbitant first-class travel expenses paid for by taxpayer dollars during her tenure on the Clark County Commission, she had thin skin when criticism was directed her way. Once, when questioned by reporters regarding action she took as a county commissioner, she pitched a fit that revealed total contempt for the public when she snarled in a holier-than-thou tone, "Don't the people know? Didn't they go to school?" Her disdain for the common person was evident in both her career and personal life.

On the Clark County Commission, a governing body with a long, sordid history of ethical lapses, she became a master manipulator of public funds and decisions which would benefit her and her buddies, giving little thought to those who elected her. Her timing was impeccable. She always remained a step ahead of justice. Of course, she had powerful help. She seems determined to become the poster child for the "Me" generation politician: the extremely ambitious elected official who is willing to sell her soul and jump to the puppeteer's strings in exchange for advancing her own career and pocketbook.

"Airportgate" is among the more notorious of the scandals in which Hunt was involved. In 1997, it was revealed that the Clark County Commission had given friends, relatives and cronies preferential consideration for vendor contracts at McCarran International Airport over those who truly qualified under federal guidelines. It was all about power, money and special treatment for a selected few.

As Congresswoman Shelley Berkley so accurately pointed out, "That's just the way business is done in Las Vegas."

This was corruption at its ugliest, most blatant and most insensitive. Documentation shows, as a county commissioner, my opponent was right in the middle of it.

George magazine ran an article on Las Vegas in which the city's corruption was deemed to be among the worst in the nation. Additionally, the Clark County Commission earned a dead last "vote of no confidence" in a newspaper poll. A reputation like that should embarrass the city and county enough that a major house cleaning would be the next logical step. That Las Vegas' elected and appointed officials don't even blush when confronted with this says volumes. Administrators at all levels are part of the problem, so nothing changes.

When Airportgate came to a nasty head, the county commissioners backpedaled and scattered like political cockroaches the minute the light of truth was turned on. Four of them were pinpointed as main culprits, including Lorraine Hunt.

While mainstream society was too busy chasing the almighty dollar or simply too disinterested to care about decisions made by those we elect, Bob Rose, a dedicated and well-respected Las Vegas public watchdog, spent nearly every day observing government in action. If it were not for his dedication and others like him, officials would be able to run amuck without having to be accountable to the very folks who put them in office in the first place.

Rose caught members of the county commission unethically awarding airport contracts to personal friends and family members of investment partners. He blew the whistle on them. He filed complaints with the state ethics commission. His evidence was clear, convincing and overwhelming.

Hunt had close relationships with several of the people she voted to award contracts to but denied knowing them. Some of the people who received airport concession contract awards also donated to her campaign.

Two people she voted to award contracts to were the daughter-in-law of her long time business investment partner, Rodney Reber, and Judy Klein, a woman Hunt claimed she barely knew. Never mind the fact she sang at Klein's wedding; that was just a favor for a mutual friend, wasn't it?

Actually, ethics commission transcripts showed that Klein admitted knowing Hunt for 17 years. She even helped host a combination fund-raiser for the Republican Hunt and Senator Richard Bryan, a Democrat, at Hunt's restaurant. Klein remembered the amount she raised for Hunt to be around $60,000.

In late 1999, Judy Klein pleaded guilty to wire fraud for embezzling $98,000 from her employer, the International Association of Gaming Attorneys. At her February 2000 sentencing, the judge told Klein the gravity of her offense warranted more than just the minimum sentence and gave her 15 months in prison.

When even the newspapers began to publicly doubt her credibility, Hunt wrote a letter to the editor denying she knew any of the Reber family. Ethics commission transcripts showed discrepancies in what

Hunt told the newspapers and her testimony under oath. Obviously, she had only a casual acquaintance with the concept of truth.

My campaign did its own, independent investigation of the matter. Candidates are required to file a personal financial disclosure document with the state, disclosing property they own as well as other personal financial information. Our researchers found Hunt had an impressive accumulation of property. Each parcel was listed by number. The researchers took the document to the assessor's office and pulled up all the parcels listed on her disclosure. One came up to Rodney Reber, the long time partner with whom she co-owned property but whom she claimed not to know.

When Rose's complaint was filed with the ethics commission, it was rewritten. The complaint, as rewritten, bore no resemblance to the one submitted by Rose. The ethics commission completely ignored the charges in Rose's complaint. Instead, they substituted a minor charge regarding Judy Klein that was never even mentioned in Rose's original complaint, one that could be easily dismissed. Correspondence between the ethics commission, the deputy attorney general and counsel for Hunt showed corroboration.

The "games" got even rougher.

Rose did not receive notification to present evidence within the required timeframe. As a result, when he arrived for the hearing, he was not prepared and requested the ethics commission grant him a postponement. They denied his request. Under the circumstances, he did his best to present his evidence but the ethics commission badgered and even intimidated Rose with threats of financial ruin via huge fines the commission threatened to impose upon him for filing "frivolous" complaints.

An elderly man, neither Rose's physical nor emotional health could withstand strong-arm tactics. Those masterminding the games knew that very well. Under tremendous stress, Rose finally conceded most of his evidence and complaints. Evil won.

As if Airportgate wasn't enough, Apex was even worse. Rose's original complaint also noted Hunt failed to disclose she knew investors in the Apex Industrial Park outside Las Vegas. Records showed at least three Apex investors were involved in separate business ventures with Hunt, including her old buddy Rodney Reber, whom she had known for decades, possibly as far back as high school.

If the commission had allowed anything but the charge they conjured up in their creative revision of Rose's original complaint, Hunt would have had to face the music along with her other three cohorts, who took the fall to satisfy public outrage. But Hunt skated on all the charges against her.

I was outraged at the injustice that power could beat down a citizen on a fixed income who couldn't afford to fight back. I held a press conference to submit fraud and lack of due process had been perpetrated upon Mr. Rose. I requested he be granted his voice as a citizen and a voter by asking that the attorney general appoint an independent investigator who had no political favors to grant, to review Rose's original complaint and determine if the ethics commission should reopen and review the complaint and amendments. If the attorney general declined to do so, I asked that Clark County District Attorney Stewart Bell take jurisdiction and appoint an independent investigator for the same purpose. Should all agencies fail to address the matter, I requested the FBI include it in their ongoing investigation. Nothing happened. Interestingly, shortly after the elections, the FBI director in Las Vegas resigned and received a coveted appointment to the Nevada State Gaming Commission and nothing more was heard about an investigation.

Word was out to members of the ethics panel that the same folks who pulled the strings for Kenny Guinn were also advising Hunt. It didn't take much persuading for panel members to get the message: their jobs and futures were at stake.

When Airportgate was exposed and she was about to be nailed, Hunt simply made the announcement she would leave the county commission and run for higher office. After all, she would certainly never run for a higher office if she had something to hide! Apparently, in her view, the people of Nevada would never believe she was guilty of wrongdoing if her powerful spin doctors projected the right story. She could count on lots of help from her powerful friends. It was merely an inconvenience that money and the right influence could correct.

Despite clear evidence to the contrary, the ethics commission decided Hunt barely knew Klein and dropped the charges. With the help of powerful friends on and off the ethics commission, Hunt picked up the proverbial rug while the dirt of her involvement was swept out of sight beneath it. Smug in the knowledge that she was untouchable, she arrogantly turned her attention to getting the hell out of Dodge before the hounds got too close and focused instead on waltzing away from the mess in Clark County and into an office in the Capitol.

It certainly appeared Hunt's case received special treatment at the hands of the state ethics commission. The commission failed to fully investigate charges against her. Her case was dropped while the remaining commissioners were held accountable for charges nearly identical to Hunt's in original form.

It made one wonder what was really going on. Could it be the power mongers wanted Hunt in a state office and in a position to better serve their needs?

The clear message from the state ethics commission was that elected officials could do whatever they want, secure in the knowledge that agencies that were supposed to make them accountable to the public, won't do their job because they cave in to pressure from power at a higher level.

It appeared they were there for one reason: to help cover up and excuse the actions of public officials when they got caught with their fingers in the cookie jar. Too often clear evidence was ignored that would nail wayward bureaucrats and make them accountable for their actions. Instead, the accused were sent out to continue their dishonest behavior at the taxpayers' expense.

Actions and decisions by the state ethics commission made a mockery of any implication that the commission felt the slightest responsibility to the public. A revamped commission was needed that would be accountable to the public instead of those in power in Nevada. We need a commission with the backbone to close the escape route for errant bureaucrats and encourage rather than punish public watchdog input.

The papers were filled with juicy details of the ethic's hearings day after day and the cover-up that happened right before their eyes, yet there was no public outcry. Other than a few letters of disgust to the editor, no further legal action was taken. Power won, at least for Lorraine Hunt.

For our government to work, we must all be accountable for the actions of those in power. Just because an agency or bureaucrat says something is so, doesn't mean it is. No one is supposed to be above the law but sometimes things go amuck. Intimidation, selective memory, badgering, cover-up, lost documentation, changing the rules to suit government's needs, emotional and/or financial blackmail in the form of threats and fines, and downright strong arm tactics all run rampant.

Responsible watchdogs like Bob Rose in Las Vegas and Sam Dehné in Reno are being browbeaten into silence by the very organization that was supposedly created to bring wrongdoing to light. When those who are doing their civic duty for the rest of us no longer are granted due process by organizations with hidden masters, we no longer live in a free America.

Betrayal by those elected or appointed to represent our wishes and protect our rights is too high a price to pay. Corrupt government can exist only when citizens permit it to. In private enterprise, if employees failed to do their job, they would be fired. It is our obligation as Americans to challenge any appearance of corruption in government and bring to justice the thieves of integrity who circumvent that process. We must take a stand and demand the facts be heard and let the truth speak for itself.

At a political event in Genoa, state Senator Joe Neal and I discussed the frustrations we both shared as honest, candid advocates in a game of deceit. Neal, a well-known critic of the excesses of Nevada gaming interests, was running for the Democratic gubernatorial nomination at the time. He is the only elected official in the state with the backbone to take on the casino industry and point out that they are not carrying their fair financial share when it comes to taxes. For his trouble and dedication to the everyday citizen, he was shut out of the process and lost in his primary. When his North Las Vegas senate seat is up for re-election, you can bet the moguls will go after him again. They will do whatever it takes to get rid of a thorn in their side and silence a voice of conscience. If we allow that to happen, we deserve whatever we get.

You can't make integrity, honesty, courage or honor magically appear in those appointed to the ethics commission any more than we can expect those traits from puppets who do the bidding of cunning, devious behind-the-scenes political manipulators. When a campaign is only about ripping off a person's wallet instead of providing for the best interest of statewide neighbors, then we will inevitably elect people who lack any trace of decency or integrity.

Until campaign reform eliminates the ability to funnel soft money to party favorites while depriving all other candidates of equal opportunity, we will continue to struggle with the same problem. Soft money is funneled through special divisions or even off-shoot branches of the state party and reaches only candidates selected by a handful of top party officials.

Big money contributors continue to call the shots in choosing those whom voters will hear about during campaigns. Choices at the polls are dictated months in advance by starving out those candidates that special interest knows won't further their agendas and by promoting only those who will.

A logical first step with an already proven success rate would be to enact a law similar to New Jersey's which mandates no one with a connection to a gaming license can contribute to a political campaign. That shuts down the puppet show in a heartbeat. No strings equates to independent decisions and actions on the part of those running for office.

If all candidates had a set spending limit that they could not exceed, it would level the playing field for everyone in a race and prevent the practice of starving out the less funded campaigns.

Campaign reform would be extremely difficult to turn into reality because those already in office would be the ones to initiate the changes. They don't want to bite the hand that feeds them. Special interest got them elected and special interest can see that they're returned or replaced at the polls in favor of someone who is more willing to play their game.

While public funding of campaigns would be the most effective avenue to neutralizing the influence wielded by the rich and powerful, it will never happen because gaming and big business lobbyists would intimidate legislative representatives and threaten the financial support needed to get them re-elected. If the proposal were to be put on the ballot, it would fail because the public is so fed up with politics they won't vote to spend a dime on a process that would benefit them in the long run. It's a good idea whose time has not yet come.

If we ever hope to begin to kick corruption out of Nevada – or the nation for that matter – we should begin with our voting process, supposedly the most sacred right of all.

Replacing the Sequoia voting machines with tabulators that are tamper-proof and provide a paper trail, as well as instigating an open primary and a set campaign spending cap would be huge steps toward cutting down on a corrupt political process. Neutral monitors at the polls are also needed to follow ballots along their entire route beginning with the ballot box voters deposit their ballot into, all the way to the final verification process.

Ironically in Nevada, along with the registrar of voters, Clark County commissioners are responsible for verifying election results. This, in my view, appears to be a conflict of interest considering many of them may be in a political race themselves. Asking them to verify a vote count that may also include their own run for office appears to be asking the fox to baby-sit the chickens. On a state level, the example of improprieties and history of Clark County Commissioners raises a concern that a more neutral avenue of verification needs to be explored for future elections.

One way the election outcome is controlled is to keep the primary partisan where it is more easily manipulated. An open primary would list all candidates regardless of party affiliation for a particular office on the ballot. The entire voting population, with no restriction to party association, would choose from that list. The top two contenders for each office would fight it out in the general election.

It's time our government has representatives who come from other than the privileged class with their rich and powerful connections. It is time we quit being duped and manipulated. It is time we again make our government, "of the people, by the people and for the people."

We found very little of that philosophy when our researchers began to scratch the surface of Hunt's associations with various high level Las Vegas shakers-and-movers. They found the common denominator to be that they all apparently knew each other from area high schools. The anointment picture began to make sense. Las Vegas has a very incestuous political community.

With that in mind, it was no surprise to find Hunt's huge campaign coffers were padded by upper echelon folks whose assistance she had nurtured over the years. According to one of Hunt's financial statements, contributions to her campaign came mainly from developers and casinos, belying her claim she was not bought and paid for by the gaming industry.

A campaign is hectic enough without having to deal with dirty tricks. Political pranks can be expensive as well as irritating as the cost of signs add up in a hurry in a statewide race. I began receiving calls from my volunteers all along my opponent's route in the north and rurals about the time she did her "rural tour," advising me that my signs were disappearing. Sure enough, every single sign was gone and replaced by governor and lieutenant governor, side-by-side "ticket" signs. To add insult to injury, some were even put up on my own distinctive sign support rebar. I was well known in the north and she wasn't, so the intent appeared obvious.

I filed a complaint with the secretary of state which resulted in no action without a witness who actually saw my signs being removed. At a later event my opponent and I were scheduled to address, we cornered her campaign manager and asked about their connection to the missing signs. He arrogantly smirked that it had to have been the people they hired to put up their signs and they would advise them not to do it again. The consequence of the missing signs and insight into a lack of funds necessary to replace them certainly occurred to both my opponent's manager and us. A candidate is ultimately responsible for actions of those involved in their campaign, however. I was proud of the fact I was surrounded by decent folks in my race.

Hunt carried the "in your face" sign crusade to extremes in Reno by placing two and three of her signs together, eliminating space for other candidate's signs. She also attached them to Nevada Department of Transportation fences and right-of-ways in violation of state law. The lieutenant governor is one of the main board members who oversee the state transportation department. It seemed to be a bad example for the person hoping to be among those heading that division to disregard the very rules that govern state property. Again, as Leona Helmsley had so often done, Hunt demonstrated total disregard for everyone but herself. I called NDOT and asked about the illegal sign placement but, apparently anticipating my opponent might be one of their next bosses, nothing was ever done.

She made many mistakes but the most potentially damaging to the average working family in the state was Senate Bill 549.

Hunt and her husband, Blackie, are the founders of the Nevada Restaurant Association. Blackie was chairman of the board and Hunt was exchange director the year SB549 was introduced by the association's lobbyist. The bill would have saved employers money by providing credit for tips against minimum wage, which meant the law would allow the employer to pay a tipped service provider up to one-half of the minimum wage, thus denying employees full wages and full tips and creating a situation which would push the working class into a class of working poor. Just like Leona Helmsley, in an effort to put more money into her own pocket, her tips bill demonstrated total disregard for employees.

As a county commissioner, she callously suggested removing cows from the one remaining ranch in Las Vegas and charging the rancher in order to please special interest developers building up around the ranch.

In an article written by Mike Zapler for the *Las Vegas Review-Journal*, he reported, "Clark County commissioners are having a cow over a herd of cattle living on the valley's only livestock farm."

The Robert Combs family has owned RC Farms for generations. As a result of the population boom in Las Vegas, the farm is no longer on the outskirts of the city. Housing tracts have been built up around it. Buyers knew the farm was there when they bought. Regardless, new residents now object to the smell of cattle. The Combs family was there first and simply wants to continue a way of life that has been in their family for a long time.

Sounding a lot like Leona Helmsley again, Hunt suggested that, in addition to daily citations, the county remove the cattle and make the Combs family pay for it.

Stan Parry, who represents the farming family, stated the county commissioners, "are trying to run the valley's last farm out so they can build a house on it."

Hunt is a long time urban Las Vegas elitist who is now making decisions for the rurals as lieutenant governor. Her decisions as a county commissioner make it difficult to believe she has any interest whatsoever outside the neon lights of her beloved metropolis.

These were examples of defining issues that showed the difference between how each of us would have run the office of lieutenant governor and how we would have treated the public.

If anyone doubted the "team" effort of the governor and lieutenant governor during the primary election, all hesitation was erased when Hunt was caught calling a former co-commissioner in Las Vegas *after* her election to the state's second highest office. She called to pitch awarding a lucrative $8 million airport advertising contract to the company that handled her race for lieutenant governor *and* the company which had direct ties to the governor and his then chief of staff. She not only was repaying favors granted during the campaign, she also just couldn't seem to keep her fingers out of airport issues.

The prevailing attitude displayed during these required paybacks showed she was still up to her "keep the big money within the cronies and cut me in" perspective. It made a mockery of the governor's newly unveiled "ethics reform package."

The prior ethics commission had given her a ceremonial slap on the wrist as county commissioner for similar unethical behavior. The naughty girl was now convinced she was above the law. As lieutenant governor, with the guv and all the power brokers behind her, she didn't even make an effort to be discreet anymore. She blatantly imposed her will on everyone, quite like the hated elitist Leona Helmsley.

I thought about both of our lives and the value system each of us employs in our day-to-day dealings with others. One a former legal prostitute; the other a career politician. It occurred to me that both Hunt and I made ourselves available to the highest bidder. The difference was, I didn't hurt anybody in the process and I did it with honesty.

Integrity – Las Vegas Style

That's just the way business is done in Las Vegas," Shelley Berkley advised her boss, Sheldon Adelson.

A former Boston cabby who created the COMDEX computer trade show, Adelson came to Vegas with a plan that would make him one of the richest and most influential men in town. Rather than building fancy hotels that would focus on gambling and entertainment, he would concentrate on convention business, developing a huge center that would accommodate any size gathering.

To that end, in 1996 he closed and imploded the historic Sands Hotel on the Strip – a property he owned for several years previously – in order to build the Venetian Hotel, an ambitious project which claims to eventually boast 6,000 suites, making it the largest hotel in the world. Somewhat behind schedule, Adelson partially opened his resort in May 1999 amidst great fanfare. The Venetian, interconnected to the Sands Expo Center, seeks to be a one-stop destination for conventioneers. Everything is there: rooms, convention space, entertainment, shopping and, of course, plenty of gambling. Guests won't have to fight traffic going all over town for business purposes, hotel stays or entertainment. It's all offered to them on his property.

At the time of her remark, Berkley was legal counsel for Adelson's business affairs. She knew Las Vegas and its particular brand of politics well. It was her job to guide her boss through the maze of permits and paperwork required to make his dream a reality. Bluffing would not accomplish that. Telling her boss the truth would.

The truth is, corruption and pay-offs are a way of life in this nasty town, especially in politics. If Adelson wanted certain permits in a timely manner, Berkley would advise him which commissioners he should accommodate and the particular favors he should afford them in order to get his project pushed through expediently. She was simply being realistic and prudent.

When the media got a hold of her comment, they had a field day. For weeks, everyone in town had an opinion. Some praised her for having the courage to tell it like it was; others crucified her for giving "immoral" advice. Adelson did damage control by firing her.

It appeared most were inflamed because they preferred tourists to think Vegas is a terrific place with wonderful values. Others defended Berkley's frankness, noting the foundation of corruption on which Vegas was built and which exists to this day. While elected officials and business people shuffled the money and looked the other way, she was one of the few people in town who told it like it was.

The media bedlam created high name recognition for Berkley. Already active in the civic and political communities, she made the decision to run for the House in the Las Vegas-based Nevada First Congressional District. Poll results would determine how residents felt about her now infamous statement.

The First's incumbent congressman at the time, Republican John Ensign, had recently announced he would run for Senate against Harry Reid, leaving his House seat open. He was the GOP's golden boy. All hopes were pinned on the veterinarian. Total focus and resources were placed at his disposal. He is good looking, ambitious, charismatic, has two terms in Congress under his belt, and an ego that pushes him to put his own career advancement before the good of Nevada residents.

He sat on the powerful Ways and Means Committee in the House of Representatives. Ensign's seat on that committee gave Nevada clout in Washington that as a small state it would not usually have. More than a few residents felt he betrayed them by giving that up. But the party stroked his ego until he felt invincible.

Ensign lost his bid for Senate by a slim margin. Berkley, a Democrat, won the congressional seat he vacated. Voters showed they understood the reason behind her candid advise even as local politics tried to play it down. Her now famous comment would be heard again and again. Like a mantra, it would indicate the true nature of business in Las Vegas.

When Nevada became a state in 1864, Las Vegas didn't even exist as a city. In fact, during Nevada's first three years as a state the Las

Vegas area was actually part of the Arizona Territory. As recently as 75 years ago, Vegas was just another small desert town. But that all changed in 1931 when the state, deep in the throes of the Great Depression, legalized gambling. By the time Benjamin "Bugsy" Seigel opened the doors to the Flamingo Hilton in 1946, all levels of government and big business were well on their way in learning the magic of money shuffling.

I had no clue the practice had become such a cancer. I ran for office out of naïveté. I love this colorful state with its rebel reputation, where old timers live and let live, where folks don't conform to authority and live by their own rules of humanity. That is outside the limits of Neon City and before all the newcomers, however.

Reality hit me between the eyes when I came to Vegas to spend time building a political base. While the history of the Battle Born State remains something to be proud of, I will never again view so-called leaders and influential business icons through innocent eyes.

My own venture into the seedy world of Nevada politics pulled back the curtains that prevent the majority of people from seeing the sordid activity that goes on behind-the-scenes. I was hard pressed to find an agency that wasn't soiled by greed and lack of integrity. Men first came to Nevada for gold and silver. Today, money is still the ruler. People come second, and it causes a lot of casualties along the way.

Any statewide candidate with serious intentions of winning has to make an impact on voters in Las Vegas and Clark County. Over two-thirds of the state's population lives there; as do the vast majority of party VIPs that can assist or destroy a candidate's future.

The lieutenant governor of Nevada chairs the state's Commission on Economic Development, which includes the Nevada Film Office under its jurisdiction. I chose to file for this race because my film industry experience was a perfect fit to this part of the office's job description. I also knew I would be an excellent ambassador for Nevada as a result of my love for the Silver State and my knowledge of the history and people that make the state so unique.

There was no denying I was a renegade Republican. I am a populist advocate, independent, and outspoken with no masters. The party would not be able to mold me. Not one cent of party money or assistance would be directed toward my campaign. I was on my own.

Our life savings, donations from working class supporters and Michael's paycheck would be the backbone of the campaign's financial survival. Michael is a saint; he supported me 100 percent without a single complaint. He knew a candidate with goals like mine was the only hope for the everyday Nevadan. He was dedicated to helping me try to make a dent in the iron fist of control that gripped the state in which he was born.

His union dispatched him to a long-term project that would support us while I tried to infiltrate the closed off and tightly guarded compounds of the Las Vegas political machine.

Rank and file Republicans in northern Nevada are wonderful. Men's organizations, women's groups, individual voters and central committee members genuinely welcomed me to the party and into their midst. I had no problem obtaining volunteers and friends who were willing to do whatever was necessary to get a candidate who wouldn't be bought into office. I love the rurals and northern Nevada. The residents there truly made me feel I could fight and win for them. There was a world of difference, however, between the north and the "Nation of Las Vegas."

We rented a place and began putting out feelers. Party headquarters for the state and Clark County are next door to each other in the western section of the city. I didn't want to go through the torture of visiting either one but it had to be done. I decided on the state office first.

Brochures in hand, I stood before the desk of a fellow redhead. Robin was really helpful and made a true effort to make me feel welcome. She would be the only one who did.

She took me into the office of executive director Dan Burdish. A small man with an evident ego, I would find out many times over that he also had a volatile temper. The state chairman, John Mason, was out of state a great deal of the time on business, so Burdish was the official in charge of day-to-day operations.

I had met Burdish before. He attended a Lincoln Day dinner in Winnemucca shortly before I announced I would run for lieutenant governor. He was making the rounds of each county's dinner and tried to discourage me from running.

"We already have a candidate picked out for lieutenant governor," he informed me, confirming the fact that, like the Democrats, the Republicans also select their own choices and exclude everyone else.

"That makes voter's choices for them when you give total support to only your pals and starve out other competition," I complained.

"Why not include everyone who wants to run for an office and support them all equally and let the public make the decision instead of a few control freaks pulling the strings for the party?" I asked.

I knew the answer of course. Their pals would further the agenda of those who run the party behind-the-scenes and renegade candidates wouldn't.

"Hey, do what you want," Burdish snapped. "You're free to run. We just won't support you," he replied as he walked off with a cocky smirk on his face.

Yes, I remembered Burdish. He would go out of his way to say the acceptable thing in public and then cut me off at the knees in private. My hooker instinct had him pegged.

He was superior and obnoxious and had no qualms about his bad treatment of others. Worst of all, he had a fair amount of power that he loved to flaunt. He made no pretext of diplomacy if he felt no need to kiss butt. His acid tongue could wilt even the most tough-skinned victim. He was a real piece of work.

Standing in front of his desk, I forced myself to be pleasant. We exchanged brief chit-chat and then he dismissed me with his usual "too important" demeanor. I went next door.

The county office was no better than the state office. In complete chaos, it was run by another former cabby turned rich entrepreneur. It was beginning to look like a person wanting to be a rich successful businessman in Las Vegas had to start out driving cabs. Thanks in part to Aaron Russo's influence, the Clark County GOP organization had no control over itself. That showed during the screaming matches that erupted at every meeting. The county party was so fractured, they couldn't even agree on a motion to adjourn a meeting!

When I got back to the office, there was a message from Burdish on the answering machine.

"Jessi," he said in a tone denoting I was his newest best friend, "I hear your husband is a union member. We need his help with an issue the party is going to make its primary focus during the remainder of the campaign. Please call me as soon as possible."

In addition to being a flamboyant businessman, Sheldon Adelson is also a well-known fat cat contributor to political campaigns. He is also notoriously anti-union and fights tooth and nail against union members working in his hotel. Therefore, Adelson would support and fund Republican candidates if the party did his bidding with an anti-union scheme called the "Paycheck Protection Initiative," a harebrained proposal which sought to prevent unions from contributing to political campaigns without the permission of its members. The idea was to curtail union power to the point where it became irrelevant, allowing big business to do what it pleased. Needless to say, the Republican establishment was only too happy to cooperate. The bartering system sounded familiar; it just wore a less honest label.

In an ideal world, employers would pay their workers a fair and livable salary that would prevent them from having to work two jobs simply to keep their heads above water. In return, employee morale would be high and they would contribute 100 percent effort to their employer and work even harder to make their employer's business a success. Everyone would benefit. The success of Southwest Airlines is proof this theory works. Unfortunately, this is not a perfect world.

Michael is a longtime union member. He knows the reality of poverty wages paid employees whose bosses are not bound by a collective bargaining agreement. In the early days, unions were necessary to force employers to pay livable wages. To a great extent, that enforcement is still necessary. He understood union mentality and was a member of his union's PAC committee. That was why Burdish wanted to pick his brain. In total ignorance, Burdish wanted to use Michael as a public example of union defection to their cause. That alone showed how little Republican leaders knew or understood unions or the working man and woman.

Twenty-six percent of registered Nevada Republicans are union members. As they become more and more frustrated and disgusted with the totally clueless approach in which their party deals with the issue, those numbers will more than likely dwindle.

We listened to Burdish with no intention of fulfilling his request. He obviously viewed us as the hayseed cowboy and the bimbo hooker. He thought we would be so grateful that he wanted to "include" us, that we would do anything the party wanted. But we were neither stupid nor desperate. After Burdish finished his spiel, we asked him why we should help the party when the party didn't intend to help us. He had no answer. We erased any further messages from him.

Under the direction of Mason, Burdish, Nevada GOP communications director Chuck Muth, and Nevada GOP finance director George Harris, this grand plan failed miserably, not even coming close to getting the initiative on the ballot. Not that it mattered; the courts ruled it unconstitutional anyway. Despite previous support of the initiative at the urging of the party, many candidates suddenly became afraid of having to face angry union voters in November and began quickly ignoring and no longer discussing the matter.

In an embarrassing aside, Kenny Guinn demonstrated immense visible discomfort when pressured by AFL-CIO officers to sign a pledge against the initiative in front of their 1998 candidate endorsement convention held at the Silver Legacy hotel/casino in Reno. Huge sums were poured into a useless drive that could have been put to better use with direct assistance to candidates to help them get elected. It became clear that not only would the party not help alternative candidates like me, but that it actually preferred to waste money on ludicrous, politically damaging schemes which only a tiny minority of zealots supported.

The party was run by idiots that had no clue how the everyday citizen thought or felt. As an executive director, Burdish needed to go back to business school for a refresher course, with special emphasis on people skills. No such course could bring him in touch with the common person's reality though.

Muth was even worse. One really had to wonder where the party found these people and why they would put them in a position of authority. It didn't speak well for any level of party decision making.

A totally arrogant and egotistical man, Muth was a perfect bookend for Burdish. Party decisions were carried out by these two with the force of a tornado. If you were in the eye of the storm, you were simply wiped out.

Muth was ambitious, obnoxious and absolutely certain no one possessed the superior intellect he was blessed to have. Like Burdish, he also had an acid tongue that would annihilate anyone who disagreed with his views. If anything, he was even more rigid and small-minded. No one I spoke to even remotely came close to liking or trusting the man. Certainly no one wanted to be on the receiving end of his continual venomous tirades in the public and private publications in which he wrote. Personal experience with the man left me convinced he is a revolting human being, void of any concern for his fellow man.

To his credit, John Mason at least tried to maintain a civil relationship with as many party members as possible. We clashed on several occasions but tried to build a working relationship that would be civilized at public functions.

Apparently he was instructed by the puppeteers who controlled party strings to monitor and censor me, because he continually called or sent letters explaining that my brand of candid disclosure regarding fellow Republicans was unacceptable. I understood he had to kiss ass in order to keep his job. I had no masters and nothing to lose, so I had the luxury of being as candid as I wished.

I was clearly on my own. My only hope was to address as many civic and political organizations as possible, become involved in civic activities, encourage media coverage and go directly to the people. All this proved to be impossible in a town of tightly controlled cliques. It soon appeared evident Las Vegas should become a state by itself and let the rest of Nevada get on with a life where one human being cares about another.

Our first Clark County fundraiser was modest but a start. State election laws dictate that as soon as $100 has been donated toward a campaign, the candidate must open a separate bank account to be used only for campaign purposes. That proved to be quite an experience all by itself. Vegas seemed to be a place obsessed with slapping a label on everyone and making them fit into a tidy little compartment.

Labeling people can be very hurtful. Realistically, I knew I would probably never shed the first name of "former" and middle name of "prostitute" as far as the media was concerned and, frankly, I gave up trying long ago. My bordello background is old history and something I never tried to hide in the first place. I didn't understand why it should be such an issue for the press.

There were times, however, when the prostitution label appeared to be the preferable one. I found that out when I went to a major bank to open my campaign account and was told they wouldn't accept my money because I was a politician. Another label!

"I'm NOT a politician," I protested. "I'm an advocate for the people."

"No difference," the woman behind the desk declared. "We've found too many politicians are crooks and we no longer open political accounts."

I stared at her in disbelief and exasperation. "I used to work in the bordellos," I stated. "If I came in as a working girl to open an account, would I encounter the same reception?"

The woman just smiled and replied, "Of course not, dear. Working girls are a cut above politicians."

I couldn't believe what I was hearing but the bank clerk was serious. I had to go to a different financial institution which opened an account for me, but even then only reluctantly, taking my fingerprints and asking for additional identification.

Clearly, this is an indication voters need to clean house and fire elected officials who create this kind of label for those who are honorable. Like hypocrisy, labels were part of the landscape when it came to politics.

There was no question the label I clearly did not wear was that of anointed candidate. During the congressional race two years earlier, after the primary I sincerely considered Jim Gibbons to be preferable to Spike Wilson. But it was a pleasure as well as a payback to actively and publicly support the Republican during the general election. That really frosted and embarrassed the Democrats. It also gained respect from many Republicans.

People came up to me at Republican functions and welcomed me to the party. They were rank-and-file party members, not party brass, but at least I had a base to work from within the Republican Party. The congressional race and its aftermath established me as a viable, if unorthodox, candidate.

In spite of it all, Jim Gibbons helped make my party transition easier. He was every inch the gentleman and consummate politician. He was the person Central Casting would have sent to play the part of a congressman. Tall, slender, erect, handsome, impeccably dressed, dazzling smile, hand extended for endless handshakes, he always said the right thing to each person with grace and the ability to make that person believe he was sincere. Most of the time in the beginning, he probably was. It also didn't hurt that he had a wife who was his best campaign asset. Everyone loved Dawn.

At his victory party election night, Gibbons acknowledged my effectiveness in turning a good number of rank-and-file Democratic labor votes his way during the general election. When others made disparaging remarks about me, Gibbons balanced their remarks with positives. Before long, the public recognized the congressman respected my grasp of the issues and potential for leadership and the snide "hooker" remarks began to disappear. I owed him a debt of gratitude for validating me at the risk of being criticized himself. In the cutthroat atmosphere of politics, two people had broken the nasty cycle of personal attacks to forge a friendship and mutual respect the public admired. We both benefited. His public courtesy toward me helped set the tone and paved the way for acceptance I was granted by Republicans.

One of the few party officials in Las Vegas who made any attempt to actually include me was the outgoing lieutenant governor. Lonnie Hammargren is a fascinating personality. An eccentric genius, he is a brilliant physician. Always outspoken, he was often shunned by those of both parties because he spoke his mind and didn't worry about being "politically correct." I admired that. He reminded me of myself.

I think his uptight cohorts were also a bit jealous of him because he was unorthodox enough to let down his hair and have fun with little regard to whether he was saying the right thing. Folks accepted him into their midst because he was genuine and could relate to them in a way other officials couldn't. He was a popular man of the people.

He is one of those rare people who don't let their privileged status or intelligence separate them from the everyday person. He can converse with the most elevated political figure and just as easily relate to an everyday laborer. He has a rare talent for genuinely caring about and relating to people regardless of their status in life.

That was probably why he and I got along so well. Even though I was running for his seat, he not only was always gracious, he and his equally kind wife, Sandy, even included me in social events they hosted.

He had a volunteer appreciation party at the top of the Stratosphere and invited Michael and me. When we arrived, Lonnie gave me a peck on the cheek and introduced me to his staff.

One of his volunteers, Geri, was a make-up professional who had worked at the same Hollywood studio in which I had worked. We had a wonderful visit and our friendship resulted in Geri helping my campaign as well.

Lonnie's chief of staff was a warm woman who expressed support and friendship, as had several other members of his staff who had already become friends many months prior to the event. I've always felt a person's caliber can be gauged by the people surrounding them, and Lonnie had a warm and caring staff. I appreciated the gestures of acceptance and told him so.

Later I would learn to my dismay that his friend of many years informed him at this function he would end their friendship if "that woman" soiled the celebration with my presence. Lonnie told his friend to open his mind and get to know an interesting person. This individual's wife, an extremely petty, superficial, self-absorbed woman, participated in the Mrs. Nevada pageant with me. I went over to say hello as a courtesy. She looked me up and down and then both she and her husband turned their backs and walked off. A modern version of the gold rush "proper" women.

Lonnie's home is a true museum to Nevada history and one of the most fascinating places one could visit. The Strip is a tourist attraction designed to fleece wallets, but the miniature replicas of famous Nevada landmarks and authentic souvenirs from memorable events in Nevada's background make Lonnie's home a priceless tribute to Nevada history. Three consecutive lots have been joined together to house this burgeoning museum inside his home. It's a perfect place for a party, and Lonnie loves to party. He told Michael about the birthday party he was throwing for himself at his home and invited us. The "copper" invitation was as unique as the host.

Michael went over to Lonnie's house on several occasions to fix his electric gate. His wife, Sandy, is as genuine and down-to-earth as Lonnie. Her work as a nurse has kept her in touch with what is really important in life. Through it, she has learned a special way of relating well to others. Nevada's Second Family was a really nice couple.

When we arrived, Lonnie gave me a hug. Michael and I mingled with hundreds of guests, exchanging chit-chat with political figures who finally accepted that I was included in social events whether they liked it or not.

I always try to look professional and am grateful my mother instilled good manners and social graces as part of my childhood upbringing. Never a witch, I am always baffled by the games catty people play.

Many thinly disguised insults have been slung at me through false smiles at numerous events. The feeling of betrayal and hurt never goes away. I always find something nice about the person I am talking to and offer genuine compliments even if the only nice thing I can find about them is a hairdo or piece of clothing. I was raised to believe if you treat others well, they will do the same with you. It took the nastiness of the congressional race to change that view. A lot of people suck and I'm not willing to take it any more. If someone is catty, insulting or nasty, I am simply going to dish it right back.

In this crowd, it didn't take long. As I stood in Lonnie's kitchen visiting with a state assemblyman, Pat Schaefer, a former congressional opponent came up to me. He is an obnoxious fringe type who thinks he is "all that" because he is a lawyer. He is a known troublemaker and lives up to his reputation. He introduced his companion to both the assemblyman and me.

Then he turned to his friend and said in a loud voice, "You'll never guess where *she* worked!"

I could see where this was going so before he could complete his sentence I quickly injected, "I worked for many years in the movie industry in Hollywood. Nice to meet you."

That would have shut a balanced person up, but Pat didn't fall into that category. He ignored my cue to leave it alone and replied in a voice everyone within a hundred yards could hear, "She was a whore in a cathouse!"

"Boy, you have real class, Pat," I replied as I glared at him.

He just laughed and walked off. I never got used to that type of narrow-minded attitude and insensitive abuse.

Lorraine Hunt, then only my rumored opponent for the upcoming lieutenant governor's race, was also a neighbor and personal friend of Lonnie's. She arrived and flitted around like a queen taking center court. Then she dramatically presented Lonnie with a Clark County Commission proclamation regarding his birthday. After all the gushing and gooing, he thanked her and declared to the crowd that Hunt was a dear friend and just might be "the next lieutenant governor." I was crushed.

"Belittled even by other outsiders," I thought.

I looked right at Lonnie, who scanned the crowd and met my eyes. One could see his blunder dawn on him and he suddenly began stumbling over his words. Had it been intentional or did he truly forget I was present? I wanted to believe he wouldn't be that cruel and thoughtless but my faith in the goodness of human nature had been tried to the max over the past few years and I no longer felt people were basically good. Michael and I left.

* * *

That was the last straw. Something changed inside me. My over-achieving, my workaholic nature, suddenly shifted. "To hell with all of them," I thought. "I guess the adage that there are no friends in politics is really true."

I loathed the system by the time the state convention was held in Las Vegas. During the festivities, Burdish would give me even more reason to be fed up with the games they played. Everyone was kiss-ing butt. Like the Democratic convention two years earlier, I knew I would be the only one with balls enough to say what everyone else silently thought. It didn't matter, because also like two years earlier, I wasn't the anointed one anyway.

We asked for an agenda a few days prior to the convention. As the Democrats had done, we didn't receive it. It seemed the schedule for these events were top secret.

I went into the state office and asked them to verbally explain the sequence of events so I would have a clue where I should be and when. Burdish gave me an extremely vague itinerary. He mentioned a demonstration event but blew it off as simply an introduction of the candidates. I didn't think much more about it until two days before the convention.

My staff called other candidates to try and get more information on the demonstration event. Only one office gave us decent infor-mation. No speeches were allowed but candidates would be intro-duced and they could sing or present a patriotic reading if they liked. I was furious with Burdish. He intentionally withheld information from me so I wouldn't show up. He knew what he was doing. I stormed down to his office and confronted him.

With a straight face, he said, "You can come if you like but all we're going to do is ask the candidates to stand and be recognized. It's no big deal."

Confused, we had absolutely no idea what to expect. The office that did give us information indicated that if they attended, they were simply going to drop balloons from the ceiling when their candidate's name was announced. They weren't even sure at that point if they would participate.

We called the balloon companies to inquire about a drop, but it was too late. I thought briefly about making a grand entrance in one of my 1800s gowns and reciting a brief statement from a female political pioneer of that era. I didn't want to make a fool of myself though in case that wouldn't have been appropriate. Besides, I simply couldn't get any reliable information about the event. We decided to take Burdish at his word that it was no big deal and skip it. Michael and I were really tired anyway.

The morning of the main convention day, I was putting my banners and signs up in the convention hall. Burdish came in. I cornered him again about the demonstration event. Suddenly, he began to fling his arms and scream at me.

"I'm sick of dealing with you, Jessi," he yelled as everyone else who was also putting up their campaign signs stopped to watch. "You are too difficult and I'm sick of you. Just get the fuck out of my face and leave me alone!"

My mouth hung open as he stomped out of the room. I knew he never liked me but his unprovoked outburst was really a shock. Several people came over and wanted to know what the heck was wrong with him. We decided he forgot to take his medication, but I was tired of watching him kiss the anointed butts while treating outsiders like cow pies.

I took a lot of heat when it was my turn at the podium and I started my speech out with, "In light of shameful conduct and questionable character on the part of some Clark County commissioners, the good news is ... I'm not involved in any scandal or under investigation by the ethics commission and I am an honest person." Although four county commissioners had been under investigation and I had not mentioned anyone by name, everyone looked right at Hunt.

The crowd was shocked I would take someone head-on and call a spade a spade when the very top power figures were behind her race. The room became totally silent. Expressions on faces in the crowd changed from shock to broad grins. Like a Jerry Springer audience, they were waiting for Hunt to jump out of her chair and rush me, arms pummeling. They wanted to see me grab her wig and toss it into the audience. They were dying to chant, "fight, fight, fight." They came for a party, confident both Aaron Russo and I would break the boredom.

Just like it was at the Democratic convention when I publicly took on the powers that be, party loyalists were aghast but outnumbered. When I completed my address and turned to go back to my seat, I glanced at Hunt and her buddy Kenny Guinn. Both looked straight ahead with absolutely no expression. I knew they were pissed. I looked at Michael and had to quickly avoid his face or I would have started laughing right on stage.

Several northern delegates grabbed me the second I descended the stage stairs. Las Vegas newspapers were distributed only halfway up the state, so they had little information about Hunt and her encounters as a Clark County Commissioner. They wanted details about the circumstances surrounding her participation in the ethics circus. My assistant rushed up and grabbed my arm.

"People are ignoring everyone else's booths, Jessi. They are lined up three deep at yours. You have to get out there," she said in a rush.

The side door would be faster. As I dashed through it, I nearly ran into Hunt and Dawn Gibbons, arm in arm. The second their eyes met mine, Dawn jerked her arm free and abruptly turned and left. Hunt turned around and swiftly went back into the convention hall.

Of all the people to stab me in the back, I didn't expect it from Dawn. It was clear she intended to kiss the butt of whomever could best serve her needs. Ambition won out over friendship. I felt she was a traitor and told her so in a short note a few days later. I couldn't dwell on it at the moment, however. I needed to get to my booth.

My assistant was right. As I rounded the corner, there was a sea of humanity at my booth. I was overwhelmed. I didn't know if I would be lynched or given a medal. Ultimately, the only people who criticized my honesty were state treasurer candidate, Brian Krolicki, and his pious wife. They were ladder climbing yuppies anyway so I didn't waste time being upset with their annoyance of my partisan criticism.

After all the months of working hard 12 hours a day, seven days a week and enduring endless abuse from the party and media, it felt good to hear the voters themselves congratulating me on having the brass balls to say what everyone else was thinking. And I said it in front of a convention filled with delegates from all over the state who would go back to their communities and recommend which candidate appeared to be the most qualified for the office they seek.

"Now if they will just break with the herd and go back and say what they really think," I thought with exasperation. Experience told me it wouldn't happen though.

The following morning was the day of the demonstrations. After brunch, everyone gathered in the convention hall where each candidate was introduced. Hunt did a full fledged floor show complete with her rendition of patriotic songs and a ceiling full of red, white and blue balloons dropping on the crowd. Burdish lied. It was a big deal.

He must have taken extreme delight in announcing my name knowing I wasn't going to be there. That deliberate act of pettiness was designed to embarrass me by indicating to the delegates that I didn't care enough to attend. When I heard afterwards what happened, I had a very foul taste in my mouth toward party officials and their intentional manipulation. Especially Burdish!

It seemed the bigger the stakes, the more clandestine the mind games became. Kenny Guinn and I never saw eye-to-eye. Among other things, he wasn't pleased that I nailed Hunt on her ethics charges in front of the party faithful. It was blatantly obvious they were running as a team despite party rules which said everyone was to remain neutral during the primaries. Guinn and Hunt campaign signs could be found side-by-side all over the state. Their paper trail even showed they apparently had the same string pullers.

The photo of Guinn as a teenager in nice clothes and with his fancy new car made it hard to believe his tear-jerking version of how dirt poor he was growing up. All the candidates were telling a similar tale in an effort to gain the vote of the everyday resident. My hooker radar was on full tilt; I had met his kind many times. I cornered him.

"As you well know, Kenny," I began, "I am the kind of woman who tackles things head-on. I've been hearing rumors and it is my policy to go right to the horse's mouth rather than listen to gossip. That's why I'm here," I said. "I've been hearing from my volunteers in the rurals that you are assisting Lorraine a great deal in the north and rurals by opening doors for her since she's unknown there. I've seen for myself your 'team' signs all over the state. Are the two of you working together?" I asked point blank.

He looked me right in the eye and adamantly denied it. He claimed he wanted to be equally fair with both of us. Nevertheless, everything for months afterward pointed to the fact he had not been forthcoming with me when he answered my question.

* * *

Our plan to concentrate on metropolitan Las Vegas this time rather than the rurals seemed to have similarities with trying to get from one side of the swamp to the other through quicksand. The more we struggled, the further we sank. Nowhere in Nevada do party controllers form a tighter circle around their ranks than in this particular city. No matter what we did, we found ourselves on the outside looking in.

The first few weeks after Hunt entered the race, polling showed us to be very close – within single digits. Despite the negative publicity surrounding her ethics investigation, the lead was comfortably in her favor now thanks to the help of the political machine. We continued along our own charted path but it was clear we were not going to make much in-road in Las Vegas. Hunt and her buddies had the city locked up. Further obscurity was created by the fact that Aaron Russo's plant in the race was also from Las Vegas and getting media coverage. Any rebel support I might have received was going to him. Nevertheless, the majority of voters were in Clark County so it was imperative that we stay and continue to try.

We held regular volunteer meetings to brainstorm how we could best utilize their talents to reach the most voters. Phone polling gave us valuable information and familiarized our name with the continually new stream of residents. Alternative newspapers were great about doing articles on a candidate blackballed from mainstream Las Vegas press. Radio shows seemed to be our best option. I had never worked so hard in all my life and yet every day felt like I was doing a marathon on a hot day up a 90-degree grade.

This campaign was different from the congressional race. Both were frustrating as far as the party itself. This time, however, I was no longer having fun – even at public events. It was difficult to maintain an optimistic and positive attitude in this never ending sea of piranhas and injustice. I longed for the rurals and home.

The Political Waltz

During the 1800s, Nevada was a Mormon way-station for mail routes in the northern and southern parts of the state, as well as for families traveling west. Many families settled in various parts of the territory rather than continue their strenuous journey. Consequently, a large percentage of the Silver State population remains Mormon.

Not surprisingly, politics in both the 19th and 20th Centuries were largely run by men of that faith. A majority of the big-money backers and primary influence molders who called the shots behind-the-scenes were Mormon. They didn't want women running their state.

I initially entered politics believing everything I had been taught in high school government. I truly thought an average person could compete and be elected. Looking back just four short years later, I found it amazing how much the public is not allowed to know and how naïve I had been.

A campaign involves much more than simply smiling for cameras and shaking hands with voters. While anointed candidates can start late because they rely mainly on TV ads during the final month, renegade candidates have to begin nearly 18 months prior to election day.

The journey is easy for chosen candidates. The parties know exactly how to funnel unreported soft money to the favored ones. They also make sure the outside candidates never get a dime of it.

Among other things, soft money helps buy an election through huge blocks of purchased media advertising, which is in effect buying name recognition to get votes. The average voters make their ballot choice the final two weeks prior to an election. Leaders are chosen based on 30-second sound bites as opposed to the public getting to know candidates personally. Anointed candidates don't have to leave the comfort of their homes and don't run the risk of voters talking to them one-on-one and discovering their flaws. Outside candidates go directly to the voters the way it was meant to be and tell them about their background, where they stand on issues, learn concerns of the district they hope to represent and present their solutions to concerns.

Reaching voters as an outside candidate takes a tremendous amount of time. Volunteers are vital to any grassroots campaign. They are the heroes that walk the precincts and get the message to residents so they can make an informed choice. Developing a corps of volunteers takes months. They are college students majoring in political science who want to see what is involved in running a campaign. They are civic minded businesspeople who are contemplating a run for office themselves and want to see what sacrifice is involved before they make such an important decision. They are working people who want a more direct influence over decisions that affect their lives. They are retired folks who have the time to give back to their community. They come from all walks of life. Some work hard the duration of the campaign. Others think it's glamorous work, but quit when asked to stuff envelopes or answer phones. All view a campaign differently after working on one.

In Nevada, state and county party organizations have been known to assist their preferred choices with mass mailings by covering the cost to print thousands of copies, providing volunteer time and paying the postage. They do phone polls to obtain data for their candidate and further establish the name with the public. By denying the same services to other candidates within their party, they know the public will only recognize the name and slogan of the party favorite and therefore will vote for the pre-determined choice.

The party makes sure preferred choices are introduced to all the right people in order to receive generous donations for their coffers. Contributors are told other candidates "aren't viable." Outside candidates must invest their own personal funds in an attempt to keep up with big-money choices who receive the funds they need elsewhere. The result can be tremendous personal debt for those who aren't party choices and a decision by potentially good leaders not to run for office when they discover the anointment process.

"Forgetting" to inform all candidates of meetings and events results in only the party-preferred choices being presented. Debates often are stacked with panel interviewers who further the agenda of the power mongers in order to curry favor and keep their jobs. They ask questions of anointed choices that bring out only the best and reverse the process with outside contenders. A lot of backstabbing and dirty tricks go on behind the scenes. Politics is big money and big stakes for the boys.

Voter manipulation exists nationwide, but powers in Nevada control the process with a particularly unforgiving iron grip. Every time I tried to expose it the politicians and media closed in to stifle my efforts.

I knew the plan by now. I also knew I was helpless to do anything about it. No one cared. The public didn't want to hear about it. The power brokers are the same type of men who are the first ones through the bordello doors on Saturday night and then the first ones into church the next morning. I just shook my head.

If they were going to play biased games, I decided I'd better learn to dish it right back.

Sweat poured down my face as I held my picket sign and walked up and down the sidewalk of a busy Las Vegas street in front of the newspaper building. Temperatures in southern Nevada are miserable during the summer, easily breaking the 100-degree mark day after day for months.

The *Las Vegas Review-Journal* and its local television affiliate issued a joint poll that showed the chosen candidates far ahead of the outside contenders. Despite the fact I was the only announced candidate for lieutenant governor in my party, I was not even mentioned.

My staff members called the pollster, who advised them the newspaper tells them what actual or potential candidate names to include in a poll and which areas to canvas. No wonder the numbers come out the way they wanted them to!

The *Review-Journal* had already endorsed Lorraine Hunt, despite at the time having been undeclared and only rumored to be running. They did something similar to me during the congressional race. I wasn't going to be silent this time around.

I called the paper. I had made numerous efforts to meet with the editor, publisher and political columnist. If they would take the time to get to know me and then decided they didn't like me or felt I would not be a good leader, I could understand. Judging me blindly was not fair to readers or to me. No one at the *Review-Journal* would meet with me.

With "Biased Poll – Selective Reporting" painted on a placard and nailed to a stick, I walked off my anger in front of the paper all morning. Before long, media were everywhere. I spent the afternoon doing the same thing in front of the TV station. I was really pleased this kind of injustice would be covered on the six o'clock news. Here was a way for the public to see manipulation in action and protest it.

Later that evening, I turned on the news. Not a word. A major party candidate for statewide office picketing on busy streets in 115-degree heat and not a word about it in the media. Nothing in the paper next day either. It was a total blackout. Citizens were only allowed to hear about candidates the power base in Nevada wanted elected. If only there was a way for the public to see how they were being manipulated. Dejected, I still had to continue with my regular schedule of speeches.

* * *

The Las Vegas Republican Men's Club is a collection of some of the city's most powerful bosses. As I looked around, I saw a sea of solemn faces in conservative business suits.

"Forget opening with a joke," I decided. My address in support of the working man and woman was sure to rile them; it was a mystery why they asked me to speak in the first place. I thanked them for inviting me, asked them to check their tomatoes at the door, took a deep breath and plunged in.

Sure enough. One of the wealthiest businessmen in the city sprang to his feet when I suggested employers had a responsibility to their rank-and-file employees to pay a wage that would prevent employees from having to work two jobs just to keep their heads above water. His boot-licking cohorts took the cue and jumped to their feet to join in. I fielded questions the best I could and got out of there as quickly as possible.

I had addressed groups before that disagreed with me but it had resulted in a healthy exchange of ideas and opinions. I had never experienced a group so hostile and so close-minded. I would find this to be typical of the attitude in this city.

It was quite ironic considering what Lonnie Hammargren told me about a later luncheon with the same group. Lonnie attended a Republican Men's Club meeting that featured *Las Vegas Review-Journal* publisher Sherman Fredrick as keynote speaker. After his address, the publisher was asked if the paper would cover all candidates for office. Fredrick told them all but "that hooker from Virginia City." All hell broke loose. The very men who had treated me with such disrespect earlier were the same ones who jumped all over Fredrick for denying me the same opportunities as other candidates. I couldn't believe my ears, but I was proud of them.

Again I called the paper and asked Fredrick to meet with me to discuss his unthinkable remark. Again, he refused. A radio personality who had also attended the club meeting called and invited me to spend an hour discussing my frustration with the political process in general and the *Review-Journal* in particular.

The switchboard lit up. It was such a hot topic that they kept me on the air for another hour. Callers were enraged at the paper. The station called the paper to give Fredrick the opportunity to present his side but his office advised he was not at work that day.

Soon after, an anonymous caller who was a *Review-Journal* employee told us that Fredrick's car was in the parking lot as she spoke. She gave the license plate number and vehicle description as verification. Listeners began calling to say they were canceling their subscriptions and pulling their ads.

The show led to several others and became a main talk radio topic for the next few days. Finally, there had been a small way to let residents know that what they see and hear during elections is preselected by a powerful few. We wind up electing a purchased network of puppets for gambling, developers and special interest.

Gaming is too pervasive and controlling in Nevada for honesty in government. But by my 1998 race for lieutenant governor, gambling was clearly going nationwide, no longer centered in Nevada and Atlantic City. Today, a Las Vegas type casino exists within 200 miles of just about any residence in the continental United States. While that is bad news for Las Vegas economics, it is wonderful news for the future of state politics. The time might yet come when gambling no longer controls the legislature and honest representatives begin to infiltrate the hallowed halls of deception. That time had not yet arrived, however.

Las Vegas pundits were not the only journalists who gave me grief. On one occasion, the *Reno Gazette-Journal* called to tell me my ads had been pulled. The ad representative's message clearly showed power's influence over the media.

"But they're all paid for," I said in disbelief. "Why were they pulled?"

"Because you poke fun at attorneys and the paper received complaints," the ad director informed me.

"That's unreal," I exclaimed. "Some of my opponents are attorneys. The attorney joke I put in each Sunday's paper was simply a way of presenting a political ad with humor. The paper offends someone in some way every single day but you still have the right under the First Amendment to express your views. Why am I not extended the same right?" I asked.

"You're paying for the ads and we reserve the right to eliminate any we find offensive," replied the ad director.

"Yeah right," I thought to myself, "Offensive to whom?" The boys were at it again.

That made me even more determined to remain in the fight right up to election day despite not having anywhere near an equal playing field with big money candidates and having to endure media blackouts designed to give publicity only to the anointed choices.

A great deal of time is spent traveling from community to community in a statewide race. While on the road, I called my children several times a week. My youngest son, Reed, had introduced me to his latest girlfriend during our last trip home. Jennifer is an incredible girl: tall as a model, slender, shiny black hair down to her waist, huge liquid eyes, thick pouty lips and very, very feminine. She is drop-dead gorgeous. Even better, she is just as beautiful inside as out. She is genuine, sensitive, gracious, and possesses a class reminiscent of Jackie Kennedy. People are instantly drawn to her and mesmerized by her charm. I like her a lot.

I was campaigning in Fallon, a military town an hour east of Virginia City, when Reed told me he and Jennifer were going to get married in two weeks. Two weeks! In the middle of a statewide campaign! Running for office teaches a person to be extremely flexible. I could do this.

Two weeks later we arrived at the chapel in Reno. A beautiful bride walked down the aisle to join her beaming groom. I hosted a reception for family and close friends afterwards and they honeymooned in a castle themed room. Before leaving, Jennifer hugged me and told me how happy she was to be part of our family. It was the beginning of a really nice mother/daughter-in-law relationship.

Both agreed to attend a Kiwanis dinner in Yerington, 80 miles away, for which I was the keynote speaker. Nestled in the heart of Lyon County, I love the remote Mason Valley area because it reminds me so much of my childhood. This is ranch country, a lush green agricultural area. I was right at home and looked forward to seeing old friends. Jennifer would be a perfect campaign companion. I would give them talking points, she would charm them.

She is wonderful. I passed on to my children the manners my mother pounded into me as a young girl. Jennifer's manners match Reed's; I am so proud of them. New to political events, they had not heard any of my speeches before. Reed looked at me like he was seeing me for the first time. The grueling effects of the campaign were all worth it to see the pride on my cherished son's face. He beamed. It made me feel very proud. I introduced the two of them and they received an extremely warm welcome. Afterward, every man in the room rushed over to shake Jennifer's hand. She was a marvel to watch. The thought occurred to me, as I watched her, that the wrong family member was running for office.

The Mason Valley folks made us feel right at home and we hated to leave. We drove slowly, inhaling the fresh country smells. The fields are so green it hurts to look at them. One of my favorite sights is bales of hay lined up in artistic rows in the field left to dry. When I was little, I used to ride on the tractor with my father while he baled hay. Bales sitting in a field brought back the same wonderful childhood memories rain on a tin roof created. I wanted so badly to take a week off, let my long hair hang loose, go barefoot, ride horses and go see a rodeo. I'd been wearing these damn suits too long. For a few brief moments, I felt at peace with the world. I was in the country with my children.

The biggest sacrifice for families to make during campaigns, especially statewide races, is constantly being apart for long periods of time. A candidate has to grab time with loved ones at any opportunity. A couple weeks after the Yerington dinner, I was again scheduled as a keynote speaker for a Lake Tahoe women's organization.

Another son, Steven, and his two boys live nearby. My grandson Cody had been begging me on the phone for weeks to come see him. Used to me being part of his life on a weekly basis, he was only seven and too young to understand why life got in the way of his time with Gramie. I asked Steven if Cody could be my escort to the luncheon. Cody was ecstatic.

A shy little character with a cherubic face, Cody is smart as a whip. He is already reading two grade levels ahead and has an unquenchable curiosity about everything. All of us talk to the boys in adult fashion and they are always included in all discussions. Cody is wise beyond his years.

He looked over my brochure and asked a lot of questions about why we were going to the luncheon. He knew it gave him the chance to dress up and he took full advantage of it. He insisted we go shopping. He let me pick out his suit but was adamant about choosing his own black dress shoes. He put everything on to show his dad how he looked in his "very important suit." He was ready.

The luncheon was expected to be quite large. I was afraid Cody would be overwhelmed and become extremely shy so we blew up a couple dozen "Jessi for Lieutenant Governor" balloons and put them on sticks. I figured he wouldn't have time to be shy if he was busy. The bouquet of balloons was so large Cody couldn't even be found behind it.

Instead of being intimidated by the crowd, he worked the room like a pro. With his dazzling little smile and mischievous little eyes, not a soul could resist a balloon from such a charmer. I didn't need to worry about him being shy; he loved it. He and Jennifer should run as a team.

Steven taught Cody the same manners I taught him. He is a very impressive table companion and quite the flirt. When it was time for my speech, he asked to go with me. Taken off guard, his wishes were more important to me than protocol. I took his tiny hand in mine and put a chair next to me at the podium. Cody climbed up on it and looked out at the crowd like a monarch surveying his kingdom. I told the guests how difficult it was to find time for family while traveling all over the state and that was why my grandson was accompanying me. Then I introduced him.

As if on cue, he reached for the microphone and in a steady clear voice, said, "Vote for my gramie." Then he got down and went back to his chair at the table. The crowd loved it. I knew it would do no good to tell them his impromptu message was totally unrehearsed or expected. No one would have believed me.

After my address, he crawled up on my lap and promptly fell asleep. Campaigning is hard work when you're only seven years old. On the ride home, I asked him how he liked politics.

"I like it, Gramie. When do we do our next speech?" he asked expectantly.

* * *

I was an old fashioned campaigner who traveled all over the state meeting and addressing voters. The majority of candidates cater to the elite, as they count on large contributions to fund their campaign. Few speak up for the working class.

My campaign donations were modest, usually comprising of checks of less than $100 from private citizens. The Republican establishment made sure I never received any money or help from their interests. They knew they could starve me out of the race. I was only one little fish swimming among sharks trying to make a small bit of difference. Nevertheless, I continued to pursue projects that would benefit the state.

When I did a speech in Hawthorne during my congressional race, residents desperately asked the candidates how we could help save nearby Walker Lake. I didn't have an answer then. But that question haunted me as I spent more and more time in Hawthorne. I was determined to find a workable answer that would save towns all over Nevada like Hawthorne. It began a two-year search for a permanent solution to the water crisis in our state.

A major ammunition depot, Hawthorne was a bustling military town during World War II. The ordinance was stored in bunkers that dotted the terrain as far as you could see. At the time Walker Lake was so large the Navy could use it to train submarine personnel. Vacationers came from all over to boat and fish.

Like many other military installations across the country that became victims of cutbacks and closures in the early 1990s, the base is a skeleton now. The bunkers are still there but the military is gone except for a few security posts guarding the remaining munitions. As one drives around the lake, one can see where the shoreline used to be. Evaporation, irrigation and the unforgiving desert climate have left it dying. The boat docks sit nearly empty. Rod and reels are nowhere to be seen anymore because the fish are dying.

Nearly every other store window in Hawthorne has a "closed" or "for sale" sign in it. Rural Nevada is becoming a series of ghost towns for two reasons: lack of water and lack of economic diversification.

The water crisis is not a problem unique to Nevada, but many outsiders – even some Westerners – still don't understand how utterly important it is. Large segments of the population in the rural Western states are economically dependent on irrigation. Rapidly expanding Las Vegas is located in an arid desert where its immense population boom and enormous development depletes available water supplies. Although the Pacific coast cities of San Francisco, Portland and Seattle get more than enough precipitation, the climate east of the Sierra Nevadas is notoriously dry. Without a diverse economy to fall back on, water becomes a virtual life-or-death matter. The issue is such an important concern in neighboring Idaho that based on a single lawsuit the state created an entire court system devoted solely to adjudicating water rights.

Nevada's water crisis will never be solved with Nevada water, so we formed a water task force to study various plans including a desalinization project and a water plan called the Columbia Diversion Plan that had already been engineered and presented to the private sector years earlier.

The desalinization plan proved to have too many hurdles and was too costly but the Columbia Diversion Plan remains a cost effective and very workable plan that could bring tremendous relief to a water starved state. Unfortunately, when it was originally proposed it was too early for folks to take a water crisis seriously. Now the time is right to pursue this very workable plan further.

The task force included some of the original principles of the Columbia Diversion Plan as well as many water related specialists. In a nutshell, pure water that would normally wind up in the Pacific Ocean would be diverted from the Columbia River below the Bonneville Dam in Oregon and pumped to the 5,000 foot elevation in the Cascades where generating costs are significantly lower than Nevada rates. It would then be gravity fed to Nevada to fill Pyramid and Walker Lakes in the north, both of which would serve as natural reservoirs, continuing on down to Lake Mead and on through Hoover Dam to be shared by California.

This "end of the hose" concept means none of the 12-million acre feet moved yearly would be taken from any entity to give to another and when possible a considerable amount of water would be pumped during flood stages when there is excess water and generating capacity. The amount of diverted water would be like discovering another Colorado River.

Cost of the project would be shared by Oregon, California and Nevada and amortized over 30 to 60 years. The plan is already engineered, water rights are not affected, environmental programs would have only a nominal effect on the total cost of the project, and thousands would be put to work in construction, maintenance, support and service. The real beauty of this natural process is its simplicity, cost effectiveness and permanence.

Michael was the spokesperson. He met with Congressman Gibbons on an official basis regarding federal participation and a feasibility study. Gibbons said he liked the project and would have his researchers look into it further and then set up a meeting with the task force, but he never called back.

Las Vegas City Life, an alternative newspaper, did an excellent story on the project, pointing out that it was not only workable, it was affordable and impacted the entire state as opposed to just southern Nevada. They called Gibbons' office for comment. Neither he nor his staff offered any comment or support.

Numerous follow-up calls by our campaign staff proved fruitless. I faxed Gibbons at home to tell him his Washington office would not return our calls and that we were told by his Reno office that a *receptionist* had been given the water project to handle and no further appointments would be available to anyone in our campaign. We never received a reply to the fax sent to his private number either.

"Politics is a facade; all smoke and mirrors," I thought wearily.

I felt really betrayed and incredibly hurt. I liked and had trusted both Jim and Dawn. Our exhaustive efforts on his behalf during the general election two years earlier apparently were immaterial and had been long forgotten. Without his assistance on a federal level, the water project died, along with the prospect of providing water to a state that desperately needs it.

I was disappointed in Jim. He won the congressional seat with his seemingly genuine concern for the everyday citizen, yet his House voting record demonstrates a shift to special interest commitment after only one term in Washington.

The gaming industry has always called the political shots in Nevada. The most influential hotel/casino mogul in the state even has his own lobbyist who is so powerful, he was able to postpone the adjournment of the legislature, which meets only once every two years, until it passed a bill giving a special tax break to his boss.

Many residents of the state, including state Senator Joe Neal of North Las Vegas, feel the industry doesn't pay its fair share in taxes and are consistently the recipients of special favor.

When the federal gaming commission recommended restricting campaign contributions from the gaming industry in order to "reduce undue influence over officials," Gibbons quickly sprang to the defense of those capable of putting big bucks into his campaign. His response was that the restriction was a "misguided proposal that would unconstitutionally limit the industry from participating in public policy." Ka-ching.

I wrote a letter to the editor nailing him on his failure to protect those whose voices go unheard. Also included was the fact he sided with racketeering business practices of credit card companies when he voted to revise the bankruptcy laws to benefit big business, thereby pushing the working man and woman further into a corner. Ka-ching.

One of the state's most listened to talk radio shows made my letter an issue on their program. When they called the congressman for his response, Gibbons said mining and gaming were the state's largest industries and must be "protected." Yeah, right. As if a lobbyist who can bring a dead bill back to life and keep legislators in their seats past the closing deadline wasn't protection enough! I made it clear I felt my former friend had sold out and was now part of the problem instead of part of the solution.

It was becoming abundantly clear that Republicans were mainly about money. Nowhere was raw greed and undisguised ambition more evident than in Kenny Guinn's two-and-a-half year quest of the almighty dollar in order to intimidate any potential opposition right out of the running against him for governor. John Ensign operates in a similar fashion and now it appears he may get his US Senate seat after not only one but two expensive campaigns.

Ensign's arrogant disregard for the best interests of Nevada citizens and unquenchable desire to climb the political ladder was revealed in an Associated Press article that showcased his cold, calculating nature. When asked about an event casino mogul Steve Wynn held for him at Wynn's Bellagio that put Ensign's fundraising efforts over the $1 million mark, Ensign bragged, "People like to be with a winner. The money creates that atmosphere."

A member of the Christian men's organization Promise Keepers, Ensign's halo appears to have slipped. Creeping out around the tarnished edges of his pseudo-pious public face is an elitist double standard hypocrisy and a very disquieting lack of humility.

In a risky political maneuver, Ensign temporarily relocated his family to northern Nevada several months before the election in a calculated plan to win over the rural and northern vote. Las Vegas may view his actions as a slap in the face and a betrayal to southern Nevada. Since both Ensign and Bernstein are Clark County residents, Ensign is gambling on his move to endear him to northern counties over Bernstein and carry him into office on election day. While a strategy like that may work in Clark County where the population is constantly renewing itself, the north is made up of long time residents with a short tolerance for artificial allegiance.

In sharp contrast to Ensign's tunnel-visioned monetary view of the fleecing of Nevada is Democratic attorney general Frankie Sue Del Papa, who was for a time looking at the open Senate seat herself. The same AP article quoted her as saying, "I want every Nevadan to search their souls about whether this is a race about money or a race about issues and Nevada values."

Values. What a concept. While her "people first" view is admirable, her history of selling out to the Feds on land use issues is widely known and that was "walkin' on the fightin' side of me" as a rancher's daughter. As it turns out Del Papa decided not to run, which in effect may give Ensign the Senate seat in spite of himself.

But then again – maybe not.

Edward M. Bernstein wants the Senate seat too. Bernstein is a long time, well known Las Vegas attorney who has a chain of offices throughout Nevada and a popular statewide television show, "The

First Step," that has featured legal, political and familiar entertainment personalities over the years. His recognizable face is on
numerous billboards throughout Nevada as well as on frequent television ads for his injury law practice.

   While wealthy in his own right, it is expected the Democratic Party
will pour mega-money into Bernstein's campaign in an effort to beat
Ensign. Bill Clinton is an old college buddy of *Las Vegas Sun* publisher Brian Greenspun, who himself was touted as a possible candidate, and Clinton has made several fundraising trips to Las Vegas
that will benefit Bernstein.

   There is no question the Democrats have the soft money needed
to give Ensign a migraine headache. In Bernstein's favor, Clark
County is also predominately Democrat. In typical Democratic fashion, they will more than likely wait until the final weeks and then
bring out many of Bernstein's former celebrity guests and present a
tremendous advertising blitz. Don't hand Ensign the crown just yet.

   I was completely turned off with constant demands for money
every time I turned around. Democrats have their faults, but at least
they don't charge their candidates to attend functions and address
them; Republicans do. It appeared the candidates themselves were a
prime opportunity for others to make money. I found myself constantly shelling out $50 here, a door prize there, all the time wishing
the club in question would actually try to help me win by donating
to my campaign expenses. It never happened. By the end of the race,
I was burned out with always giving and never receiving.

   A fashion show sponsored by the Henderson Republican women's
organization was the last straw. As an outside candidate and a north-
erner to boot, it was extremely difficult to find organizations in Clark
County that would give me the opportunity to speak to them. For
decades there has been a north-south rivalry in the Silver State. The
south wants everything to be centered around Las Vegas. The north
is resentful that they are always left to become more destitute. The
media feeds the feud. While I was the princess of the northern
women's groups, I was the bastard child in Las Vegas. Getting inside
Fort Knox would have been easier than walking through the doors of
Clark County political clubs.

   I was surprised when the Henderson club included me in their
event. It was a fashion show luncheon in which the candidates mod-

eled. A cute enough idea, but it required me to find time out of my hectic schedule to visit a boutique so I could be measured and select a wardrobe, followed by a return visit shortly before the luncheon for a final fitting. The social butterflies who present these events don't have a clue how chaotic a statewide candidate's schedule is, nor do they care. Politics is simply a social club for them. To drop everything and go for repeated fittings for a benefit fashion show was asking quite a bit, but inconvenience came with the turf. What really riled me was the fact the show tied up half a day of valuable campaign time and the club actually had the audacity to charge the models for lunch! These functions were putting me in the poor house.

Most statewide office-seekers have at least one person on their staff whose sole responsibility it is to book events and make sure the candidate gets to the right city and the right event at the right time. My schedule was filled every day of the week; some days I was lucky to have time to wash my hair. It was not unusual to address an early morning breakfast meeting, tour a facility before lunch, give a speech for a noon crowd, travel to a nearby town for campaigning after lunch, sit in on meetings in late afternoon, be a keynote speaker for a dinner event and then attend a social function later in the evening. This type of schedule was repeated many times over in cities and towns all over the state. Many nights I fell into bed absolutely exhausted.

"Instead of making money to allow me to get my message out to more people and help me get elected," I told the Henderson chairwoman, "I am constantly paying in. I can't afford the time or the money. I don't think it's fair to charge participants."

In a stuffy voice, she snapped back, "Our functions raise money for the candidates, my dear."

"Then why have I never received a dime?" I inquired, "Not a red cent is ever given to me for my campaign, either by a club or by any of the individuals belonging to the clubs."

She got huffy. I was fed up with phony pretense and greed. I told her I could no longer afford to give my time, provide expensive door prizes and pay to attend dozens of functions. I declined to model. She didn't care. This "palm's up" routine was repeated time after time. There seems to be something wrong when candidates are seen as cash cows for the party instead of the party helping their hopefuls get elected. The longer I observed the political process, the more disgusted I became. In the country, it is a common sight to see vultures circling around dead animals. Politics, especially in Las Vegas, just had a different type of carcass and a different form of vulture.

It would be good to get out of this place and back home for a few days. The Veterans Parade was coming up before long in Virginia City. We rented a convertible for the parade and put my banners on the side and decorated it in red, white and blue. The morning of the parade was cold and overcast. It can get bone cold up there. Even so, Virginia City has one of the largest and best veterans parades in the state.

My father was a World War II veteran. He also taught night school twice a week to Korean War vets when I was little. I remember well his intense dedication to all our country stands for and to the men and women who preserve our rights and freedoms. Patriotism was, and still is, a big deal in our family.

Veterans were an important segment of my campaign. Their issues are too often overlooked. It made no difference if my efforts were spent trying to establish a ceremony at the Veteran's Cemetery in Fernley or donating part of the Bordello Ball funds to the new chapel at the Boulder City Veterans site. Each year, a portion of the funds raised from my Ball goes to a veterans' drop-in center, a veterans hospital or a special cause such as the new veterans' home or chapel. I feel it is important for our upcoming generation to see public events that honor the sacrifices of our military personnel and learn respect for our flag and everything it symbolizes. Too little remains sacred today and our young people have little to direct their respect toward.

Entries came from all over northern Nevada. The route started at Fourth Ward School at the south end of town and stretched for nearly half a mile. It included bands, military formations, political entries, historical costumes, an equestrian review and lots of civic pride. The narrow street was lined with people holding small children's hands and waving tiny American flags.

The sun was hidden by huge dark clouds so the mountain cast a large shadow over main street. Cold blasts of air swooped over Mt. Davidson and wrapped around all those walking the long distance through town. My teeth chattered. It was an awesome sight to look out over the valley and see billowing dark clouds as far as the eye could see, casting shadows over the hills and giving the ancient buildings in town a dramatic effect. It set the stage perfectly for the fly-over.

Promptly at noon, the jets flew low overhead in perfect formation. Everyone stopped. The town was silent. Men saluted. I wondered if I was the only one to get a lump in my throat and wipe away a tear. Flyovers are always intensely emotional for many, including me. The pride I feel in America all comes to a head during a moment like this and is a main reason I ran for office. I just wish our government officials on all levels shared the same feeling of honor.

The following week my daughter sent me the local gossip rag. There were several letters to the editor criticizing my participation in the parade. How dare a prostitute join a patriotic parade, they said.

I wrote a rebuttal pointing out I am an American first, this is my hometown, the veterans asked me to participate and I did so as a political candidate, not as a prostitute. Small minds were still at work. Like Lottie Johl, I would never be accepted in my community. My heart was heavy.

It is hard for Becky to deal with the vicious superior attitudes of most Virginia City residents towards me. She is one of the foster babies my first husband and I took into our home. Hard to place because of her rare medical condition, we were blessed to legally make her our daughter.

Becky is a special young woman with a kind heart, sunny outlook, stubborn determination to be as independent as possible and a precious human being. She is active within the community and has blended well and been accepted by most people. A few residents keep a watchful eye out for her. Some treat her badly knowing she is the daughter of "that woman" but the majority accept her for who she is without thought to whom she is related.

Virginia City isn't all bad. For every vicious resident, there is one that cancels the others out. The bookstore owner is one of them. A former policeman, Joe Curtis has a wonderful store on the main street filled with books on local history. He and his wife are two of those special people sprinkled around the planet who give of themselves and watch over those less fortunate. I think they are angels in disguise. They have counseled, guided and helped Becky in so many wonderful ways.

Becky is happy and for the most part loves living in the tiny mountain town. Her disability keeps her from driving the 20 minutes down the mountain to the nearest town, Carson City. Virginia City has no proper medical facility, and there is only one very tiny convenience store where she can get a few groceries. Daily life has become more difficult for her now that we have moved "down the hill."

My battle with the Storey County Commission over brothel ordinance revisions and town fury over my participation in an A&E television show which depicted the county's brothel history as it is instead of the rosy but unrealistic version of history that town fathers wanted, has spilled over into how she is now being treated. Kind folks still remain but more than a few have begun to make life uncomfortable for her. She wants to attend classes at the community college in Carson City. Her church is there as well. She feels she has blossomed and the time may have come where she has outgrown the attitude in the Comstock and is ready to move on. In recent months, she has been giving serious consideration to relocating near us in Carson City.

* * *

Sometimes, being a public figure can take a bizarre and even dangerous turn. I was a scheduled speaker at a remote rural event. Michael and I drove several hours to reach a tiny community in Pershing County and enjoyed talking with residents who were very involved politically and sincerely desired the opportunity to have a say in decisions that affected them. They wanted to know their ballot choices on a personal level.

When the evening was over, we were among the last to leave. We walked out into the dark deserted parking lot headed toward our truck. Suddenly a man stepped out from the shadows of the building. He walked up to us briskly and flashed a gun.

"Don't be alarmed," he barked, "I'm not going to hurt you. I have to carry this for protection because 'they' are everywhere," he explained as he looked around. "I have information only you can help me with," he said as he pointed toward me. "We can't talk here. Get in your truck and drive 'til I tell you to stop," he demanded.

I was terrified. Michael was frantic. The janitor locked the auditorium door behind us, so we couldn't make a mad dash back into the building. Only a couple of vehicles were in the parking lot. No one was around. We were the only three people standing out in the dark;

me, Michael, and an evidently unbalanced individual with a gun. We got in the truck.

He rambled on and on about crazy things that made no sense. We drove for several miles before he indicated we should simply leave the road and drive into the desert. The Nevada desert is filled with bodies and we were sure we were about to join them.

We never learned the man's name. He was too busy telling us "top secret" information that he wanted me to bring out in order to "save" the nation from being annihilated. Hooker instinct kicked in with a plan.

"I'll take notes so I don't miss anything that is important to you," I offered, trying to calm him and gain his confidence. "But you have to show good faith by putting down your gun. I can't concentrate knowing you are holding a gun."

To my complete surprise, he did as I asked. Placing the gun on a rock beside him, he explained again that he didn't intend to hurt us and that the gun was for protection against those who were out to get him.

He rambled on for over an hour. Finally Michael told him we had a long drive and needed to go. I assured him I would do what I could to investigate all the charges he had outlined. I felt we had reached a cordial rapport.

In a heart stopping moment, he reached for his gun. While we held our breath, he put it in his holster, wished us god speed and simply disappeared into the darkness.

Really breathing for the first time in an hour-and-a-half, we jumped back into the truck, locked the doors and drove in the direction in which he disappeared. We hoped to follow him at a distance to see where he went so we could notify authorities, but he was nowhere in sight. We waited for a few minutes and then decided to get the hell out of there. We had been lucky. I had a bodyguard for months after my story broke. I called him again. He remained with us from then on whenever we had to travel.

* * *

I spent a lot of time talking to various Nevada people associated with film. Bobbi Hughes, the Nevada Screen Actors Guild executive director, is a charming and very capable woman. We talked at length in her office and found we had mutual industry contacts. The vice president I worked for in Hollywood was one of three high-level executives who came to Las Vegas to explore the possibility of building a permanent studio. She was his guide. We discussed avenues the lieutenant governor needed to pursue in order to assist Nevada production. I liked her. She is good for the industry.

I had lunch with several producers that live in southern Nevada and learned their frustrations with promoting film production in the state. It was like old times, talking about people we all worked with. Nevada has a rich resource of creative talent, both in front of and behind the camera. It needs to be marketed; we need to put our own talent to work.

One agency in particular, IATSE, International Alliance of Theatrical Stage Employees and Motion Picture Technicians, is involved in all phases of film production. I met with their business agent, Tom Walker. He proved to be a most visionary, knowledgeable and dedicated person in promoting Nevada talent. His people skills were impeccable. In addition, he was pleased to discover my husband was also union. We became fast friends.

I could always expect a call whenever a premiere was scheduled or a major shoot was being done in town. Tom escorted me to the premieres, bringing back pleasant memories of my days in Hollywood. Valuable networking was done during these events. I valued the friendship offered to me by IATSE.

The local went above and beyond professional courtesy and that alone showed me how production companies were treated. IATSE is a perfect ambassador in encouraging Hollywood to film right next door in Nevada. Tom introduced me to their training program and invited me to attend one of their meetings so I could meet some of their members and hear their concerns.

I spent a lot of time with IATSE. Tom told me of their frustration with becoming signatory to Hollywood collective bargaining agreements. Many feature films are produced on location in Toronto, where special financial incentives are offered to make filming less expensive and a more attractive site than many other locales. The same can be said of the east coast, where production costs are a fraction of what they are in Hollywood. Tom felt there should be no reason for them to go any farther than Nevada. It is certainly closer.

We can offer all the needed amenities for cast and crew for the duration of their shoot, but the state needs a full service studio that could accommodate a production— from providing the perfect shoot site to post-production services. We also need to offer financial incentives similar to what's done in Toronto that would make shooting in Nevada financially attractive. If elected, I knew Tom and I could do so much to increase film production in our state.

According to their collective bargaining agreement, Hollywood studios have to bring their own crews with them on location if there is no signatory agreement with local agencies. In order to be signatory to Hollywood collective bargaining agreements, IATSE Local 720 in Las Vegas needed to include film and agree to the same terms Hollywood contracts followed in order to allow location productions to hire Nevada hands. Tom wanted to put our own people to work. He pointed out that the film division is a responsibility that falls under the lieutenant governor. Since I was running for the office and had worked in Hollywood, he asked if I would tape an infomercial to assist him in making Nevada signatory.

We taped outside during one of the coldest, windiest days Las Vegas had seen in a long time. I was frozen. It made it difficult to remember my lines. They filled me with hot coffee but my teeth continued to chatter.

Ken Richardson was the producer. He has a string of hits, such as *Kojak*, on his resume and is not only wonderfully patient, he has a great sense of humor as well. Take after take, I flubbed my lines because I was so darn cold. Take after take, he offered patient encouragement until we finally did it right. The man is a saint. He probably went inside and drank his lunch after our shoot. In the end, however, IATSE became signatory and able to give our own folks a paycheck during location shoots.

Tom knew I was being shut out by the political puppeteers and decided to put his money where his mouth was. He was one of the few people I met in all my campaign experiences who was more than lip service.

He and Ken taped all my TV commercials as a training exercise in an effort to help me get elected. Unfortunately, funding sources that would provide the means to air them were not available to me. The hard work of IATSE would not be seen on TV. Even so, their kindness and loyal friendship will forever be remembered.

* * *

The final sweep through the rurals marked the end of a long and discouraging but hard fought campaign. The exclusion and obstructions repeated again this second time around validated my findings that election victories are not a coincidence or a fluke; they are premeditated. As in my previous campaign, I loved the voters and will treasure my visits with them. I felt good about completing the race and doing the best I could do under the circumstances. I held no illusion, however, about not being able to prevail against tremendous financial and influential odds within the political process.

I reflected on my battle against government invasion of individual liberties and then thought about the persecution visited upon so many of those who signed the Declaration of Independence. Residents were British subjects at the time the document was signed and to give us a free and independent nation, many of the signers faced capture, torture, destruction of their homes, fortunes and families – even death. Forms of that treatment continue today for many who still seek representation with integrity.

Key periods in our history should make us hang our heads in shame and prompt us to take a firm stand of change that will grant America a new status of decency, pride and honor.

Why have we not learned from events such as the Trail of Tears, one of our government's darkest moments when President Andrew Jackson defied the Supreme Court by stealing Southeastern American Indian land and forcing the removal of 60,000 members of the five Civilized Tribes resulting in the death of 4,000 along their forced march to Oklahoma.

Or the notorious Wyoming Johnson County Wars of the late 1800s which was one of our nation's most despicable range wars pitting powerful cattle ranchers against struggling newcomers simply seeking to settle and establish a better life for themselves. Cattle barons began building an exclusive society around their elitist lifestyles taking vigilante action, even murder, against the settlers to run them off. Concentrated power and political corruption was so deplorable and pervasive that when the settlers rebelled, the pompous cattle barons, who now saw themselves as above the law, simply brought in mercenaries to exterminate remaining settlers. The elitists, after all, controlled government, media and the courts of Wyoming and were able to buy their own version of justice in a governor who contacted President Harrison with an untruthful account of events in Johnson County imploring military troops to assist them in prevailing over the settlers and halting the advance of Democracy, which they shamefully were able to do.

Volumes have been written about Prohibition and the Vietnam War, both of which were artificial crises created by corrupt government to augment private pockets and further disturbing political agendas. Unfortunately, as in the case of Prohibition, when choice is eliminated and an entity is declared illegal it opens the sinister door to exploitation and enhancement of criminal activity. Vietnam was pure and simple greed. War became big business and resulted in the outright murder of innocent pawns.

The 1986 War on Drugs is a complete and total failure. The explosion of criminal activity in order to obtain the next high has culminated in current day gun violence. Guns are not the problem; they have simply become the tool for minds controlled by and obsessed with obtaining drugs. Government agencies certainly share culpability and are now helpless to cure a population consumed by substance abuse.

William Jefferson Clinton, in my opinion, is without a doubt the worst president we have ever had. Besides being a man with little regard for women or wedding vows, he is a president who consistently ignored the oath he took to uphold the Constitution, allowed atrocities such as Waco and Ruby Ridge to unfold under his watch, permitted out-of-control federal agencies to view themselves as above the law and protected the employment of ineffective agency heads such as Attorney General Janet Reno whose sole assignment appeared to be to cover up and prevent prosecution of any wrong doing on the part of those in power.

Rather than defend America against foreign enemies, the Clinton-Gore administration allowed a hostile power (China) access to national security secrets in exchange for illegal campaign contributions during the 1996 reelection campaign. The Democratic National Committee sold their soul by taking huge sums of money from

Chinese operatives and then allowing them to sleep in Lincoln's hallowed bed of history.

Clinton's road to impeachment was a low point in U.S. history. Arkansas is taking steps to disbar Clinton, which appears to send a message that once returned to citizen status, the Clintons could very well finally have to answer for activities surrounding their unrestrained pursuit of power. Perhaps, finally, the American public will get the justice we deserve.

The price of two terms in office under the Clinton-Gore Administration is beyond calculation or repair and will be felt for generations to come. Despite the revolting and criminal nature of this president, his wife and his administration, we the people are the real culprits. We reelected him.

The Declaration of Independence, states the Creator – not man – has endowed us with "unalienable" rights to life, liberty and the pursuit of happiness. Black's Law Dictionary defines unalienable as "incapable of being sold or transferred." Those rights are secured by consent of the governed – we the people – whose voices are supposed to be heard via representation of those few who are elected to give a voice to those who put them in office.

By the time we realize our freedoms have been quietly stripped from us one by one, our guns may be gone, a national ID card may regulate our every move, bureaucratic tyrants may have legislated the right to seize everything we own without due process, DNA may be mandatory, most misdemeanors may have become felonies and a disproportionate number of our population may be incarcerated as a result, transponders may track our every move, protesters may be discredited and labeled as radicals or terrorists and rounded up, and we could wind up a nation under siege. That time is not that far away. By then, power in our country may be so invasive and dangerous, it may simply be too late.

When national representation breaks down into mass corruption within our government and it is so pervasive as to no longer represent the voice of the people, the Declaration of Independence declares it is our *duty* to dissolve that form of government.

Perhaps that time has come.

***

The time has come for me to pass the baton to another freedom warrior with the fresh energy needed to tackle the political trenches. In the end, I placed surprisingly well for being outspent 30-to-one, receiving no party assistance nor a single advantage enjoyed by chosen favorites. Considering the circumstances, I was pleased to finish third in a field of nine in the primary.

Our savings exhausted and credit cards maxed, it certainly proved one thing: only the rich or anointed can afford to run and get elected in the State of Nevada.

A Time to Debrief

One of the highlights about doing my civic duty is that when my life comes to a close, I'll never have to wonder "what if?" All my life I've been a risk taker. My personal philosophy is that a person doesn't really live if he or she hides in safe corners and never takes chances. I've never been afraid to fail. Not having the courage to try is much sadder than failure. I'm proud I made the attempt.

President Theodore Roosevelt said it best when he observed, "It is not the critic who counts. The credit belongs to the person who is actually in the arena … who, at the best, knows in the end the triumphs of high achievement and who, at the worst, if they fail, at least fails while daring greatly, so that their place will never be with those cold and timid souls who know neither victory nor defeat."

My firsthand experience with the political process was a combination of worst nightmare and best memories. The hardest part was slowing down after four years of non-stop, blinders-on, full steam ahead hectic pace. My work in the political arena is finished, at least for the present. Now it's time to debrief.

I wasn't elected but I didn't fail. The system failed me. There may be only one winner in each race but there are no losers. Those who brave public scrutiny and make the enormous sacrifices it takes to run for office are all winners.

The races in which I participated were not about me. I was only the vessel. They were about freedom and giving a voice to the everyday working person who is the backbone of this nation and who is losing representation more and more with each election.

In hindsight, it amazes me that I was so naïve. I will never again view politics through the eyes of an innocent. I was just an average citizen who believed in the system. I felt strongly about trying to help my statewide neighbors and friends. I thought I could do that by running for office where I could make significant changes that would benefit others.

We all learned in high school government class what a right and a privilege it would be to serve our country in that manner. We also were taught America has a political process that is fair and decent and equal.

I knew it would be a sacrifice but I felt certain the political process and the honorable leaders involved in it would assist each person who was willing to brave the extreme physical, emotional and financial sacrifices that result from becoming a candidate for public office. I had every confidence I would not be abandoned.

I felt I had to run in one of the major parties if I had any realistic hope of winning. I tried them both. I simply didn't know then that it doesn't matter what party an outside candidate belongs to; if I didn't have the financial backing and wasn't the party choice, I wouldn't win anyway.

In the course of observing and participating in the election process, I found that those in high and powerful positions behind the scenes make our national, state, and local decisions for us. We voters have little to do with it. High school political science classes may have been good in theory and may even have had some basis in fact in times past, but today's reality is that we are no longer a Democracy or even a Republic. The rules have changed. Camelot is gone – camouflage is in.

Edmund Burke is right. An apathetic public is allowing our country to be controlled, manipulated, and run by those who don't hold the good of the people in mind. Lack of integrity in leaders has trickled down to all levels of government. It will continue silently to creep into our lives one lost liberty at a time so we don't notice – until it is too late. These are the very people our Founding Fathers warned us about.

It's time to get back to patriotism –- where one's word stands for honor and pride instead of the negative militia undertones contrived by government agencies and the media to discredit patriots.

Our children need heroes who actually abide by the vow they took when they entered office to defend and protect the birth certificate of our nation –- the Constitution of the United States – instead of following a path of treason in trampling the Second Amendment and blatantly doing the very opposite of what is clearly defined for us in this important document.

Our children need to learn national pride and what it means for their hearts to swell and their eyes to fill with tears of emotional fulfillment when they hear the strains of our national anthem at ball games.

Our children need to know a state flag that has symbolized the rebel attitude of the south and the independent spirit of fallen Confederate soldiers is a symbol to preserve rather than turn into a target of hate by the media and a few manipulating agitators with hidden agendas.

Our children need to cherish history by not falling prey to those few who feel major athletic teams should change their names to become "politically correct" and not "offend" any ethnic group. They need to understand history twisted actual perception of certain cultures and made them out to be something they weren't and team names were meant to pay respect to the competitive character that has always existed in our nation.

Our children need to develop courage of their own convictions, maintain an independent mind, be willing to explore all avenues of an issue, and avoid becoming part of the herd mentality that is leading us blindly down the road to ruin.

When we are old and gray, our children will be the ones to take care of us and protect our way of life. We'd better have trained them to be competent!

Charlton Heston said it most effectively when he addressed Brandeis University and stated, "Political correctness is tyranny with manners."

The word patriot denotes people who feel pride in their country, their leaders, and their actions but the government has contrived it to mean militia, thereby providing themselves with a scapegoat for any view they do not sanction. The fabric of our society has been torn away, one thread at a time. We need to unite and stand up against those who would destroy our way of life. America's two major political parties have lost their way. It's time for us to wake up and get back to patriotism.

Even as far back as the first years of the 1900s, we had influential people bailing from the major parties because the parties couldn't come to grips with the reality of what was actually happening in the real world. For instance, Woodrow Wilson and the Democratic Party buried their heads in the sand in an effort to avoid dealing with the reality of America's apathetic reaction to the affect of European conflict on the United States. This subsequently led America directly into World War I.

One of Wilson's opponents in the 1912 presidential election was Teddy Roosevelt. That year, the colorful former president defected from the Republican Party to form the Progressive Party, better known as the "Bull Moose" Party. He did this because the GOP of his day refused to look at national issues in a realistic manner. Conservative factions within the Republican Party were alarmed at Roosevelt's attempts to direct policy towards the more progressive measures he had long championed. With many key Republican constituencies siding with Roosevelt, the GOP suffered its worst defeat in its history that year.

Not much has changed in nearly a century. What would cause a viable GOP presidential candidate to defect from a party at a crucial time in his political career? Pat Buchanan defected from the Republican Party to run on the minor Reform Party due to lack of unity within the GOP, irreconcilable differences in principles, and the GOP's inability to deal with the reality of issues.

The 2000 presidential race demonstrated an even clearer picture of dysfunction within the Republican Party in the campaigns of George W. Bush and John McCain. Most people know that Bush's father is a former CIA director and a former president. Did the elder Bush really do anything remarkable for the working class American, or did he simply carry on Ronald Reagan's legacy of watching out for privileged cronies and ensure the next generation continued in his footsteps?

George W. has been less than memorable as governor of Texas and certainly not forthcoming about his past substance abuse. He has made public remarks that are downright ignorant and presents an attitude that is emphatically arrogant and elitist. As a former president's son, he inherited the prestige and influence of his father's former office, the clout of his father to call in chits, and a name that automatically grants him the backing of the political machine. He's a dragon the average person can't hope to slay. He may not have the best interest of Americans in mind and may not be the best choice for president, but the machinery that moves politics is clearly in his bloodline and on his side.

Senator McCain was, in my opinion, by far the better choice. But the Republican Party had already bestowed the throne to Bush, and in their usual manner simply discounted McCain. McCain surprised the party by becoming a real threat to Bush when he attracted a following of mainstream folks who were fed up with a system bogged down in lip service and no action, as well as independents and third party supporters. In the end; however, herd mentality on the part of voters and pressure visited upon electoral voters forced McCain to bow out of the race.

McCain received little help from his party even though, unlike his opponent, he was a contender who was less concerned with his own ambitions and, instead, represented citizen concerns rather than his own. His years as a POW certainly gave him a compassion and empathy lacking in those of the silver spoon set. His selflessness, courage, and loyalty to his fellow prisoners-of-war were displayed when his captors discovered he was the son of a high-ranking military officer and feared retribution. They tried to convince him to leave captivity, but McCain refused to leave those that had been there longer than he had and stayed to the end, even though it meant several more years of torture and hardship. That degree of dedication to his fellow man and courage in the face of extreme torment is the kind of integrity not earned by country club candidates.

He listened to voters, was very much in touch with all strata of Americans, and was determined to make changes, such as campaign finance reform, that would alter the face of elections and help eliminate corruption derived from special interest money.

GOP arrogance and dysfunction in general, and Bush in particular, disrespected this decent and honorable man by ignoring and treating him in a shabby manner. Bush even lacked common good manners by refusing to personally call McCain along the campaign trail or when McCain "suspended" his participation in the race. America has been cheated of a very human choice for president.

A principal factor for me in deciding to leave the Republican Party is the undue influence of the extreme Christian Right on the party. I have precious little patience with witch hunt attitudes and those who feel their opinion is the only one that matters and they are superior to others. The Christian Right feels they can dictate policy whenever they want, and very often they do.

A vicious smear campaign by WWCR, a worldwide Christian short-wave radio station out of Nashville, effectively ended America's most popular overnight radio program, which had reached 15 million listeners over many years.

As a short-wave station, WWCR does not fall under the same regulations as commercial radio stations and therefore got away in 1997 with broadcasting false rumors that popular talk radio host Art Bell molested his own son, when in fact the boy's substitute teacher was convicted of the charges. Bell is tainted for life by the false accusations. As a direct result, in April 2000 Bell ended his radio career, which had covered controversial topics such as exposure of political corruption, CIA and FBI conspiracies and covert government operations.

While not all religious organizations engage in such spiteful behavior, it is this kind of intolerance that has become more and more pervasive in Republican politics. An organization such as WWCR that claims to be so pious but deliberately destroys the lives of others has no business influencing political decisions. Hypocrisy at the most disgusting levels was a final straw for me in my decision to defect from the GOP.

The most damning evidence of all which convinced me I had made the right decision to *flee* – not just run – from the major party system, was the Clinton Administration-initiated article in the December 1999 issue of the FBI Law Enforcement Bulletin entitled, "Vehicle Stops Involving Extremist Group Members." Along with Clinton's anti-gun stand and Al Gore's pledge that he intends to make America a gun free nation, the article is clear proof major parties have crossed the line into downright Stalin type tactics.

The article cautions law enforcement officers that a vehicle bearing pro-gun bumper stickers is a sign of extremist organization involvement. Really? You mean we no longer have the right to express simple frustration, humor, or disillusionment? When were Clinton and Gore given the right to retract our freedom of speech? When did America become a dictatorship?

I have two bumper stickers on my truck. One says, "I love my country but I fear my government." The other is a tongue-in-cheek humorous expression of aggravation: "Stop honking, I'm reloading." Does this mean I can now count on harassment stops or a trip to the slammer every time I venture out to get groceries? I don't consider myself an extremist but articles like this certainly don't soothe me into a passive mode. I am really fed up with bullies, control freaks and intimidation tactics where First Amendment rights apply to them, but not to us. I'll be damned if these punks in Washington – or anywhere else – are going to frighten me into removing my bumper stickers.

The article goes on to reveal even more appalling, frightening, and reprehensible instruction: a sitting president, a presidential candidate and many among the faceless Beltway bureaucracy consider possession of a Bible or a copy of the Constitution as proof of an "extreme" attitude. Even though I have the Constitution memorized, I still carry a copy in my purse and I consider that document a source of pride instead of a threat to total control by twisted minds.

Possibly the most sinister assault on individual freedom is the change in procedure in which search and seizure is carried out. The Cato Institute reports government has found a way to circumvent the Fourth Amendment. Skirting this safeguard permits law enforcement to seize property and enforce forfeiture laws and actually keep whatever they confiscate. In a quiet and subtle manner, they simply bypass criminal court and take their case to civil court instead where they present the illogical *theory* that since the *property* may be involved in a crime rather than the person, it entitles them to keep confiscated effects regardless of whether a person is convicted, or even charged. Constitutional rights don't apply since a civil court is one of administrative law where the burden of proof is not as stringent and is switched instead to the owner, who must try to convince the court the property should be returned. Taking criminal matters to civil court to sidestep Constitutional protection is the single biggest threat to individual freedom we face today. We *must* put a stop to it.

Law enforcement was originated as a service agency to protect the public but seizure has turned it into a lucrative business of profit. Incentive is high for authorities to engage in confiscation, as they keep much of what they seize without having to account to the public. This policy instills fear, anger and distrust in most citizens because anyone can become a target in law enforcement's quest for more. Police officers take an oath to uphold the Constitution. Intentionally circumventing the law of the land blatantly, arrogantly and knowingly violates that oath. How can they expect citizens to respect their authority when they break the law themselves? Congress has the power to amend forfeiture legislation to make it more difficult for authorities to entrap innocent people and "rip off the wallets of Democracy." As representatives "of the people," it makes one wonder why this has not been done.

Cops have adopted an us-against-them view towards the citizens they are sworn to protect. With the encouragement of the Clinton-Gore regime, they consider the public the enemy, frighteningly reminiscent of Hitler's Germany and Stalin's Russia. The intention and direction of these two men is abundantly clear and I want no part of a political party which condones such people.

Voters make their ballot choices the final two weeks before the election and then for strange reasons known only to them. In addition, people are so disillusioned and turned off by politics that only a very small percentage of citizens actually get out and vote, and those are usually the hard core party loyalists who have a vested interest in the status quo. Rarely do we see a surprise as astounding as the election of then-Reform Party candidate Jesse Ventura.

Ventura brought mainstream credibility to third party candidates, but he certainly isn't the only one. On the same night Ventura shocked the world by winning the Minnesota gubernatorial race, Maine voters quietly yet decisively sent their independent governor, Angus King, back to the statehouse for four more years. Not far away in Vermont, independent House member Bernie Sanders was returned to Congress by his constituents. The successful elections of these and other alternative candidates discounts the erroneous theory that casting a ballot for an independent or a minor party contender is a wasted vote. Obviously, under the right circumstances, it is not.

As a successful third party pioneer, Ventura is a trendsetter with a heavy responsibility to be a good role model thus bestowing credibility on minor parties that may encourage voters to consider them in future elections. It's worth noting that according to one exit poll over 90 percent of people who voted for Jesse Ventura in 1998 said they wouldn't have voted at all if he weren't on the ballot. Not surprisingly, Minnesota led the nation in voter turnout that day. Without those votes, Ventura would have lost in a big way. If we want to shake up the system, we need to bring people back into the process. It's that simple.

Investigation into minor parties left me with one clear choice: the Libertarian Party. It is an alternative whose focus is on defending the Constitution of the United States, protecting individual rights and liberties, promoting individual responsibility, reducing taxes, and diminishing government intrusion into private lives.

The Nevada Libertarian Party has hired a full-time professional organizer to give the party focus, refine its organization, recruit winnable candidates, and move the party into mainstream acceptability. It is an alternative to the fractured major party system that appeals to weary voters and gives hope for the individual fed up with seeing their rights disappear on a daily basis. National political climate and timing make the fledgling Libertarian Party an alternative worth examining when one realizes the mainstream system is crumbling from within. The party has promising potential but there are still a lot of dues to be paid, a lot of insight to be uncovered and a lot of lessons to be learned before they're ready to do battle with the big boys.

With few exceptions, Libertarian candidates run a paper only race and typical ballot results consistently run around five percent. Since I had already run a bona fide race with each of the major parties with substantially higher vote results, it was felt my experience could be beneficial to the party.

One concern I expressed was my reservation in using the candidate training seminars put on by former Republican communications director Chuck Muth. Shortly after I lost the Republican primary, Muth sent a vicious letter to Nevada newspapers attacking me personally and disrespecting my effort to become elected. He did the same with another northern female candidate. I thought back to when the state chair admonished me as a Republican for criticizing a fellow GOP governor for taking the lion's share of tobacco settlement money for his pet project instead of putting it toward health care issues as was intended. It was doubtful Muth had also been chastised for criticizing me as a fellow Republican. In the good ole boy state of Nevada, it was a safe bet the guys were just "expressing themselves" while the gals must have been suffering PMS.

In time, Muth was removed from any position of authority with the party and began instead, to present candidate training seminars in Las Vegas. Among others, he pursued Libertarian Party officers in a bid to find another political niche. I shared my experience and observations of Muth when I ran as a Republican with the Nevada Libertarian director and state chair. I was concerned that in training inexperienced and unsophisticated candidates from a third party, the end result would be Libertarian candidates would be molded into carbon copies of two-party system candidates thus causing the Libertarian Party to NOT be an alternative after all.

I received a very male dominated response from the state chair which made me realize leadership differed very little from Democrats and Republicans. I told him Muth was the one person I could not work with because there was every reason to believe destructive behavior already exhibited with Republicans would be repeated with Libertarians. His disinterested and unprofessional reaction to a legitimate concern resulting from first hand experience was surprising. He simply dismissed the issue and made it clear my input had no value. He was quite willing to allow a candidate that could win for them to walk away rather than consider information that might save the party trouble in the long run. His territorial posturing and disrespect made me reconsider any active role in the party.

I have great respect and admiration for Chris Azarro, the state director who is always willing to listen but whose hands are often tied by restrictions placed on him by the state chair. The party's principles and goals are commendable so I find it unfortunate that despite themselves, they will not find the party in a position to advance an agenda that is good for all of us with that type of leadership attitude.

I ponder the futility of running for public office again and yet a nagging voice in the back of my mind keeps reminding me that change starts with one small step and if I don't fight for what I believe in, then I must go quietly to the ovens when the knock comes on my door. The most successful avenue toward change may not be in public office, however. The written word is a powerful communication tool. Additionally, I have been offered the opportunity to host my own national talk radio show on the Liberty Works network (also heard on the Internet). These options may prove to be a more effective venue.

* * *

In politics, I discovered one never knows who their friends are and has to assume everyone is an enemy. Trustful by nature, I had a hard time accepting the fact others judged me harshly for choosing to work in an occupation that was not against the law rather than accept welfare. My first name was always "former" and my middle name "prostitute" in the newspapers. It was never mentioned that I also spent many years working for the vice president of a major movie studio in Hollywood. That didn't sell papers.

But I also came away with a valuable gift. Despite society's small-minded labels, I learned a person is only confined by the boundaries of their own mind and their worth is not measured or defined by small minded hypocrites, elitist power brokers or media bias. I discovered my strengths, held my head high and walked down a road of pride. I found good and decent people everywhere and they outweighed the counterfeit humans.

I've moved on past the labels. It is my nature to help others. I believe things happen for a reason. Politics as usual was not meant for me: I'm too honest. There's another path I was meant to take and when the time is right, I will find it.

Unlike anointed choices who receive soft money from the party as well as other advantages, we had to rely on and invest all our own money in order to compete. As a result, my financial situation as an outside candidate is one of shambles. I would never recommend anyone else put themselves through the agony of becoming an outside candidate. There is simply no incentive for anyone other than the anointed choices.

Even my final official action as a candidate was irritating. It would have been funny had it not projected such a profound message. Closing my campaign account proved to be far from entertaining, however. They wanted my social security number to close the account. Why? It's unnecessary, as well as an invasion of freedom and privacy. It was only through tricking the bank officer into giving me my balance and writing a check to zero out the account that I got my money.

Closing the account was as frustrating as opening it and only confirmed my growing belief that the less a person has to do with "the system," the better off – and freer – they would be.

That type of attitude never occurred to me growing up in the country. We worked hard, raised food for ourselves and others, never turned our backs on our neighbors when they found themselves on hard times and treated everyone the same. We were all poor but we were rich in family, friends, good neighbors, living in the best country in the world and for having dreams that might be possible to reach some day. We pulled together and we were all better off for it.

Somewhere along the decades, we lost that precious gift. The spoiled baby boomers grew into selfish greedy adults who ruined our way of life with their self-concerned lifestyles. Money and material possessions became more important than people. We are paying for that now. A nation built on shifting sand cannot remain solid.

I learned some interesting and at the same time disheartening facts while I campaigned in Las Vegas. The city is a constantly changing melting pot. The very nature of the town's sick value system places premium value on money, not people. City residents don't pull together. The dynamics of this fast growing city where people come from everywhere else is a great part of the problem. Another part rests squarely on the value system on which the city was built. Money and power hover over this metropolis like dark clouds before a storm.

Everyone is out for number one which has caused the breakdown of a feeling of community. Together, each of us contributes to part of a whole. We are human beings; mortals who all came into this world equal. Along the way, pathetic power seekers bestowed labels on others in an effort to make themselves feel superior. Labels serve only to hurt and stifle the success each of us aspires to. Most of us go through our daily lives simply trying to exist. We all struggle at one time or another. We are no more nor less than the person next to us. Especially in Sin City, we should be wary of those who throw stones. It has been my experience they are the ones who usually have the most to hide.

While Las Vegas was more typical of the baby boomer mentality, I found the rest of the state to be rich in values that count.

I had the rare privilege of meeting thousands of extraordinary people in my campaign travels. People who live everyday lives but touch others in exceptional ways. Human, caring people who know the true value of life. They recognize what's really important is not material wealth, greed or power … but human beings. Family, treasured friends, dear acquaintances. I have been blessed to meet and live among the most courageous and wonderful residents in the world – Nevadans. No road worth traveling is all good or all bad. The combination allows us the contrast to appreciate each. I'm a rich woman.

When I worked in Hollywood, one of my favorite sets was the house featured in the old TV series *The Waltons*. It was a big comfy house built with the architecture and character from the early part of the 20th Century that housed a large close knit family with it's daily problems and all it's love. It was nestled under a big tree that provided shade for the porch.

A tree house was lodged securely part way up the shade tree. It was irresistible to a former tomboy. Big enough for an adult, I sometimes got my lunch to go at the studio commissary and climbed up into the tree house where it was peaceful.

I often wandered around the house, stepping over cables, ducking wiring and watching for loose floor boards and remembering a time when I grew up in a house very much like it. I loved the show. It reminded everyone of a time, not that long ago, when families and neighbors cared about one another and were always there to help each other.

I still saw that way of life in the rural communities of Nevada. Ranches are miles apart, towns are small, everyone knows everyone else, many have lived in their communities for generations. The rurals aren't transient, constantly changing or superficial like Las Vegas. Their most important resource is people. They pull together and help each other in order to survive. In the process, they map out a way of life that places premiere importance on human relationships. That's really as it should be. It makes an observer feel good inside and have hope for the future.

The hardest part after two back-to-back statewide races was slowing down, learning not to fester on corruption I could not change, and becoming centered again sinking my feet firmly into the common sense soil of life. It was time to rediscover what was really important in life's scheme of things and discard the rest.

I needed to feel Cody's tiny arms around my neck and see his innocent little face break out in a big smile because Gramie was going to spend time with him again. I needed a long hug from each of my grown children and time for long talks. I needed to have a Chinese food lunch with my new daughter-in-law and get better acquainted. I needed to walk hand-in-hand with the wonderful man I married and watch a heart stopping sunset over the open landscape of the country. I needed time to get the petty life of politics out of my head and bury it forever. I needed my life back.

Now that I am simply another faceless citizen, I'm free to admit that in the future, I will vote my conscience with no mindfulness of party affiliation. Old Nevada has always been fiercely independent, refusing to be bound by party lines and voting for the person as opposed to the party. I fall firmly within that description.

Leaving politics also gave me time to check on my sisters. We needed to breathe fresh air, see open spaces, smell the sage and talk to real people. We took a week and covered the state, stopping to thank loyal supporters for their trust and confidence. We also stopped at the bordellos. It was good to be home.

The brothels will remain status quo now that their voice has been silenced on a political level. I'm not nearly as effective as I could have been had I been elected. I would have attempted to make changes that would have been good for brothel owners, the ladies who work in the houses and for our state. Some of my efforts will still be directed in that area as an advocate but I'm realistic enough to know not much will change.

It was fun to catch up on what the girls had been doing during my absence. Amber was the proverbial "hooker with a heart of gold." While visiting her at one of the ranches, she told us about Paul.

Amber lived in town and went home after her shift. She got off around 3 a.m. and didn't want to drive when she was tired, so she normally took a taxi. One night as the taxi drove past the casino, she saw a man lying in the gutter. People stepped over him or went around him but no one stopped to help. She didn't hear sirens either, so apparently help had not been called. She instructed the driver to pull over.

It was evident the gentleman was not hurt but was so drunk he passed out on the sidewalk and rolled into the gutter. Afraid he would be run over, Amber and the driver put him in the back seat of the car and drove him to the hospital.

He remained in the hospital until he dried out and they could send him to a rehab facility. Amber not only visited him regularly, she paid his entire bill. He was homeless, so she arranged for him to have a small apartment to go home to. The only thing she asked in return was that he attend AA meetings, stay sober, look for work and get his life back on track.

Today, thanks to a hooker, Paul has been sober over a year, has a good job, just put a down payment on a condo and is now a contributing member of society instead of one that taxpayers must take care of. He considers Amber his guardian angel and they are best friends.

During a recent trip home, I ran into Kevin at the store. Normally when a prostitute sees a client out in public, she pretends not to notice and never says anything to them. Kevin is different. The minute he spotted me, he came right over and swooped me off my feet and twirled me around and around. After putting me back down, he grabbed his wife's hand and pulled her over to where we were standing and introduced us. She knew all about me and was very gracious. We had a wonderful visit and I was thrilled to be able to spend a few minutes holding their new baby daughter. Happy endings like Kevin's made me feel good about my work.

It had been quite awhile since we had enough time at home that we could go down to Fly's pub and visit with locals. It was Saturday night, so we knew a good many of the folks we knew would be there.

We climbed the back stairs and opened the door. A girl who sounded like Bonnie Raitt was singing. She was really good. Above her head, monopolizing a good part of the wall, was the print of my painting, smiling down on everyone in all my naked glory.

"Hey, girl," the singer said into the microphone as we sat down, "I almost didn't recognize you with your clothes on!"

Everyone laughed. Fly shook Michael's hand and gave me a big hug. We sat down at a small table and suddenly everyone was crowding around us.

Hazel evidently had forgiven me for removing a print of the painting from the Washoe Club since Fly now had his on display. She was there with John, the artist, and began talking to us like no hard feelings had ever occurred. John gave us both a big hug. It was good to have the fences mended.

The editor of the paper eyeballed Michael. Like two gunslingers at opposite ends of the room, they stood in a silent standoff. The editor knew Michael would kick his butt at the slightest provocation. The editor was really out of shape after years of excessive food and lots of booze. He decided it was late and time for him to go. Michael was disappointed.

A few of Virginia City's infamous holier-than-thou types sat at the end of the bar, giggling and gossiping while looking our way. They were too pitiful to worry about, so we didn't. There were too many others in the room that were genuinely glad to see us back home for awhile and we intended to have fun for the evening.

We caught up with what everyone in town had been doing during our absence. We looked around at the cowboys and country women who filled the room. Taking a deep breath, Michael and I looked at each other and smiled. Despite the small minded hypocritical puritans in town, we were among friends at Fly's and it felt good to be here.

We stopped down the hill at the brothel to check on Porche. She wasn't there. The madam told us she went back to Phoenix and remarried her ex-husband. They had always remained friends. He simply waited for her to get the houses out of her system. She was only a year away from obtaining her college degree in physical education, so she went back to school and got it. She teaches girls' PE in a junior high school.

Jillian was an airline stewardess before working in the houses. A gorgeous girl with waist length blond hair, big blue eyes and an incredible body, she looked like a Barbie doll. She had worked the houses for many years and vowed she would stay until her quarter-million dollar home and BMW were paid for and her son's private school tuition was paid in full. She accomplished her goal but had a really hard time leaving the business. Most people think "hooker" refers to the girls "hooking" in the clients. In reality, it's the girls who get hooked. On the money, the independence the lifestyle creates and on the bonded friendships developed among the girls themselves. Jillian tried going back to the airlines. It didn't last. She was happier in the house.

Michael and I are returning to a quality of life in the best part of the state, with family and friends and time to ponder where we go from here.

I have a path to find. Whatever road I travel, it will involve the most precious commodities of all: people and freedom. Ironically, one of the best quotes I've heard comes from a politician. Former Senator Bob Dole, a man I admire a great deal, summed up how I feel about politics and life in general when he said, "When it's all over, it's not who you were, what you did or how much money you had. It's whether you touched anyone and made a difference." He's right – we must get back to putting people first.

* * *

My father died six months before the congressional primary. He and my mother retired to southern California to an adult community where the weather was warm. Daddy had been active all his life. Their house was situated on the golf course and he played golf nearly every morning well into his 70s. Then Parkinson's Disease began to take its toll.

Toward the end, he was in his 80s, frail and confined to bed. He was trapped in a fragile body that hurt all the time but his mind was still sharp until pain medication confused him during his last few months. I felt tremendous guilt that my campaign schedule prevented me from visiting him often.

During my last visit, he was on pain medication and drifting in and out of consciousness. He always had the most vivid blue eyes. As long as I can remember, they reflected his sweet, kind, innocent nature. Looking at his face was like looking at a child. I saw the same thing in his eyes that I see looking into my little grandson's. Life was full of wonder for him.

When he woke up, it took a minute for him to recognize me but I could see the realization dawn on him. It spread across his face and in those precious eyes. He was no longer able to talk but we had no trouble communicating.

I told him about all the memories I had about him from my childhood. Especially my favorite memory of being in the machine shed when it rained and listening to the rain on the tin roof while he sang

"You Are My Sunshine" to my sister and me. His eyes sparkled. I began to sing the song to him.

And then the most amazing thing happened. This dear man who was in such pain and could no longer speak, listened while I sang. Suddenly, I heard humming that went along perfectly with the song. I stopped and listened to my father. Together, we finished the song. It was our bittersweet goodbye.

I didn't have proper time to grieve. I just knew my world was so much more lonely now. Every once in awhile something would trigger a memory and I would have a good cry but usually the campaigns kept me so busy, I had little time to think about the fact he was gone.

He was a phenomenal man and such a special parent. I will have time now to think about him, put my thoughts and feelings in order and celebrate his life and the extraordinary way in which he touched and influenced others. I was so blessed to have been his little "sugar."

It has come full circle. My father was staunchly political. Loyally Republican. I wanted so much to dedicate an elected victory in his memory. He would have been so proud.

In the end, he would have been proud anyway. The hooker was the one who wound up with principles. I remembered the values he taught me. I fought for what was right and decent and honorable.

About the Author

Jessi Winchester is a former prostitute in the legal Nevada bordellos who ran for US House of Representatives in 1996 as a Democrat and Nevada lieutenant governor in 1998 as a Republican. Although she has no immediate plans to run for public office again, Ms. Winchester continues to be an activist on behalf of bordello sex providers in Nevada, as well as a political advocate for individual rights as defined under the Constitution of the United States. Ms. Winchester lives with her husband, Michael, in the Carson City, Nevada, area.

Visit the author's website at www.jessiwinchester.com

W. Lane Startin is a former president of Idaho Young Democrats and a graduate of Idaho State University. Mr. Startin lives in Philadelphia.